planet earth

as you've never seen it before

Alastair Fothergill

Vanessa Berlowitz, Mark Brownlow, Huw Cordey,
Jonathan Keeling, Mark Linfield

Foreword by
David Attenborough

UNIVERSITY OF CALIFORNIA PRESS
Berkeley   Los Angeles

foreword **6**

the whole earth **10**

the great plains **90**

the great sands **116**

fresh water **196**

rainforests **224**

frozen poles **32**

the great forests **62**

mountain heights **142**

the underworld **170**

shallow seas **252**

open ocean depths **280**

FOREWORD

Today our planet has been photographed with a degree of detail, thoroughness and technical virtuosity that would astound photographers of a previous generation. Within the past few decades, we have acquired the ability to take pictures of an entire continent from a satellite out in space and to explore the microscopic world inside a drop of water. We can photograph in what is to our eyes total darkness and expose film so briefly that it freezes the beat of a hoverfly's wing. We have taken cameras to the tops of the highest mountains and put them in unmanned probes that descend into the abyssal depths of the ocean. The cameras themselves have become so small that we can attach one to the back of a bird so that it photographs as it flies or insert one down a long burrow to photograph an animal in its nest hole without the occupant being in the least alarmed. And most recently of all, we have acquired yet another ability that has produced breathtaking results. We can photograph the head and shoulders of a wild wolf in close-up from a helicopter so high in the sky that the roar of its engines in no way disturbs the animal beneath and the downdraft from its rotor blades doesn't batter the vegetation like a hurricane. So it is indeed true that this book – and the television series which it mirrors – can show you the world as you may never have seen it before.

But – alarmingly – it is also the case that, within the next few years, the world itself may never look the same again. That great, shaggy, double-humped camel – one of the hardiest of all mammals and which once wandered in huge herds across the Gobi Desert in central Asia – has been reduced in the wild to fewer than a thousand individuals. No more than 40 or so wild Amur leopards still survive, and their numbers continue to fall.

And the world's remote and unspoiled places that are the homes of our planet's wildlife are also in danger. Oil pipelines are being built across the Arctic tundra and highways driven across the Amazonian jungle. Rainforests are being felled by the square mile to make way for plantations of oil palms, and coral reefs are being poisoned by marine pollution. Even those parts of the wilderness that have so far escaped such despoliation may very soon become radically changed in character as a result of the global warming caused by humanity's activities.

So this remarkable and beautiful book should stand not just as a revelation and celebration of the wonders that our planet still retains at the beginning of the twenty-first century. It surely must also be seen as an eloquent rallying call to all of us who care for the Earth's welfare to redouble our efforts to protect those wonders that still survive.

Davie Attenborough

DAVID ATTENBOROUGH

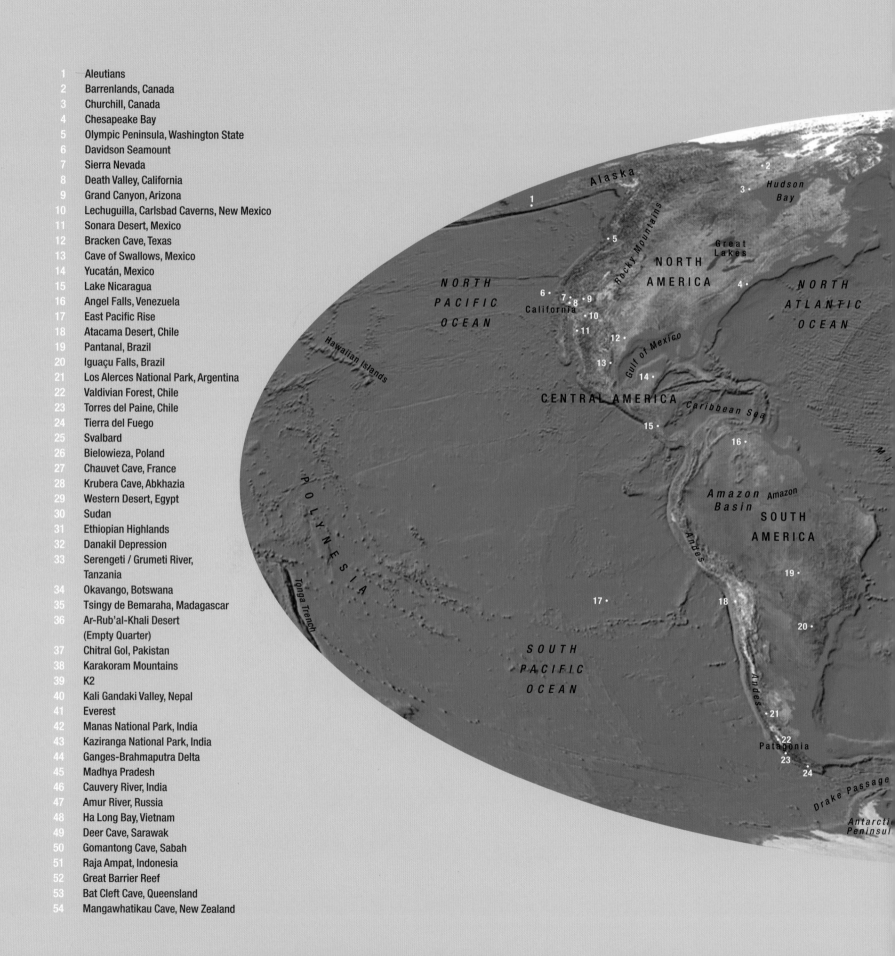

1 Aleutians
2 Barrenlands, Canada
3 Churchill, Canada
4 Chesapeake Bay
5 Olympic Peninsula, Washington State
6 Davidson Seamount
7 Sierra Nevada
8 Death Valley, California
9 Grand Canyon, Arizona
10 Lechuguilla, Carlsbad Caverns, New Mexico
11 Sonara Desert, Mexico
12 Bracken Cave, Texas
13 Cave of Swallows, Mexico
14 Yucatán, Mexico
15 Lake Nicaragua
16 Angel Falls, Venezuela
17 East Pacific Rise
18 Atacama Desert, Chile
19 Pantanal, Brazil
20 Iguaçu Falls, Brazil
21 Los Alerces National Park, Argentina
22 Valdivian Forest, Chile
23 Torres del Paine, Chile
24 Tierra del Fuego
25 Svalbard
26 Bielowieza, Poland
27 Chauvet Cave, France
28 Krubera Cave, Abkhazia
29 Western Desert, Egypt
30 Sudan
31 Ethiopian Highlands
32 Danakil Depression
33 Serengeti / Grumeti River, Tanzania
34 Okavango, Botswana
35 Tsingy de Bemaraha, Madagascar
36 Ar-Rub'al-Khali Desert (Empty Quarter)
37 Chitral Gol, Pakistan
38 Karakoram Mountains
39 K2
40 Kali Gandaki Valley, Nepal
41 Everest
42 Manas National Park, India
43 Kaziranga National Park, India
44 Ganges-Brahmaputra Delta
45 Madhya Pradesh
46 Cauvery River, India
47 Amur River, Russia
48 Ha Long Bay, Vietnam
49 Deer Cave, Sarawak
50 Gomantong Cave, Sabah
51 Raja Ampat, Indonesia
52 Great Barrier Reef
53 Bat Cleft Cave, Queensland
54 Mangawhatikau Cave, New Zealand

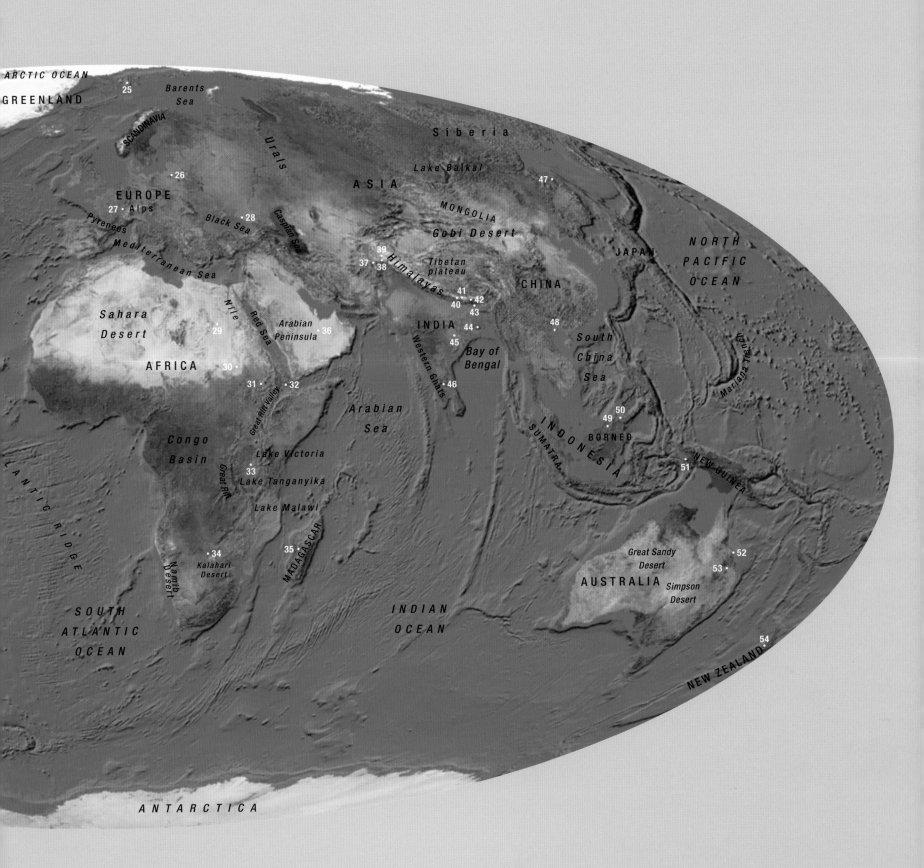

the whole earth

1

The Big Bang, cosmic dust, gravity, nuclear fusion,

electrostatic forces, sunlight, liquid water, a collision

in space, a moon, a tilted axis and, in the end,

a world that is uniquely fit for life.

Consider our planet as a whole and all the living,

breathing consequences of plain good luck.

Some 35 years have passed since anyone has been able to look back at the beautiful sphere of Planet Earth, alone in the darkness of space. The Apollo 17 mission in 1972 was the last time humans visited the Moon and stood far enough away to get this particular view of our home planet. Since then all our exploration has been in low Earth orbit, where from an altitude of just 350km (220 miles) the 12,700-km (7900-mile) diameter Earth is too close. You can see our planet's curvature but nothing more. From the Moon, though, you look back at a solitary blue sphere wrapped in white clouds. Between the clouds are glimpses of green on the land. These are the colours of life, and as far as we know, our planet is unique in the solar system. It alone supports life, and more than anything else, this seems to be down to chance. When the cosmic dice were thrown, our planet came out with a double six.

THE LUCKY PLANET

Our solar system was created between 4.5 and 5 billion years ago. The Sun and planets were formed from a huge cloud of dust and gas produced in the Big Bang. Gravity caused the cloud to collapse towards its centre and begin to rotate. At the centre of this spinning disc, temperatures rose to a point where hydrogen fused to form helium and our Sun was born. Further out, dust particles were drawn together by electrostatic and other forces and gradually grew into larger and larger rocks. Gravity drew these rocks together, and slowly these bodies grew to form the planets. The four planets nearest the Sun – Mercury, Venus, Earth and Mars – were made up largely of solid material with high melting points, rocky planets with metal cores. Further away from the Sun are the gas giants – Jupiter, Saturn, Uranus and Neptune.

Early in its history, our planet began to sort itself into a number of different layers. The natural decay of radioactive material at its centre generated enormous quantities of heat, which melted most of the rock, forming a liquid 'mantle'. Around this mantle – and no thicker, relatively, than the skin on a peach – formed the cooler solid crust. Then, as still today, the molten rock regularly erupted through the thin surface layer. This volcanic activity was accompanied by the release of gases such as nitrogen and carbon dioxide that formed the basis of our planet's atmosphere. With the gases came water vapour in such

ABOVE *A continual stream of lava pours into the sea from Kilauea Volcano, Hawaii. It lies over a hotspot in the Earth's thin mantle and is one of the most active of volcanoes.*

OPPOSITE *The Earth seen from the Moon – a planet orbiting at just the right distance from its sun and the right angle to support life as we know it.*

large quantities that when it condensed it formed the oceans, and it was in those oceans that the first simple life forms evolved 4 billion years ago.

Volcanic activity and the release of gases and water vapour were also happening on Earth's near neighbours, but as far as we know, no life has evolved on any of the other planets in our solar system. The main reason for this seems to be simple cosmic luck. Planet Earth happened to end up orbiting the Sun at just the right distance. Mercury is closest to the Sun at an average 57.9 million km (36 million miles) and has never developed an atmosphere. It experiences the largest daily temperature fluxes of any planet, with average daytime surface temperatures of 430°C (806°F) plummeting to a night-time average of −180°C (−292°F). It is hard to imagine any life form that could survive these extremes, let alone the daily variation. Venus is 108.2 million km (62.7 million miles) from the Sun and has a thick atmosphere rich in carbon dioxide. The strong greenhouse effect of this thick atmosphere ensures that Venus stays hot around the clock, with an average surface temperature of 480°C (896°F).

If Venus is too hot for life, Mars is probably too cold. It is 227.8 million km (141.6 million miles) from the Sun and has a thin atmosphere with very little carbon dioxide. Average surface temperatures are always −50°C (−58°F), and any water that might exist beneath the planet's surface or at its poles remains permanently frozen.

Our planet, though – orbiting at 149.6 million km (93 million miles) from the Sun – seems to be at just the right distance for life. Our medium-thick atmosphere has contained just the right amount of carbon dioxide to help keep Earth at a perfect average surface temperature of 17°C (63°F). We live on the 'Goldilocks' planet because, just like the porridge in the fairy tale, Earth is neither too hot nor too cold but 'just right' for life.

LIFE FROM THE MOON

Looking back to Earth from the Moon, the astronauts may not have fully realized the vital role the satellite they were standing on has played, and still plays, in creating and maintaining life on Earth. It has been the architect of evolution, and without it, we probably would not be here today. Again, cosmic luck was on our side. It is generally believed that the Moon was formed about 4.5 billion years ago, when a planet about the size of Mars collided with the early Earth. The huge impact threw into space an enormous quantity of the Earth's crust, which orbited the planet before gradually coalescing to form the Moon. By chance the planet that hit Earth also had a liquid-iron core. In the heat of the impact, this joined up with Earth's existing liquid iron, and our planet ended up with a much larger

iron core. It is this core that produces the Earth's magnetic field, which itself acts as a defensive shield from the particles that stream out of the Sun as solar wind. At both poles of our planet, the magnetic field is less strong, and solar particles break through into the atmosphere to create the spectacular coloured light shows of the aurora borealis and aurora australis. For the most part, though, the Earth is protected from deadly ultraviolet radiation that otherwise would scorch the surface and destroy all life.

The impact was to have other profound influences. So much of the Earth's surface was thrown into space to form the Moon that only about 30 per cent of the original crust was left. What remained was so thin that the continental plates moved around more easily. This continental drift has played a key role in driving evolution. Over the millennia, the freely moving landmasses have continually shaped our planet's surface. Their collisions have created great mountain ranges such as the Himalayas and ripped apart wide trenches such as Africa's Rift Valley. In the process, new and different habitats have constantly been created, and a wide variety of life evolved to exploit these new and changing environments. Without the collision that created the Moon, the plates would be locked together as they are on Venus, and there would be far fewer habitats on Earth today.

The collision had one other dramatic effect. It knocked our planet so that it was no longer spinning on a straight axis with respect to the Sun. The angle of tilt it created was roughly 23 degrees off the perpendicular, and that tilt remains today. Without this, life on Planet Earth would be very different. Day length all over the world would be the same all year round. The Sun's warming influence would also remain constant throughout the year and there would be no seasonal change. Without the warmth of summer, the poles would on average be far colder, and their frozen influence would extend further towards the equator. There would be no cycle of wet and dry seasons in the subtropical regions, and the world's deserts would be far more extensive. There would be no need for animals to migrate, and life would probably be far less diverse.

Ours is the largest moon relative to its mother planet, and this gives it a powerful gravitational influence. It is the pull of the Moon's gravity that plays the dominant role in creating the oceans' tidal cycle. Less well known but equally important is the dampening and stabilizing effect the Moon's gravity has on Earth's angle of tilt. Without such a large moon so close by, Earth would be at the mercy of the gravitational influence of the Sun and Jupiter. The power of this pull would vary as Jupiter circled closer or further away. Without the Moon acting as a stabilizing gyro, the Earth's angle of tilt would vary chaotically and at times reach as far as 90 degrees to the perpendicular. This would leave the North Pole pointing directly towards the Sun, causing the whole ice cap to melt and widespread flooding of our planet. The Moon then is a vital climate regulator on Earth, providing the stability for life to evolve.

SUN PLUS WATER EQUALS LIFE

All life on our planet ultimately depends on two vital ingredients – energy from the Sun and liquid water. This at least was the accepted view until 1977, when deep-sea explorers discovered a completely new ecosystem of animals around hot volcanic vents on the floor of the ocean abyss. It is totally dark at around 3000m (10,000 feet), and for a while nobody

OPPOSITE *A full moon rising over boreal forest in the northern hemisphere. Our Moon is the largest in the solar system relative to its planet and has a gravitational pull that stabilizes the tilt of the Earth. Without it, the tilt would be chaotic and the planet would be a different, less hospitable place.*

BELOW *Water is another unique ingredient of life on the planet. Here a California sealion plays in a forest of kelp – giant algae fuelled by sunlight and a rich supply of nutrients.*

could work out how this community, as productive as the richest coral reef, was getting its energy. Eventually they discovered that specialized bacteria were fixing energy from the sulphides pouring out of the vents. But even the animals in this food chain are not living totally independently of the Sun's energy. They all use oxygen to burn the compounds supplied by the fixing bacteria or obtained by eating the bacteria themselves. This oxygen is created in shallow, sunlit waters by plants that are themselves dependent on the Sun for their energy. At first sight the vent communities seem to live independently of the Sun, but ultimately they could survive only on a sunlit planet.

THE SOLAR PUMP

The enormous variety among the different habitats on our planet, from the rich tropical jungles to the barren polar wastes, is shaped principally by the differing availability of the vital ingredients of sunlight and water. The amount of the Sun's energy that reaches the planet is not evenly spread. More of it is available around the equator because there the Sun's rays have to travel through less of the Earth's atmosphere than they do at the poles. At higher latitudes, the lower angle of the Sun also means the energy is spread over a wider area than in the tropics.

The amount of water available to life on land has a more complex distribution, but even that is largely influenced by the Sun. Ninety per cent of the world's fresh water is created by evaporation off the ocean, and most of that occurs near the equator in warm tropical seas. The other 10 per cent comes from the surface of lakes and rivers or is released by plants. The water vapour is carried high into the atmosphere on rising warm air, and in the process it cools and forms clouds, which are blown round the world by winds. Exactly where these clouds release rain depends on many factors, but mountains play a key role. They cause the clouds to rise and cool, and their water vapour condenses as rain. Because most of the Sun's energy falls around the equator, it is here that you find most of the rising hot air that carries moisture into the atmosphere. As it rises and cools, it produces torrential downpours. Having lost its moisture, this air is deflected by the spin of the Earth and flows north and south away from the equator. As it reaches cooler higher latitudes, it sinks, and this dry air creates the bands of desert lands found along both tropics.

In the oceans, the variety and quantity of life is also determined mainly by the availability of energy from the Sun. The top 100m (340 feet) or so of sunlit, shallow waters contains 90 per cent of life in the oceans. Here it is the availability not of water but of vital nutrients, especially phosphorus and nitrogen, that has shaped marine communities. Though tropical seas receive the largest amounts of sunlight, they are, with the exception of the coral reefs and seagrass beds, largely deserts. This is because these waters are calm, allowing most of the nutrients to sink to the depths. The ocean's greatest riches tend to be found in rough temperate seas or where upwelling currents provide a good supply of nutrients.

ABOVE *Clouds created by seawater evaporation over the tropics. Oceanic clouds provide 90 per cent of the fresh water that falls on land.*

OPPOSITE *Botswana's Okavango Delta. As fresh water pours down from the highlands, the river floods the parched land.*

EQUATORIAL RICHES AND POLAR POVERTY

With sunlight and fresh water abundant and available all year round, it is hardly surprising that the most productive habitat on our planet is in the tropical regions around the equator. The tropical rainforest is life at its most abundant, and plants grow here in greater profusion than in any other habitat. Up to 200 different tree species grow in a single hectare (2.5 acres), compared to 10–20 tree species in temperate woodland. Though tropical rainforests now cover just 3 per cent of our planet's land surface, they are thought to contain more than 50 per cent of the animal and plant species yet described. Growing conditions for plants are perfect, with warm year-round temperatures between 20°C and 28°C (68–83°F) and continual reliable rainfall that averages 2500mm (100 inches) a year.

As plants are the primary producers and almost all animals are ultimately dependent on them for their energy, the amount of carbon fixed by the plants per year through photosynthesis is a good measure of the total productivity of a habitat. Tropical rainforests are the record-breakers on land by this measure, producing 1000–3500g (35–125 ounces) of carbon per square metre (11 square feet) each year. They also win out in terms of another good measure of a habitat's productivity – the total weight of animals and plants, the biomass, which reaches 4500g (160 ounces) in every square metre.

The coral reefs that are restricted to the same tropical regions of our planet are often called the rainforests of the seas, and in terms of productivity they deserve this accolade. They produce between 1500 and 3700g (53–130 ounces) of carbon per square metre per year. This figure is particularly impressive considering the fact that the shallow tropical seas in which they grow are so low in the vital nutrients of nitrogen and phosphorus. But coral reefs and the other animals that share this habitat have reached these heights of productivity through very efficient recycling of their nutrient needs.

THE DRIER TROPICS

As you travel north and south away from the equator and towards the tropics, the climate changes. Though there is plenty of sunshine and it is warm all year round, rainfall is less reliable. Each year there is a distinct wet and dry season, and the plants that grow there have to be able to cope with these changing conditions. The monsoon forest of northern India and Southeast Asia is a good example. The evergreen trees typical of tropical rainforest are replaced by deciduous species such as teak and ebony, which save water by dropping their leaves each year. These trees are shorter, more widely spaced and have deeper roots than those in the tropical forests. This is the land of the langur monkey and tiger, which each year live through a dry season from November to April before being deluged by the monsoon rains. In drier regions such as northern Australia, trees like the eucalyptus are even better equipped to deal with drought conditions between 'the big wets'.

In the driest subtropical regions, trees are replaced by grassland – the vast open landscapes of the savannahs. This is a habitat that supports unusually high numbers of large animals. It is warm all year, but the lives of the plants and animals here are dominated by the annual cycle of wet and dry. For much of the year, the East African savannah is parched

ABOVE *Dawn over the rainforest, Borneo. Perpetual warmth and rain at the equator have created the most productive habitat on the planet.*

OPPOSITE *A garden of hard corals surrounds Bunaken Island, Sulawesi, in Indonesian waters – possibly the richest marine waters on the planet. Coral reefs are the rainforests of the sea. Though nutrients are in short supply, the complex, productive system is fuelled by recycling.*

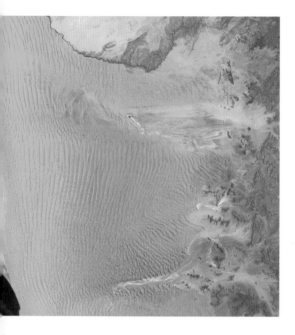

ABOVE *The Namib Desert, southwest Africa, as seen from space. Though it lies beside the sea, the desert receives almost no water, except for early-morning fog near the coast. Like other coastal deserts, it is on the west side of the continent, and prevailing winds push any rain clouds forming offshore out to sea.*

OPPOSITE *African elephants in Botswana, making the long, dusty trek in the dry season to faraway rivers and waterholes. Older matriarchs lead the way, remembering traditional routes to water sources.*

golden brown, but come the rains, it flushes with new green growth. The annual migration of the wildebeest in the Serengeti follows this new grass. The savannahs are only half as productive as the tropical rainforests, fixing 200–2000g (8–80 ounces) of carbon per square metre per year, but they achieve that with just a tenth of the biomass of plants in the tropical rainforest. Savannahs are one of the most efficient ecosystems on the planet.

THE THIRSTY LANDS

As you approach the tropics of Cancer and Capricorn, you reach the thirsty parts of our planet. These are the high-pressure regions, where warm, dry air is sinking and there is little rainfall – on average, less than 100mm (4 inches) per year, and in true desert regions, less than 50mm (2 inches). There is no shortage of sunlight, though, and because humidity levels are so low and there is very little cloud cover, 90 per cent of the Sun's radiation reaches the ground. Day temperatures frequently exceed 38°C (100°F), and at night, when heat is rapidly lost back to the atmosphere, they can drop more than 44°C (79°F) in just a few hours. Though most deserts are hot all year round, some high-altitude ones, such as the Gobi in Mongolia, can be extremely cold, with winter temperatures of –21°C (–5.8°F). Cold deserts such as the Gobi are usually far inland and in the shadow of mountain ranges, where moist air from the oceans rarely penetrates. Life for animals and plants in the planet's desert regions is about surviving extremes of temperature and very limited supplies of fresh water. Vegetation is sparse and annual productivity rates are as low as 300g (11 ounces) of carbon per square metre.

These low levels are similar to those found at far higher latitudes and way out to sea in the open ocean. The vast blue desert of the tropical oceans receives ample supplies of sunshine, but once again, lack of nutrients limits phytoplankton growth – the algae at the base of most marine food chains. Tropical oceans are the famously calm seas of the doldrums, and there is little surface mixing to bring nutrients up from deeper water. Neither do these waters benefit from the regular supply of nutrients that rivers bring to shallower waters on the continental shelf.

TEMPERANCE

Halfway between the tropics and the polar circles are the temperate regions of our planet. Here you find the grasslands and deciduous woodlands of northern Europe and the prairie and coniferous woodlands of North America. There is less of the Sun's energy here than in the tropics, but summers are still warm and moist – rainfall averages 500–1500mm (20–53 inches) per year. This is also a very seasonal part of the world, and the animals and plants that live here have to adapt to distinct winters, springs, summers and autumns. Winters, particularly in northern temperate climes, can be hard, and much of the fresh water is locked up as snow and ice.

In Europe, the oak, beech, ash and chestnut trees of the broadleaf woodland shelter wild boar, deer and squirrels. The structure here is simpler than in tropical forests, with just two canopy layers. Shafts of sunlight easily penetrate to the forest floor, where bushes, flowers and mosses flourish. This is a very productive habitat supporting an average biomass of 3000g (106 ounces) per square metre. In North America coniferous trees are also

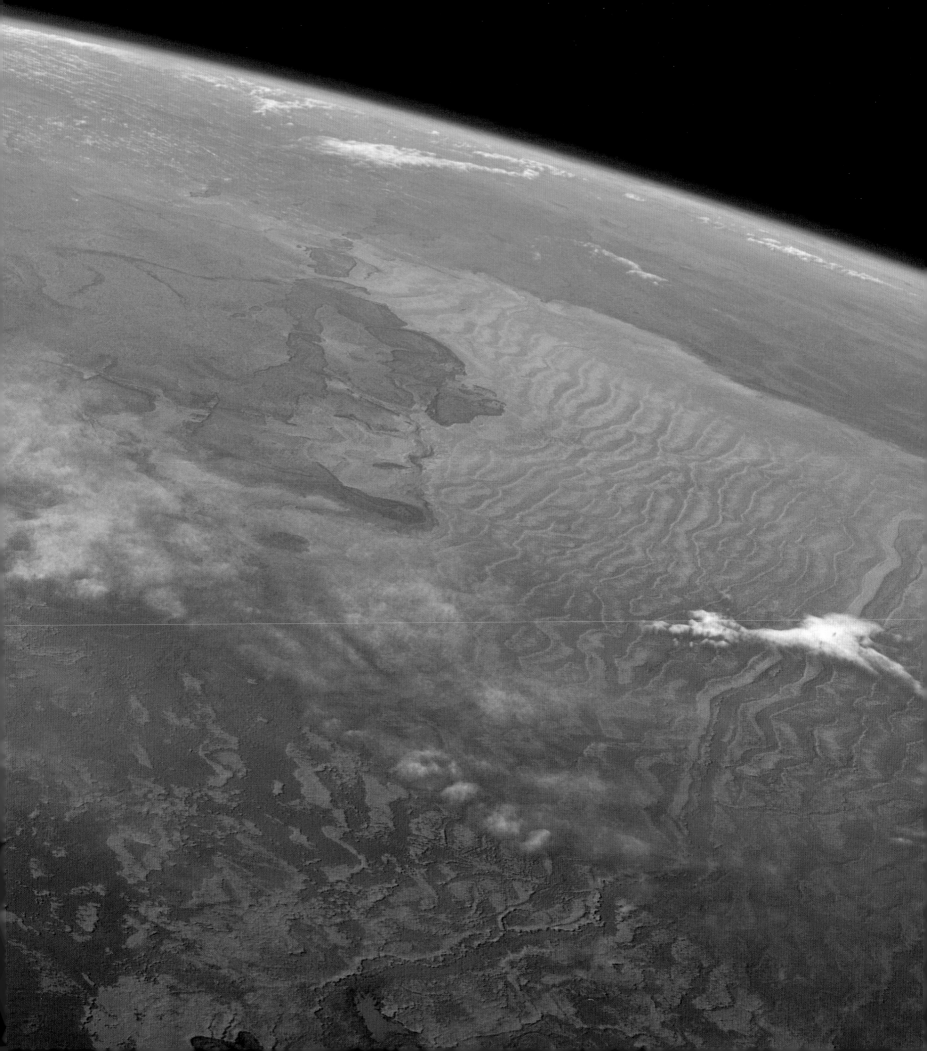

ABOVE *Kiang, or Tibetan wild asses. They thrive almost exclusively on grass and, like many plains animals, are fast runners. In summer they live in small herds, but in winter they gather where there is exposed grass.*

PREVIOUS PAGE *Seasonal winds drive a huge sandstorm nearly 1.5km (a mile) high across the Sahara. The cloud of dust may be carried over the Atlantic as far as Brazil, fertilizing the Amazon in the process.*

common. The most spectacular are the giant redwood forests of the Pacific coast, where a mild and very moist coastal climate nurtures the tallest and largest trees on our planet.

As you journey further north, coniferous trees become increasingly dominant. All across northern North America and Eurasia is a continuous belt of coniferous woodland called the boreal forest, or taiga. Every third tree on our planet is found in this forest, which is home to wolves and lynx, moose and reindeer. Winters here can be long and harsh, and for nine months of the year, most of the available water is frozen as snow or ice.

When the spring melt does finally arrive, the ground quickly becomes waterlogged, because the permafrost layer keeps moisture at the surface. Vegetation is slow to decay, and the acidic soils trap nutrients needed for plant growth. The short growing seasons and demanding conditions make it impossible for deciduous trees to grow, but conifers do well because their conical shape and needle-like, waxy leaves help them survive the cold and drought of winter. Average rainfall is just 400–600mm (16–23.5 inches) per year, and in some regions as low as 150mm (6 inches). This is no more than many semi-desert areas receive, but in these colder conditions less moisture is lost through evaporation. But productivity in these northern boreal forests is only 200–1500g (7–53 ounces) per square metre – nearly half that of the deciduous woodlands to the warmer south.

In the interiors of the vast landmasses of North America and Eurasia, you experience continental climatic conditions. Without the softening influence of the oceans and the moisture they provide, the winters here are cold and the summers hot and dry. Trees do not do well in these parched conditions and give way to the wide-open temperate grasslands.

In the northern hemisphere, there is the North American prairie with its pronghorn antelopes, prairie dogs and remnants of the bison herds that were once millions strong. In Europe there is the Russian steppe, where until very recently large herds of saiga antelope used to roam. In the southern hemisphere exactly the same habitat is found in the South American pampas and the South African veldt. On either side of the equator, north and south, there always seems to be this mirror of similar habitats created by the same conditions of sunlight and rainfall.

Productivity in the temperate grasslands is similar to that found in the savannahs nearer the equator – both depending on that great survivor, grass. Remarkably tolerant of both changing temperatures and lack of water, grass has become the most abundant plant on Earth. Today it covers a quarter of the planet's land surface and supports more large animals than any other habitat.

ROUGH, RICH SEAS

Though life on land is richest in the tropics, the reverse is true in the seas. Distribution of life tends to be patchy, influenced by local factors such as currents, but generally, the seas in temperate latitudes are the most productive. Here, air travelling up from the equator meets polar air travelling down, creating unstable weather.

In the North Atlantic, it takes the form of weather fronts that rush towards Europe, bringing dramatic storms to western coastlines. Particularly in shallow waters on the continental shelf, these storms mix up the sea as deep as 200m (650 feet). Phosphorus and nitrogen are brought up from the depths and, every spring, fuel a massive bloom of phytoplankton. By the end of the summer, the nutrients have been used up, but mixing occurs again in winter, recharging the ocean's batteries.

ABOVE *The world's second largest fish, the basking shark. It is found not in clear tropical seas but in nutrient-rich temperate waters, where it feasts on the plankton that multiply here.*

OPPOSITE *Midwinter at the South Pole. An emperor penguin stands backlit by the aurora australis, or southern lights. At the poles, the protective magnetic field produced by the iron-rich inner core of the Earth is weaker, and harmful electrons from the Sun break through, creating the southern and northern lights when they collide with atoms in the upper atmosphere.*

THE FROZEN POLES

At 65 degrees north, you cross the tree line and enter the bleak, barren world of the tundra. Here there are long, dark winters, with temperatures as low as −30°C (−22°F). This is a high-pressure region, and the chilled air delivers little rain. Winters are too cold for trees to grow, and productivity here is as low as southern deserts, with only 100–400g (3.5–14 ounces) of carbon per square metre. In the winter only a few hardy residents are left, such as the musk ox and the Arctic fox. In the short summer, though, visitors migrate from the south. Snow geese and caribou take advantage of the long days and short flush of new growth.

In both the north and the south, 66.5 degrees marks the polar circle – the line beyond which, for at least one day of the year, the Sun never sets. As you approach the poles, the number of days increases until, at the North and South Poles, the Sun rises and sets only once a year. To make things worse, the snow and ice reflect back 85 per cent of the little sunlight. The altitude and isolation of Antarctica make it colder still. Average annual temperatures are −55° to −60°C (−67° to −76°F), and only about 50mm (2 inches) of snow falls each year. Nothing grows except lichens on a few mountaintops piercing through the ice sheet that engulfs the continent. Productivity is as close to zero as you can find anywhere.

SEASONAL SHIFTS

The chance collision that created the Moon and left the Earth spinning on a tilted axis has shaped the lives of wildlife more than any other factor. As the Earth orbits the Sun, different parts are tilted towards it at different times. In the northern hemisphere, the North Pole is tilted away from the Sun in December, producing the dark, cold winter. As the Earth

continues its annual orbit, the North Pole is gradually turned towards the Sun, which with every passing day rises higher in the sky, and day lengths increase. In March, at the spring equinox, the Sun is directly over the equator and the night and day length is exactly equal.

The Sun's influence continues to increase in the northern hemisphere until, on 21 June, the summer solstice, it is directly over the Tropic of Cancer. This is the height of the northern summer, when areas north of the Arctic Circle experience 24-hour daylight. From then on, the North Pole begins to tilt away from the Sun, and day length starts to decrease. Summer turns to autumn, and by 21 September – the autumnal equinox – the Sun is again directly over the equator. Gradually, the southern hemisphere tilts closer to the Sun until, at the winter solstice on 21 December, the Sun is directly over the Tropic of Capricorn. This marks both the height of the northern winter and, of course, the southern summer.

The transition from winter to summer at the poles is sudden and dramatic. In Antarctica, for instance, the continent effectively doubles in size in just a few months as the surrounding ocean freezes. This is the most drastic seasonal change on our planet, and with the exception of one bird and one seal, the wildlife has no option but to head north with the departing Sun.

The temperate regions, halfway between the polar circles and the tropics, are where the seasonal rhythm of our planet is most obvious. Here are four distinct seasons, but none extreme, and so there are many permanent residents, which adapt with the seasons. The temperate ocean also experiences four seasons. In shallow waters, the lengthening days of spring fuel the phytoplankton bloom, which drives the marine food chain. Even in the total darkness of the deep-sea floor, a seasonal cycle exists. Through time-lapse photography, scientists have shown that the quantity of the marine 'snow' (detritus from the waters above) follows a seasonal cycle that closely tracks the level of activity in the sunlit waters above.

In the regions around the tropics, where day length hardly varies, there are only two seasons – wet and dry. But even these are produced by the Earth's orbit round the Sun. When the Sun is directly overhead, more water evaporates off the oceans and there is more rising hot air to carry it up into the atmosphere. This produces more clouds, storms and rain. In June, when the Sun is directly over the Tropic of Cancer, the northern tropical regions experience their rainy season – while in December, when the Sun is over Capricorn, the southern hemisphere enjoys the rains. Only in equatorial regions, where the Sun rises and sets at exactly the same time each day of the year, is there no seasonal cycle.

For billions of animals on our planet, seasonal change in their habitats means they are constantly on the move, following the warming influence of the Sun or the changing supplies of precious fresh water. Every autumn, some populations of red admiral butterflies leave northern Europe and fly nearly 3200km (2000 miles) to North Africa to escape the cold. Every summer, 3 million caribou undertake the longest migration by any land mammal, up to 3000km (1865 miles), in search of fresh pasture. European swifts are permanently on the wing as they migrate 18,000km (11,000 miles), following the Sun and their insect prey, first across the Sahara to West Africa and then, when food becomes scarce, on to East Africa and finally back again to Europe to breed. In the oceans, most of the baleen whales travel huge distances, from their breeding nurseries in warm tropical waters to their summer feeding grounds in the high latitudes. In fact, all the animals and plants on Earth have lives dominated by a chance cosmic event – a collision that shifted our lucky planet by 23.5 degrees and, in the process, changed the whole history of life on Planet Earth.

ABOVE *A red admiral takes flight. Like populations of many other, much larger animals, some red admirals escape the cold winters by migrating, in this case, from Europe to Africa.*

OPPOSITE *A humpback mother and her calf in the warm waters of Tonga. When the calf is strong enough to leave the tropical nursery, they will make the great migration south to krill-rich, cold waters, where they will spend the southern summer feeding. Humpbacks make the longest confirmed migration of any marine mammal, and can survive on their fat reserves for up to eight months in a year.*

frozen poles

It is in the frozen worlds of the Arctic and Antarctic

that the seasonal nature of our planet is most

keenly felt. From the total darkness and

numbing temperatures of the polar winter to

the 24-hour daylight of the polar summer – this is

the ultimate world of extremes.

ABOVE *An Antarctic summer night.*

OPPOSITE *The coldest place on earth, Antarctica, which in winter is surrounded by frozen ocean.*

PREVIOUS PAGE, TOP *An ivory gull (left) shadowed by an Arctic skua.*
BOTTOM *Emperor penguins going back to sea, Antarctica.*

September 21 is a very important day for anyone working at the Amundsen-Scott research station at the South Pole. For the past six months, the scientists and support staff have overwintered here in near-complete darkness. Now, at the spring equinox, the sun crosses the equator on its journey towards the southern hemisphere and appears above the horizon at the South Pole. Everyone living at the station rushes out to enjoy the first sunshine they have seen for a long time. The sun will not set again for six months but will circle permanently above the horizon, providing 24-hour daylight. At the North Pole, the situation is exactly reversed, with the sun disappearing below the horizon for six months every September, only to return in March. At both poles, the sun's warmth is enjoyed for one long 'six-month day', which is followed by a 'six-month night'. Nowhere else is this seasonal difference so extreme, and the arrival and disappearance of the sun each year completely dominates the lives of polar wildlife.

Despite the enormous difference between summer and winter, the South Pole enjoys the same number of hours of sunlight, taken over a whole year, as at the equator. But because the poles are tilted away from the sun, solar radiation strikes the surface at an oblique angle, which reduces its intensity. The poles therefore remain frozen wildernesses. At 60 degrees, the latitude of Oslo and the Shetland Islands, the intensity is 50 per cent that at the equator. At 80 degrees north, at the top of Greenland, the power of the sunlight is just over 17 per cent that at the equator.

We are used to the cool of early morning or late afternoon sunlight, but at the poles it is like that all day. The sun never rises high enough to produce the burning midday heat that beats down on the tropics. The effect of the sun is further reduced by the Earth's atmosphere – the greater angle means there is more atmosphere for the rays to penetrate before they reach the surface.

Finally, and most significantly, the almost complete coverage of white snow and ice means that 85 per cent of the solar radiation that does make it down to the surface is reflected straight back into the atmosphere before its warming influence is felt. With so little solar radiation available in the first place, the warmth equation at the poles remains heavily in the negative. Only in November and December, the very height of the Antarctic summer, does the South Pole actually gain heat.

ABOVE *Polar bear with its seal catch. A polar bear's survival depends on it being able to catch enough seals and seal pups in the spring and summer, which in turn depends on there being enough ice for it to hunt over. Now the ice is melting earlier and earlier each year, its extent is reducing and polar bear numbers are falling.*

Though the sun's influence is felt similarly at both poles, there are enormous differences between the Antarctic and the Arctic. For a start, it is far colder in Antarctica. The average winter temperature is −50°C (−58°F). Even on a summer day, the temperature at the South Pole can be around −30°C (−22°F), which is colder than the coldest winter night at the North Pole. The main reason for this enormous difference is altitude.

The Arctic is a low-lying basin of frozen sea ice. Stand at the North Pole, and all you have between you and the ocean are a few feet of ice. At the South Pole, you are standing 2900m (9515 feet) above sea level (twice the height of Ben Nevis) and certainly feel the altitude. Even light work quickly tires you out, and the extreme cold makes it difficult to stay outside for more than half an hour or so. In the height of summer, it can be far too cold to leave your skin exposed for long, and the moisture in your breath freezes as soon as you breathe out. In the winter, you can throw a cup of boiling water into the air, and it will freeze instantly into a beautiful puff of ice crystals before it reaches the ground.

Beneath your feet are almost 3000 metres (9840 feet) of ice, compacted over hundreds of thousands of years, which completely engulfs the highest continent on Earth. The white wilderness extends to the distant horizon as flat and level as a cricket pitch. Absolutely nothing breaks up the tedium of the view.

Submerged beneath the world's largest ice cap are massive mountain ranges. Antarctica is three times higher than any other continent. Its average elevation is 2300m (7545 feet), which compares to an average of just 720m (2360 feet) in North America. As anyone who has climbed a mountain knows, with increasing height, air temperature drops – one degree for every 100m (328 feet). It is altitude that makes Antarctica so much colder.

The other key factor is isolation. Antarctica is a frozen continent surrounded by ocean. The southern tip of Africa is about 4000km (2500 miles) to the north, while Australia is about 2400km (1500 miles) away. The Southern Ocean, the stormiest water on our planet, separates Antarctica from these continents. Intense low-pressure systems rush unimpeded around the continent, excluding warm air from the tropics and isolating it from the rest of

the world's weather. When the sea freezes in the winter, it becomes impossible for even the strongest icebreakers to force their way through to the edge of the continent. For the few hundred tough scientists and support staff left to sit out the long Antarctic winter, it is a life of isolation. Though satellites have made communication possible, even in dire emergencies it is rarely possible to escape.

The Arctic, by contrast, is a frozen ocean surrounded by land masses. The most northerly parts of Canada are just 1224km (760 miles) from the North Pole. High-pressure systems that form each summer over the land masses of Russia and North America spill warm air north over the Arctic. And in the winter, these continents act as enormous night-storage heaters, ensuring that the Arctic never gets that cold. Logistics are also far easier than in the Antarctic, and year round, specially adapted planes fly in and out of even the remotest communities.

POLAR SWINGS

The great difference in the temperatures and the degree of isolation experienced at both poles has moulded two very different animal and plant communities. The close proximity of land masses has made the Arctic accessible for repeated colonization. Each spring, as conditions improve, Arctic animals can journey north, and as the worst of the winter weather approaches, they can easily walk south again. The result is that the Arctic today is home to more than 40 land mammals, ranging in size from tiny lemmings to massive musk oxen.

Antarctica has no land mammals and, with the exception of the Weddell seal, all its marine mammals head north each winter as the sea begins to freeze. The emperor penguin is the only bird that manages to stay throughout the winter, and even it is restricted to the edges of the continent. Fewer than 20 bird species penetrate further south than 70 degrees, and all are summer visitors. By contrast, the Arctic has 8 permanently resident land birds and more than 150 visitors, at least 100 of which are found further north than 75 degrees.

Plants, of course, are firmly rooted to the spot and cannot move away when winter comes. But the conditions are so harsh in Antarctica that all you find south of 80 degrees are tiny lichens, and the whole continent is home to just two flowering plants. In the Arctic, more than 90 flowering plants are found as far north as 82 degrees.

Though the Arctic is milder and less demanding than the Antarctic, both polar regions remain the coldest, harshest and most extensive wildernesses on our planet. The real challenge for wildlife struggling to survive near the poles is the enormous seasonal difference – from 24-hour summer daylight to the complete darkness of the polar winter. Average daily temperatures can drop 10°C (18°F) within a month. Whole habitats are completely transformed by the annual advance and retreat of the sea ice.

At its winter peak, the Arctic Ocean is covered by nearly 13 million sq km (5 million square miles) of ice. But in summer, nearly 50 per cent of that melts, and with it goes the polar bear's firm hunting ground. In the Antarctic autumn, the front of freezing sea ice moves forward at a remarkable 4km (2.5 miles) per day. The penguins and seals that need access to open water to feed are driven north. By September, the ice extends 645–3060km (400–1900 miles) from the coast. More than 20 million sq km (8 million square miles) of new sea ice will have formed, and the continent will have effectively doubled in size. Nowhere else does wildlife experience such enormous seasonal change.

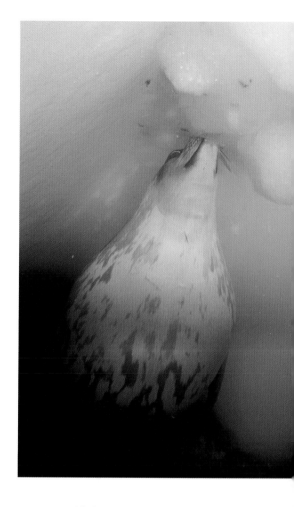

ABOVE *Weddell seal – the only Antarctic mammal that does not head north when winter arrives. Living under the ice helps it stay warm, but to survive, it must keep its air holes open by gnawing at them. This wears down its teeth and may be one reason why Weddell seals do not live as long as other seals.*

OPPOSITE *Nunataks – mountaintops projecting above a sea of ice in Queen Maud Land, Antarctica. Snow-free rocky peaks such as these are sought-after nest sites for snow petrels.*

THE POLAR SPRING

The island of Kong Karls Land in the northeastern corner of the Svalbard archipelago has one of the highest densities of breeding polar bears in the world. In just one valley, more than 40 polar bear mothers dig their winter dens into the snow-covered hillsides. For four months, while the worst of the winter weather rages outside, the mothers shelter in these dens, where they give birth. They do not eat, and as they suckle their cubs, they gradually lose weight.

By late March, the cubs are three months old and ready to leave their snowy wombs. Daytime temperatures still fall below −25°C (−13°F), and sudden, vicious storms can keep mother and cubs below ground for days. But the sun has returned above the horizon, and for a few hours each day, beautiful pink light brightens the hillsides.

A mother waits for a good calm day before breaking a small hole through the wall of her natal den. All that can be seen is the black shape of her nose as she cautiously sniffs the breeze. She has to be careful. With so many polar bears breeding in one valley, hungry male polar bears that spent the winter outside on the sea ice are attracted by an easy meal of cubs. But the female is starving, having lost at least a third of her body weight. Her twins will stay near the den, cautiously getting to know their new world, but after about two weeks the mother is too hungry to wait any longer and leads the cubs out of the valley. Her timing is perfect. The Arctic sea ice is still largely frozen, and out on this solid hunting ground the seals have just started to give birth to their pups.

The lives of most of the Arctic's seals are dominated by this large, hungry predator. Unable to give birth in the water, seals are forced to haul out onto firm ice to have their pups. Breeding in early spring ensures their newborn pups have the whole of the Arctic summer to grow and learn to hunt before the winter returns. But this is just the time when the sea ice is still extensive enough to make polar bears a real threat, and different seal species have had to develop different strategies to try to protect their pups.

Harp seals give birth far out on the unstable pack ice on the Atlantic side of the Arctic Ocean, where they are less likely to encounter bears. Their white-coated pups are, like all true Arctic seals, camouflaged against the snow. To further minimize the risks, harp seals spend as little time as possible on the sea ice. The mother's milk is 45 per cent fat, and within just 12 days, the pup has tripled its birth weight and is well insulated with blubber for an independent life in the ocean.

Hooded seals – named after the red balloon of a nasal septum that the males inflate to woo the females – also breed on precarious pack ice to avoid polar bears. But they have cut weaning time further still. With milk so rich that it contains 60 per cent fat, the female hooded seal can abandon her pup after just four days.

Ringed seals breed further north on the permanent sea ice and so can afford a much longer six- to seven-week weaning period. But the length of their breeding season and the fact that the ice is firm make them far more vulnerable to polar bears, and they are forced to hide their pups in lairs beneath the ice. These little ice caves also provide shelter – when temperatures outside are below −30°C (−22°F), the temperature inside will still be up around freezing.

All through the months of spring, seals provide most of the polar bears' diet. Polar bears have an acute sense of smell and may well be able to sniff out seals in lairs 2km (1.25 miles) away. But capturing the pup may not be that easy. Each lair has an escape hole into open

ABOVE *A hooded seal and her pup. In spring, the lives of most Arctic seals are dominated by polar bears, which eat the pups as well as adults. The strategy of hooded seals is to give birth on precarious pack ice and produce milk so rich that pups are weaned in less than a week.*

OPPOSITE TOP *A lounging leopard seal. These huge seals, along with killer whales, take the role of the polar bear in the Antarctic. When not hunting crabeater seals and penguins, they often lounge on ice 'couches'. Their sinuous bodies give them a serpentine look unlike that of any other seal.*

OPPOSITE BOTTOM *Adélies and a lurking leopard seal play a waiting game. In the sea, the greatest threats to penguins are leopard seals and killer whales.*

PREVIOUS PAGE *An emperor penguin pauses near the edge of the sea ice in front of a 'jade' iceberg. The berg has probably 'calved' from low down at the edge of the ice sheet. The colour is the result of pressure over time that has crushed out air bubbles, which are what cause icebergs to look white.*

water beneath the ice, and the polar bear needs to sneak up to its prey before the pup slips away to safety. Moving very slowly and carefully, and silently placing every massive step, a bear creeps up to where it suspects the lair might be. Then, arching its back, it makes a large and sudden leap, trying to smash into the lair and simultaneously block the exit hole. With soft snow, the bears are successful on roughly every third attempt. When the snow is hard, they manage to trap a pup within its lair only about once in every 20 hunts.

From dawn to dusk, throughout most of the short spring days, polar bear mothers patrol the pressure ridges in the ice searching for seal pups and teaching their cubs to hunt. It is a season of relatively easy pickings, and by the time the sea ice starts to break up properly in the summer, most polar bears have eaten enough to keep them going through the leaner times.

THE CRABEATER AND THE ICE LEOPARD

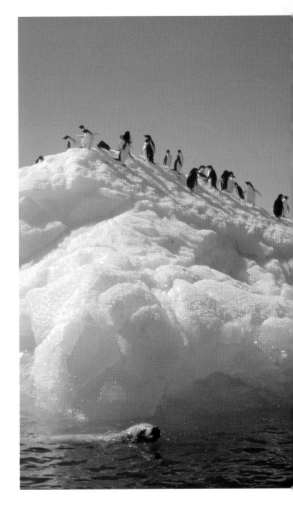

Antarctica's winter sea ice is so extensive that it conceals the breeding activity of what is probably the most numerous large mammal on the planet other than humans. The dense fields of pack ice that surround the continent are so difficult to penetrate with even the most powerful modern icebreaker, nobody can be certain of the exact numbers, but at least 14 million and possibly as many as 40 million crabeater seals breed on the ice each spring. For most of the year these animals are social, foraging together in large groups that are sometimes hundreds strong. Despite their name, they do not feed on crabs – there are no crabs in Antarctic waters. Instead they feed largely on krill (a shrimp-like relative of crabs). In September, as spring is returning to Antarctica and the outer fringes of the winter sea ice are starting to retreat, the crabeaters haul out on ice floes to give birth. The single pup weighs about 20kg (44 pounds) at birth, but within just four weeks, its weight is about 100kg (220 pounds). Its mother, by contrast, has lost 50 per cent of her body weight.

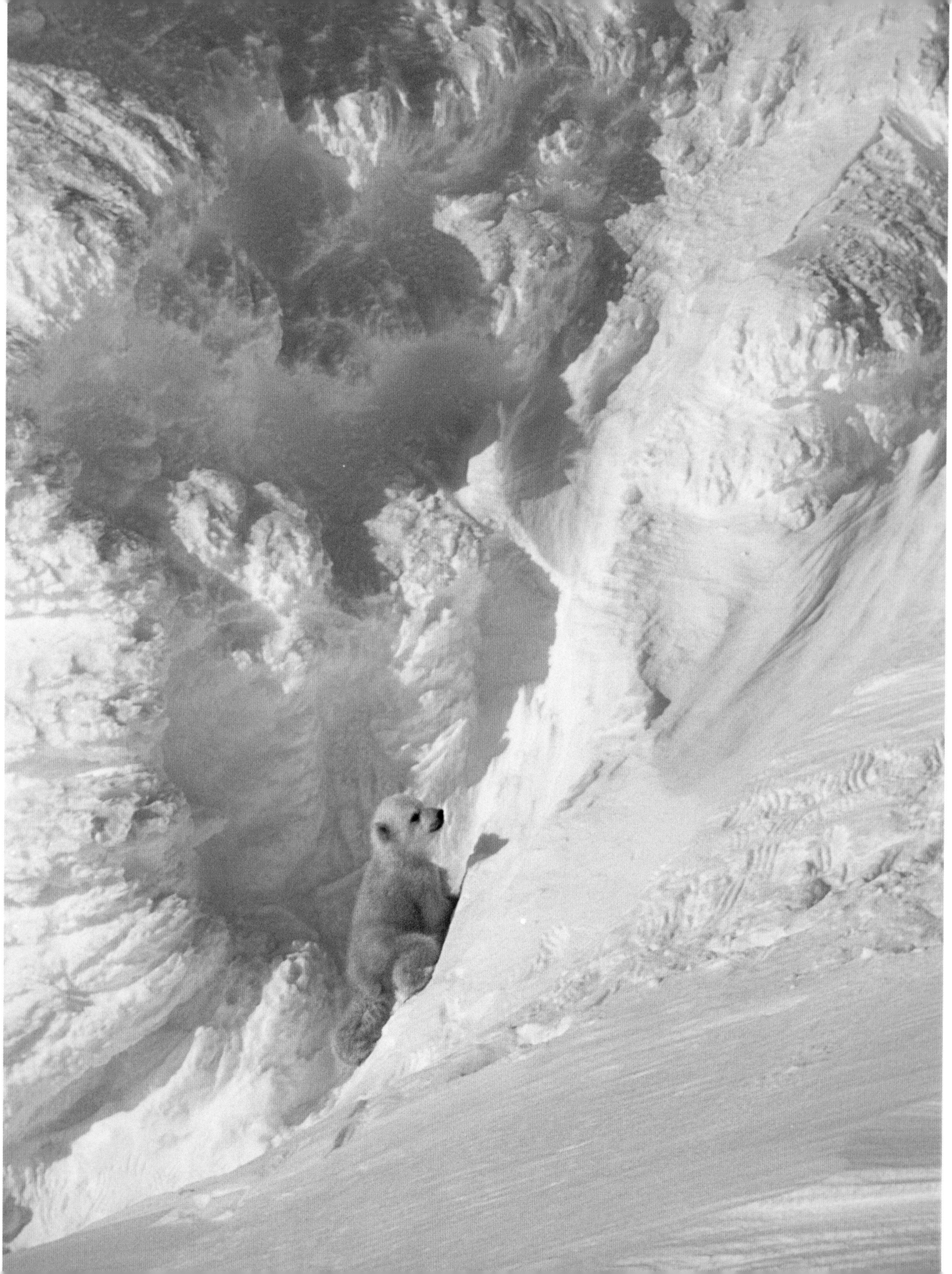

There are no polar bears in Antarctica to encourage this rush to wean the pup, but there is dreadful weather. In the water, temperatures are never below its freezing point of −1.8°C (29°F). But out on the ice floe, exposed to the effects of wind chill, temperatures in the spring can be as low as −40° to −50°C (−40° to −58°F). There are also threats from the sea. Killer whales have developed a cunning technique for snatching crabeater seals and their pups off the ice. Pods of killer whales working together will coordinate a jump out of the water on one side of the floe. Their combined weight creates a bow wave that upsets the ice floe and throws the seals into their waiting jaws. This technique requires the more open water, which usually only develops later in the summer. More threatening is the crabeater's chief predator, which can hunt among even the densest pack ice in spring.

The leopard seal is the largest of Antarctica's true ice seals, with a huge, threatening, snake-like head. For those hardy enough to brave the cold Antarctic waters, diving with a leopard seal can be an unnerving experience. It can put on a real turn of speed and suddenly appear out of nowhere, twisting and turning its sinuous body. If you are holding a camera or anything that produces a reflection, the seal may come right up and bite at what it sees to be a rival. Though this huge predator is quite capable of lunging onto the ice floe to steal a seal, it usually hides among the ice floes until a pup takes its first swim. Of the crabeater seals that survive their first year, almost 80 per cent bear the scars of leopard seal teeth.

BIRTH ON THE ROCKS

Unlike seals, all of Antarctica's birds, with the sole exception of the remarkable emperor penguin, are unable to breed on ice. They must lay their eggs on bare rock, and that is in very short supply. Even in the summer, only 2 per cent of the whole continent is free of ice,

ABOVE *A mother polar bear emerges for the first time from her winter maternal den in Kong Karls Land, Svalbard.*

TOP *She checks to see and smell that no predatory males are around. Though starving, she may wait for up to two weeks before leading her cubs out of the safety of the denning valley.*

OPPOSITE *One of her young cubs takes its first steps outside the den. The greatest danger it faces at this size is a hungry male polar bear.*

ABOVE *Snow petrels, true Antarctic-ice birds. They still, though, need exposed rock to breed on and will fly long distances inland to find suitable sites.*

ABOVE RIGHT *Brunnich's guillemots – Arctic summer breeders – flying back to the colony with fish for their chicks.*

and 98 per cent of that is found along the Antarctic Peninsula. This long arm of land extends further north than the rest of the continent, and so it enjoys slightly milder weather. When the sea ice starts to retreat each spring, the first bare rock to be released from winter's grip is on the peninsula, which is why so many breeding colonies of penguins and seals can be found here. This is the mild face of Antarctica. Certainly, on a good day in the height of summer when the sun is out, it is possible to walk around on the peninsula in no more than a thick shirt and a good fleece.

In most of the rest of Antarctica, wildlife has to wait much longer for the ice to retreat. But the world's most southerly breeding birds don't wait. Instead, they fly hundreds of miles inland each spring in their search for bare-rock nesting places. Snow petrels are true birds of the ice, and even when at sea, they never seem to be far from an iceberg. Small, elegant birds, all white bar their jet-black bills, they seem far too delicate to fly right up into the Antarctic continent. Yet each spring, they journey south as far as 345km (215 miles) from the edge of the continent to nest on remote nunataks. These spectacular spires of bare rock are the exposed summits of mountain ranges that, for the most part, are completely submerged under the vast depths of Antarctica's ice sheet.

The bare rock of nunataks is so precious that a particularly remote one, Smarthvaren, attracts hundreds of snow petrels and over half a million pairs of Antarctic petrels each spring. By October the cathedral-like spires of this nunatak are surrounded by a mosquito swarm of birds courting and preparing to lay their eggs. Southern polar skuas patrol the circling masses, stealing adults on the wing and feeding off the petrels' eggs and chicks.

The predatory skuas can only survive this far south because the petrels are here. The petrels, though, must find their food on the open ocean and have no option but to make regular 1000-km (600-mile) or so return journeys to feed their growing chicks.

Penguins, of course, are not able to fly, and most species must wait for summer and the ice to retreat far enough to give them access to the bare rock they need for nesting. The Adélie penguin, the most southerly nesting species, cannot wait and has no option but to walk over the still-frozen sea ice. The summer in the deep south is so short that late arrival at their traditional breeding sites would simply not leave enough time to complete their breeding cycle. With their black dinner jackets and comical rolling gaits, Adélies are the archetypal penguin. Their appearance on the distant horizon, some walking and others tobogganing on their bellies, is a true sign that the sun has returned to Antarctica and the short summer will soon be here.

THE POLAR SUMMER

June sees a real change in the Arctic as the ice begins to melt back in earnest. Now 24 hours of continuous daylight inject energy into the newly exposed ocean, and the phytoplankton (a mass of minute plants) starts to bloom. Copepods, small crustaceans that have spent the winter below 300m (985 feet), come up into shallow water to feed on the phytoplankton. They occur in enormous numbers and form the basis of the Arctic marine food chain.

THE BIGGEST HUNT IN THE SEA

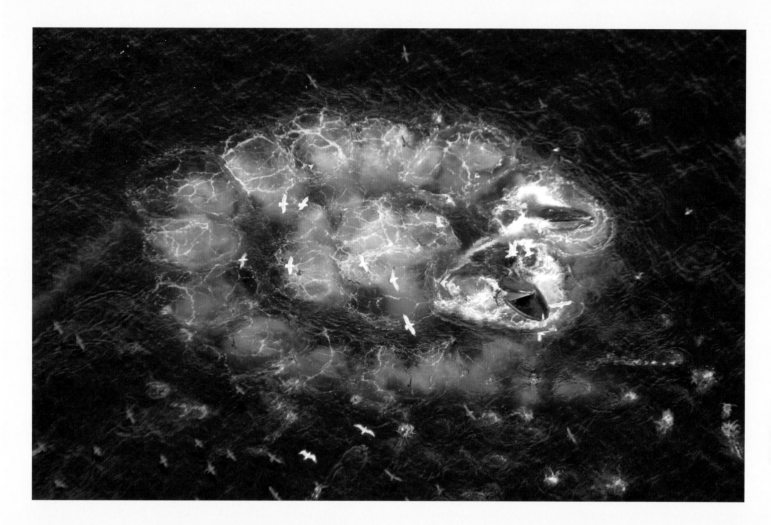

Humpbacks, the most regularly seen of Antarctica's whales, have several techniques for harvesting krill. If the swarms are dense and close to the surface, the whales simply open their cavernous mouths and lunge through the krill. Often, though, the whales will cooperate.

Working together like a row of tractors, they will all surface and lunge at the same moment, the whale in the middle possibly benefiting from the way the other giant mouths push the swarms towards the middle.

If a swarm is more dispersed and further from the surface, the whales cooperate in another way to concentrate the krill.

Diving down together in perfect synchrony, they then simultaneously release blasts of air from their blowholes. These blasts rise as columns of bubbles. At the surface, beautiful spiral patterns form as the 40-ton leviathans spiral round each other releasing their bubble nets. It seems that the krill swarms, frightened by the noise and disturbance produced by the streams of bubbles, tend to aggregate in the centre of the spiral. Finally, with mouths wide open, the huge whales emerge explosively at the surface and swallow up the concentrated crustacean soup (as above). Congregating seabirds dive down to mop up any remaining krill.

THE ICE-BREAKERS

At the top of the food chain is the bowhead whale – the only baleen (filter-feeding) whale that remains in Arctic waters all year round. Waiting out the winter in polynyas, or patches of open water at the edge of the sea ice, they are the first whales to head north again in April.

Their massive heads, protected with a layer of fibrous tissue, may be used to smash breathing holes through the winter ice. Calling to each other all the time, groups of these 100-ton giants will work together to pioneer a trail through the ice. Once in patches of open water, they open their cavernous mouths and hoover up copepods. They then sieve the tiny copepods out of the huge amounts of water they imbibe, using the largest baleens of any whale – each of these structures can contain more than 600 separate plates and be up to 4.5m (15 feet) long.

The pioneering bowheads are soon followed by the Arctic's only other resident whales – belugas and narwhals. They, too, spend the winter in open water and in summer follow the retreating ice north, using cracks, or leads, in the ice to penetrate as far as they can. Groups of narwhals have even been seen cooperating to break up the ice with their foreheads. They probably travel further north than any other whale, reaching as close as 322km (200 miles) from the North Pole. Narwhals and belugas are both toothed whales and feed principally on fish and squid rather than plankton.

ABOVE *Belugas using cracks in the ice to move north, following food. Along with bowheads and narwhals, they are the Arctic's only resident whales.*

THE KRILL CONNECTION

In Antarctic waters, there are no permanently resident whales, but as the ice retreats, six species visit: humpback, southern right, blue, fin, sei and minke. They are all baleen whales in search of the shrimp-like crustaceans known as krill, which they filter out of the water in huge quantities with their baleen plates.

Krill form the basis of the Antarctic food chain in much the same way as copepods do in the Arctic. Like copepods (also crustaceans), krill feed on phytoplankton (mainly diatoms) and occur in vast numbers. There is probably a greater mass of Antarctic krill than any other single species on Earth, with acoustic surveys estimating the total mass in the Southern Ocean at 100–500 million tons. In the summer, krill characteristically form into swarms, with concentrations of up to 30,000 individuals per cubic metre (nearly 23,000 per cubic yard), and it is these swarms that the whales are searching for. A blue whale may consume 3–4 tons of krill daily.

Having given birth to their calves in warm but nutrient-poor tropical waters, the southern whales follow the sun south to feed round the clock on krill in rich polar waters. They then migrate all the way back again in the winter. The record for the longest migration of any individual marine mammal is held by a humpback whale, which travelled 8330km (5175 miles) from the Antarctic Peninsula north to the Caribbean coast of Colombia.

Krill is also the staple diet of most of Antarctica's penguins. By mid-December, the height of the Antarctic summer, their eggs are starting to hatch, and it is essential that the sea ice has broken up far enough south to allow the adults immediate access to the sea so they can easily feed their growing chicks. The need for access means that even hardy Adélie penguins can breed no further south than the edge of the sea ice at its summer minimum. Chinstrap and gentoo penguins, which do not walk over the sea ice in the spring, are restricted to breeding further north still. All these species need to choose sites that are not only accessible from the sea but are also exposed enough for the wind to have blown winter snow away by the start of the breeding season. Such areas of bare rock are in short supply, and so penguins return to them year after year. Adélies and chinstraps can breed in enormous colonies. The largest Adélie one, at Cape Adare, covers at least 1.5 sq km (more than half a square mile) and contains an estimated 220,000 pairs. The noise and smell created by so many penguins racing to bring up their chicks in the short Antarctic summer is so great that you can tell you are approaching the colony when you are still miles downwind.

THE SOUTHERN INVASION

The break-up of the sea ice in the summer allows very few other seabirds access. Antarctica has just one visiting member of the cormorant family, the Antarctic, or blue-eyed, shag, and one true gull, the kelp, or Dominican, gull. The continent's only breeding tern, the Antarctic tern – a delicate white and silver-grey bird with a blood-red dagger of a bill – is joined each summer by its northern counterpart, the Arctic tern. Following the sun south, some Arctic terns undertake what is probably the longest of all bird migrations, flying more than 15,000km (9300 miles), if measured in a straight line, from their nesting grounds in the high Arctic right down south of the Antarctic Circle. In this way, they fit two summers at high latitudes into a single year and spend three quarters of their lives in near-continuous daylight, enabling them to feed virtually round the clock for most of their lives.

NORTHERN TENEMENTS

While only a handful of seabirds visit the Antarctic continent each year, in the Arctic, more than 50 different seabird species are busy breeding by the height of summer in June and July. Unlike the flightless penguins, which face no threats from land-based predators, birds breeding here have to deal with Arctic foxes and even hungry polar bears, which will resort to raiding birds' nests when the melting sea ice makes their usual seal prey inaccessible. The birds have developed a number of different strategies to deal with this problem. Many of the auks, such as razorbills or guillemots, nest high up on inaccessible cliff faces. These avian tower blocks are one of the Arctic's greatest spectacles, with tens of thousands of birds crowded together, using the space of every tiny ledge to lay their eggs.

Little auks, too, resort to numbers for protection – some colonies in Greenland contain more than a million breeding pairs. They also hide their nests under ground among the boulders of scree slopes, where Arctic foxes find it difficult to get at the chicks and eggs. But adults still get taken on the wing by glaucous gulls and even the occasional peregrine falcon.

LEFT *Brunnich's guillemots, breeding in their thousands on the narrow ledges of Rubini Rock in the Franz Josef Land archipelago, Russia. Surrounded by rich sea fishing, their remote basalt high-rise keeps them relatively free from predators.*

OPPOSITE, TOP TO BOTTOM
Snow bunting in full song. In spring, many northern species of birds flock to the Arctic to breed. With relatively warm temperatures, huge supplies of insects become available to feed to young chicks.

Little auks. In spring, these small birds move from the sea to Arctic islands in their hundreds of thousands to nest among the scree and in rock crevices away from predatory gulls and Arctic foxes.

An Arctic fox bringing a mouthful of lemmings back to her cubs at the den. In summer, chicks are also plentiful and will be gathered up for the cubs or stashed for harder times.

Willowherb mass flowering. Many plants survive in the Arctic by growing, flowering and setting seed, all in the space of the brief summer.

To reduce this risk, the little auks always return to their nesting colonies in dense, thousand-strong swarms of circling, calling birds. To sit in a little auk colony waiting for the birds to return together en masse has to be one of the most exciting of ornithological experiences. At one moment, all is quiet, and the scree hillside seems lifeless. Then on the horizon, you start to notice puffs of swirling smoke, which gradually get thicker. And then suddenly, thousands of little auks are all around you in a cacophony of calls and whirling black wings. It is impressive evidence that the Arctic Ocean can support an enormous amount of life.

BEAR NECESSITIES

By July, with only remnants of ice floes littering the open water, the Arctic's seabirds, seals and whales all have access to the best of the feeding grounds. But for polar bears, these times are tough. With no firm ice for hunting seals, they are forced to resort to aquatic stalking. They are strong swimmers and, using just their front legs as paddles, can keep going for many hours. Bears can easily travel between isolated ice floes in search of hauled-out seals and have been seen as far as 97km (60 miles) from the shore. Aquatic stalking relies on stealth. A bear will approach a seal slowly, keeping just the top of its head above the water, hoping it will not be seen before it makes its final grab. At this time of year, polar bears hunting on or around the ice catch seals once every five days. But as the ice continues to melt, success diminishes, and particularly in the south, polar bears are forced to feed on land. Apart from raiding birds' nests, bears will resort to scavenging for berries or almost anything edible to eke out this period of near-starvation. Some polar bears have even learnt to attack walruses, which are also forced to retreat to land when the ice disappears.

GOING FOR WALRUS

Walruses are bottom-feeders, using their whiskers to feel for clams and, occasionally, their massive tusks to plough the mud for them. Like most polar seals, they prefer the security of the sea ice as a place to give birth to their pups. But come the summer, they are forced

to retreat with their pups to land, where they moult. Even a polar bear, the world's largest land carnivore, finds it nearly impossible to wrestle with the world's largest seal – some adult walruses can weigh more than 1500kg (3300 pounds). But a hungry one may rush into the midst of a haul of walruses to try to snatch one of the relatively immobile pups. Adult walruses will aggressively defend their pups and can do real damage with their tusks. But for a polar bear near to starvation, a blubber-rich pup is worth the risk.

THE POLAR AUTUMN

The end of summer is the busiest time in penguin colonies, as the rush is on to finish breeding before the sea starts to freeze again. During the day, a colony is almost totally empty of adult birds, who are away searching for food for their growing chicks. The chicks are large enough now not to need the warmth of brooding adults, but in their parents' absence, they snuggle up together in large crèches to protect themselves from both the elements and a variety of predators and scavengers. In late afternoon, the adults start to return from a day's foraging out at sea. They appear even more business-like – seeming to hurry in the knowledge that the brief window of summer opportunity is coming to an end.

Their appearance provides more pickings for the sheathbills, Antarctica's dustmen – all-white birds, about the size of a jackdaw, with rather unattractive fleshy protuberances around the base of their bills. They are the continent's only truly land-based birds, which never go to sea to feed but get all they need by scavenging from others. Penguin eggs and droppings are an important part of their diet, but these confident, bold birds regularly intercept krill being passed from adult penguins to their chicks.

If sheathbills are the dustmen, giant petrels are Antarctica's vultures. With a powerful hooked bill and an enormous 2-m (6.5-foot) wingspan, a giant petrel is not only a scavenger but also an aggressive predator that hangs about penguin crèches looking for weak or isolated chicks. Grabbing a flipper or foot, a giant petrel will pull a squawking chick from the huddle and kill it.

After about two weeks in the crèche, the penguin chicks have reached about 70 per cent of adult weight, and their parents start to lead them to the coast, the adults anxious to get to sea to build up their reserves in preparation for moulting. But they face a final hurdle. Lurking just beneath the surface are leopard seals. Three metres (10 feet) long and with powerful teeth, they are the dominant Antarctic predators. Though up to 45 per cent of a leopard seal's diet is krill, penguins in the summer and seal pups in the spring are important to their diet. Come the autumn, when the penguin chicks start to fledge, they are waiting.

The race to complete breeding is so intense that Adélies, nesting as far south as 77 degrees, can produce fledged chicks in just 50–60 days. Gentoos are more relaxed and take 70–90 days, but they can breed no further south than 65 degrees. By the end of March, the days are quickly becoming shorter and the temperature is dropping. The sea starts to freeze, advancing north by about 4km (2.5 miles) a day – representing 103,600 sq km (40,000 square miles) of new ice every 24 hours. In front of the ice, practically all Antarctic wildlife – seals, birds and whales – is driven north and will not return until the following spring.

In the Arctic, September marks the end of the long summer days of endless sunshine and the start of the first storms. High on the cliffs, guillemot chicks ready to fledge have no option but to leap. It almost seems to be raining fledglings as hundreds take flight. The lucky few glide down and crash-land into the sea, which may be a long way below. Many more fall short and bounce across the tundra, where Arctic foxes eagerly await them.

BELOW *Musk oxen in defensive formation. In storm conditions or when wolves are about, they gather like this or in a circle surrounding the calves. In winter, they must find exposed areas where the snow cover is light enough for them to dig down to the vegetation. Protecting them against the cold is the longest known body-warming hair of any mammal, overlying an undercoat that can be up to 30cm (12 inches) thick in places.*

EXODUS

On the mainland, the short, intense growing season is coming to an end, and the Arctic's grazing and browsing animals are on the move south again. Each summer, huge herds of up to half a million caribou travel north to find good grazing before splitting up to have their calves. Come autumn, the herds form again and the caribou return south to the forest for the winter. Throughout this journey, they are harried by grey wolves, which are the widest-ranging (other than humans) of all the land predators. Like most large Arctic mammals, the wolves are larger than their southern relatives, their size and thicker fur insulating them from the cold. Packs usually consist of five to eight individuals, but when hunting is good, as many as 30 wolves work together to bring down caribou and their calves.

By the time the seabird colonies have fallen silent and the caribou have gone, polar bears that have spent the summer on land begin to gather along the coast. Churchill in Canada has the most southerly population, and each autumn, hundreds of polar bears wait there for the sea to freeze again. Males have mock fights to try out each other's strength and establish some form of hierarchy. But this enforced intimacy soon comes to an end, and the polar bears return to their usual, more solitary life hunting seals far out on the sea ice.

THE POLAR WINTER

Of the Arctic's 40 land mammals, only 12 remain year round to face the worst of the winter weather in the far north. The small ones, such as lemmings and voles, do not hibernate but survive by nibbling shoots and roots in networks of tunnels under the snow. The microclimate within the snow allows the little rodents to survive much further north than they would otherwise be able to. At the other end of the scale, huge musk oxen stay right out in the open. They are shielded from the elements by a waterproof and windproof layer of long, matted guard hairs. Beneath this protective layer is a dense layer of insulating downy hair. If the winter snows cover their summer grazing, the musk oxen move to higher, more wind-blown ground. Here much of the snow is blown away, and they can dig for partly buried vegetation. When the winter storms get particularly fierce, these 400-kg (885-pound) giants gather together in a circle like a wagon train under attack. Standing close together for warmth, and with all their massive heads and horns facing out against the elements, the oxen can brave both the worst of the winter winds and any hardy wolf packs still in the area.

Once the sea is frozen, the Arctic seals, whales and birds that get their food from the ocean have no option but to head south in search of open water. But on the land, eight non-migratory birds manage to remain year round. The ptarmigan, a grouse that turns white in the winter, survives much as the musk oxen do by rooting out shoots and seeds hidden under thinner snow cover. Tiny snow and Lapland buntings, which feed mostly on insects in the summer, revert to seeds in the winter. Along with the Arctic and common redpoll, these little birds live year round in the Arctic but tend to move further south as supplies start to dwindle. Two predatory birds remain: the common raven, which is a scavenger, and the snowy owl, which survives by taking the occasional lemming or vole foolish enough to stick its head out from the security of its winter burrow.

ABOVE *A southern giant petrel scavenges a seal carcass. A strong sense of smell helps the birds locate carrion – their main food source. But they will also hang around penguin colonies waiting to pick off stray chicks or vulnerable adults, killing them with their large, hooked beaks.*

TOP *A juvenile male eider tosses back an urchin grabbed from the sea bottom in the frozen Hudson Bay. Unlike other eiders and most Arctic birds, the Hudson Bay eider ducks don't migrate to escape winter. Instead they survive by feeding in breaks in the ice or oases of open water – polynyas – kept from freezing by tidal currents. Here they can dive for mussels and urchins, which they swallow whole and grind up in their stomachs.*

During the worst four months of winter, the female polar bears are snug within their maternal dens. Insulated by the snow, a den's temperature can be 20°C (36°F) higher than outside, and there are no problems with wind-chill. For the males left out on the sea ice, it is the cruel storms of December and January that are hardest to bear. The best they can do to protect themselves from the biting wind is to hunker down behind a ridge in the ice. To some extent, it is the polar bear's great size that helps it weather the cold, but what of the far smaller Arctic fox, which also remains on the sea ice all through the winter? It survives the dark months shadowing the bears, living on the scraps that drop from the table of the Arctic's top predator.

THE COLDEST PLACE ON EARTH

Winter conditions in Antarctica are far harsher than those in the Arctic. Arctic winter temperatures may drop as low as −50°C (−58°F) for short periods, but Antarctica's can remain a steady −70°C (−94°F) for weeks on end. Towards the centre of the continent, up on the polar plateau, no life at all remains year round other than a few tiny lichens growing on remote nunataks. Even at the milder edge of the continent, only one bird and one mammal sit out the dreadful conditions of the Antarctic winter. For the hardy few people overwintering at the research stations dotted around the edge of the continent, it is a time to batten down the hatches. Most scientific research is suspended until the following

BELOW *A young polar bear using the snow as a blanket against the extreme cold. Winter is a desperate time for polar bears. Though temperatures in the Arctic never reach the depths of those in the Antarctic, they can still be lethal. Those bears not in breeding dens take refuge from the wind behind ridges and in snow holes.*

summer, and everyone concentrates on keeping the stations safe and working. A failed generator or, even worse, a fire can quickly turn into a life-threatening disaster.

The Weddell seal breeds further south than any mammal on Earth. Perhaps the most attractive of all Antarctic seals, it is 3m (10 feet) long, with a grey coat beautifully patterned with black spots. Unlike crabeaters, which choose to live among the broken pack ice to the north, Weddell seals have opted for permanent fast ice that never breaks up even in the summer. To survive here through the winter, Weddells maintain permanent breathing holes in the ice. Their lives are split into two very distinct halves separated by a few feet of ice. Surfacing through their breathing holes, they face the worst conditions on the planet. Beneath the ice, wind is unknown, year-round temperatures are never lower than a comfortable −1.8°C (29°F) and the seals have access to a year-round supply of food. But keeping the breathing holes open through the winter comes at a price. The Weddells must constantly grind away at the ice on the edge of their breathing holes to stop them freezing over. This relentless task damages their teeth and is probably the main reason why Weddells live only 20 years, while crabeaters survive for almost twice as long.

THE EMPEROR'S TRIUMPH

In early April, just as the sea ice is really starting to form and all the rest of Antarctica's wildlife is heading north, the emperor penguin heads south. More than a metre (3 feet) tall

BELOW *Emperor penguins, the only birds in the Antarctic to weather the extreme winters. They lay their eggs in winter, the males gathering on the sea ice to incubate them. The only way to survive the cold is to huddle together – at the heart of a huddle, heat loss may be reduced by 50 per cent.*

and twice the weight of the king penguin, emperors are elegant birds that truly deserve their name. Breaking all the rules of nature, they lay their eggs in autumn and incubate them for four months through the worst of the winter weather. They are the only birds that lay their eggs on ice, usually choosing predictable fast ice, which does not break up before they finish breeding at the end of the following summer.

All these colonies are in the deep south between 66 and 78 degrees, and even today, nobody is sure how many emperors there are. So far, about 40 different colonies have been found at remote locations all around the continent, with new colonies still being discovered. The largest contain about 40,000 birds, and the total population is thought to be about 160,000 breeding pairs.

The female lays her single egg in early May but almost immediately passes it to the male. He carefully balances it in a brood pouch just above his feet, which keeps it warm at a temperature that can differ by up to 80°C (144°F) from the temperature outside. The female then heads straight back to sea to feed up through the winter. She will not return for 65 days, leaving the male to survive the long nights of winter darkness. With temperatures down to −70°C (−94°F) and winds of 160kph (100mph), the males huddle

close together. The huddle is constantly shifting slowly round so that all the penguins take their fair share of the exposed positions. At the heart of the huddle, heat loss may be reduced by 50 per cent.

It is not until mid-July that the females finally return from the open ocean. The sun has only just begun its journey south from the northern hemisphere, and the males still see only an hour or two of distant daylight each day. The sea ice is also still near its maximum extent, and the females may have to walk 160km (100 miles) back over the ice to reach the colony. They must time their return perfectly. Once the chick has hatched, the male can only give it a single feed with a special meal he preserves all winter in his gullet. He can only maintain his chick for 10–15 days before his own near-starvation forces him to abandon it and head for open water. By the time he finally makes it back to sea, he will have fasted for 115 days – a record for any bird – and lost half his own body weight.

This remarkable feat allows the emperor penguin to break all the rules. By surviving through the world's worst winter weather, a male ensures the egg will hatch out at the very start of the polar summer. By autumn, the chick will be strong enough to head off to sea on its own, and the emperor penguin will have triumphed over the greatest seasonal change on our planet.

3

the great forests

Between the poles and the equator lie huge tracts

of forest. They are fuelled by sunshine and water,

but the quantities of these vary hugely

with the seasons, which has far-reaching effects

for both the wildlife living there and for

the health of the whole planet.

The seasonal forests act as lungs for our planet. They produce oxygen that we breathe and remove carbon dioxide from the air by locking it up in wood, they convert the Sun's energy into a form animals can eat, and they regulate the supply of fresh water by soaking up what falls as rain and releasing it back into the air slowly as vapour. Though this same process happens most vigorously at the equator, where there is no variation in day length and therefore no seasons to limit the process, seasonal forests cover a far larger area than equatorial ones. The fact that these forests span such a great range of latitudes and seasonal variations means the trees and animals they shelter need to take extraordinary measures to survive the extremes.

THE GREAT NORTHERN FORESTS

In the barren wilderness just outside the town of Churchill in Canada, you can stand among shrubby, stunted trees that are lower than chest-height. They appear to grow in a belt with a distinct edge. To one side is endless Arctic tundra, to the other a motley collection of thinly spaced miniaturized trees. This is the tree line – the most northerly point where it's possible for a tree to grow – and this is where the seasonal forests begin. Most of these stunted trees are conifers, though at ankle height there will be a few Arctic willow and scrubby birch.

The position of the tree line varies with altitude and maritime influence, but it is usually at about 65 degrees. Though the composition of tree species depends on whether you are standing in North America, Scandinavia or Russia, the principle is the same. There are at least 30 days in the year when the average temperature climbs above 10°C (50°F) – the minimum requirement to build a tree. Fewer days than this, and the growing season is too short to build a trunk or for new, delicate needles to reach maturity before the brutal winter arrives.

Winter temperatures on the tree line can drop to −50°C (−58°F). The sun barely rises for months at a time, and for seven months, all water is locked up in snow and ice, leaving the area as dry as any desert. Such severe conditions require special survival equipment. The needles of conifers have a small surface area and a waxy covering that helps reduce water loss. They also contain little fluid, which lessens the chance of ice crystals forming inside them. Their dark appearance is due to the efficient pigments needed to catch the

ABOVE *The tree line marking the beginning of the great tree belt (here at Hudson Bay, Canada). Beyond this point there are just not enough days in the year when the temperature is high enough for trees to grow.*

OPPOSITE *A northern conifer forest in the grip of winter. Conifers are adapted to withstand water loss and freezing. They are also designed to bend under the weight of snow and shed heavy loads of it.*

PREVIOUS PAGE, TOP *Mixed temperate woodland, Japan.* BOTTOM *A group of golden snub-nosed monkeys, China.*

weak, low-angled light that falls on these latitudes. Even so, it's an uphill struggle: the growing season is so short that a conifer seedling takes 25 years to rise above the tundra scrub and resemble a tree, and many die long before they reach maturity.

Animals are scarce among these stunted trees and shrubs. To some extent, this is merely a place where polar creatures visit in the winter for shelter and where animals from more southerly climes only pass through in the short, intense summer. The woolly bear moth is one of the few permanent residents, and its existence says much about the hardships of life on the tree line. By the time the caterpillar hatches, only three or four weeks of the summer remain. It consumes dwarf willow at a ferocious rate but cannot eat enough to pupate before the onset of winter. So it spins a silken cocoon to hibernate in. During the winter, the caterpillar freezes solid. When the snow retreats in early June, it thaws out and starts to feed again. But the stunted vegetation is a wretched food source, and the caterpillar is unable to turn into a moth by the time its second winter approaches. Yet again it freezes solid, thaws in spring and resumes feeding. This cycle repeats itself for up to 12 years until the caterpillar can finally complete its metamorphosis. It then has just a few days to find a mate and lay eggs before it dies.

THE VAST GREEN DESERT

As you head south, the trees become larger and more densely packed, forming a swathe of green that stretches from horizon to horizon. In Canada, this is called the boreal forest after Boreas, the Greek god of the north wind; in Russia it is known as the taiga, but the words have become interchangeable. The forest is so vast that, when viewed from space, it appears as a massive green belt that girdles the top of the planet, broken only by ocean. Nearly 2000km (1240 miles) wide in some areas and almost 10,000km (6200 miles) long, the belt covers about 4 million sq km (1.5 million square miles) in total and contains a third of all the trees on Earth. Half of the forest is in Russia, a third in Canada and the rest in Alaska and Scandinavia. During peak growth in the short northern summer, it absorbs so much carbon dioxide and gives out so much oxygen that it significantly changes the composition of the Earth's atmosphere.

The view from space gives the impression of an almost endless Eden. But in many respects, the taiga is a green desert. There are frequently only one or two species of tree for hundreds of miles, and they grow slowly. Russian larches can take 60 years to add an inch to their girth – 10 times longer than conifers in temperate areas. Nor are there many animals. Conifer needles are unpalatable, and though capercaillie and blue grouse can eat the younger needles, as can porcupines, other creatures scrape by on moss, lichen or the seasonal seed crop. The situation is just as bleak on the forest floor. Instead of a rich leaf-litter crawling with creatures engaged in decomposition, there is just a thick, dry mat of needles that breaks down very slowly, leaving an acid soil. The nutrient recycling is done almost entirely by specialist fungi that surround the trees' shallow roots. The fungi digest the needles, freeing up chemicals for the tree to absorb, and in return receive nutrients from the tree that they are unable to make. If it were not for this relationship, trees might find it hard to maintain their grip on these latitudes, especially as the soils throughout the boreal zone were left by the retreating glaciers after the last ice age and are stony and poor.

BELOW *A capercaillie hen feeding on young pine needles, Finland. Very few animals can digest the leaves of northern conifers, with the result that the great forests of the north are comparatively empty.*

OPPOSITE *Conifer desert. Northern conifer forests are often composed of just one or two species – a monoculture with an almost bare forest floor.*

ABOVE *Lapland snowscape. In winter, there is little sign of life in the northern forests other than up in the treetops and under the snow blanket.*

For much of the year this is a fairy-tale land cloaked in snow. There is no better way to experience it than by drifting over the forest at low level in a balloon. The smaller conifers barely look like trees, more like stooped figures dressed in white. The larger ones are lean with a conical shape, which encourages the snow to slide off, but glistening icicles still hang from every branch. Every footprint is etched in the powdery snow and is almost unmissable. You might see the print of a hare or lynx – if you are very lucky, a wolverine – but great distances can pass beneath you without the snow being blemished by a single living thing. The overwhelming impression is of emptiness.

But prints alone can be misleading. Birds such as crossbills stay in the treetops. They survive here all year round by using their extraordinary beaks to extract seeds from cones. To work efficiently, the beak must be exact, and three species with three different kinds of bill have evolved to eat the cones of fir, spruce and pine respectively.

Some rodents, such as lemmings, stay alive under the snow, leaving no obvious sign of their existence. The ceiling of snow actually insulates them from the cold and gives them some small protection from predators, though snowy owls can still hear them moving about and come crashing, talons first, through their roofs. The lemmings survive by chewing roots or eating seeds that they stored during the summer.

THE MEMORY BIRD

Clark's nutcracker survives here by combining a special tool with a remarkable memory. It uses its powerful bill to prise open cones of trees such as the whitebark pine and remove the nuts. When food is abundant, it hides nuts throughout the forest as a reserve for leaner times. The nutcracker will cache at least 30,000 nuts each year, but instead of placing them in just a few larders, as a squirrel does, it hides them in up to 5000 small ones. One possible explanation is that the smell of a large cache would attract bears, in which case, the bird could lose a large proportion of its reserve in one hit. The nutcracker is able to remember the location of about 75 per cent of its stores – a phenomenal hit-rate, especially considering the bird has a brain not much bigger than the nuts it hides. The interesting question is whether the remaining 25 per cent is actually forgotten or whether it is deliberately not collected. Curiously, birds seem to cache 25 per cent more nuts than they normally need. Are they compensating for memory loss, or are they caching extra as forward planning in case of a particularly hard winter? Either way the pine tree benefits: its reproduction is totally dependent on the 25 per cent of nuts left in the ground. Neither the bird nor the tree could survive without the other.

GIANTS

Though the northern forests stretch right around the globe, the animals are remarkably similar throughout. The enormous deer with giant antlers known as a moose in North America is called an elk in Europe, but it is exactly the same animal. Caribou and reindeer are virtually identical. Wolverine, lynx and bear are little different from Canada to Russia. This is presumably an indication of how similar the forest is throughout its unbroken range. The exception that proves the rule can be found in Siberia, for only here can you find tigers.

The residents of these forests are not just similar but are also giants. Larger animals, pound for pound, have less surface area than smaller ones and so lose less heat. Wolverines are much the biggest kind of weasel, moose are the world's largest deer, and the Siberian tiger is easily the biggest cat alive, dwarfing the tigers that have evolved on tropical islands

ABOVE *A common crossbill. It levers open pine cones with its crossed beak and extracts the seeds with its tongue. Crossbills are among the few birds adapted to feed on conifer cones.*

ABOVE LEFT *Clark's nutcracker retrieving whitebark pine nuts stashed in bark. Whitebark cones need the nutcracker to rip them open and 'plant' the seeds by stashing them. Tree and bird depend on each other.*

THE GLUTTON

The wolverine is an animal steeped in legend. In some areas it is considered a cross between a wolf and a bear, in others a go-between with the spirit world, but throughout its range it has a reputation for ferocity and cunning.

The real wolverine is the largest member of the mustelid family (badgers, weasels and the like) and well suited for the challenges of boreal life. Opportunities to eat in the frozen north can be few and far between, but the wolverine stacks the odds in its favour. It will aggressively scavenge carrion, driving even wolves and bears from a carcass. It is also an active hunter and capable of catching anything from a mouse to a reindeer. Though its prey animals are usually rodents, squirrels and hares, a 20-kg (44-pound) wolverine is able to bring down a 150-kg (332-pound) deer by leaping on its back and biting through its neck. The wolverine's other name is glutton, and indeed it can eat a huge amount in one sitting, and whatever is left over will be cached in the snow for later. Food is scarce, and so wolverine territories need to be vast. Females can range over 500 sq km (193 square miles), but a male's range can be three times that.

such as Sumatra. Larger animals can also travel further, lay down bigger reserves of fat and go for longer between meals – all useful talents in a barren land where animals frequently need to travel great distances to find enough to eat.

SUMMERS OF REPRODUCTION

Winters in the boreal forest are long and hard, but the summers are intense. In June and July, there is no night to interrupt growth, and herb plants seem to spring up from nowhere and produce flowers almost as quickly. Insect larvae flourish in boggy pools, their life-cycles so accelerated that, within days, their adult forms are flying over the same lakes, mating and laying eggs. Groundhogs wake after eight months of hibernation, with a busy schedule – just three months in which to breed and lay down enough fat to survive the next winter. Bears emerge from a more fitful sleep, during which time cubs were born inside the den. They set to work eating the first berries to ripen. Moose can be found in the ponds feeding on water plants that are growing vigorously in the near-24-hour sunshine.

The biggest change comes with the influx of migrant birds. Finches and thrushes that moved south for the winter to feed in the deciduous woodlands are back to feed their chicks on the booming populations of insects, which are buzzing and crawling everywhere you look. Birds of prey such as goshawks and owls arrive to feast on young songbirds and the multiplying rodents. Geese can be heard overhead, en route to the extensive grazing now available on the tundra. But the wildlife is still not concentrated within the conifer forest, rather at its edges in the birch, willow and aspen that fringe the lakes and marshy areas.

OPPOSITE TOP *A bull moose – the world's biggest deer– in Alaska. To survive in the cold forests, it helps to be a giant with a small surface area compared to its bulk.*

OPPOSITE BOTTOM *Amur tiger – another giant of the northern forest. A big predator needs a huge territory with plentiful prey, and so logging of Siberia's forests and poaching of its prey, together with increased hunting of the tiger itself, mean that this subspecies is now highly endangered.*

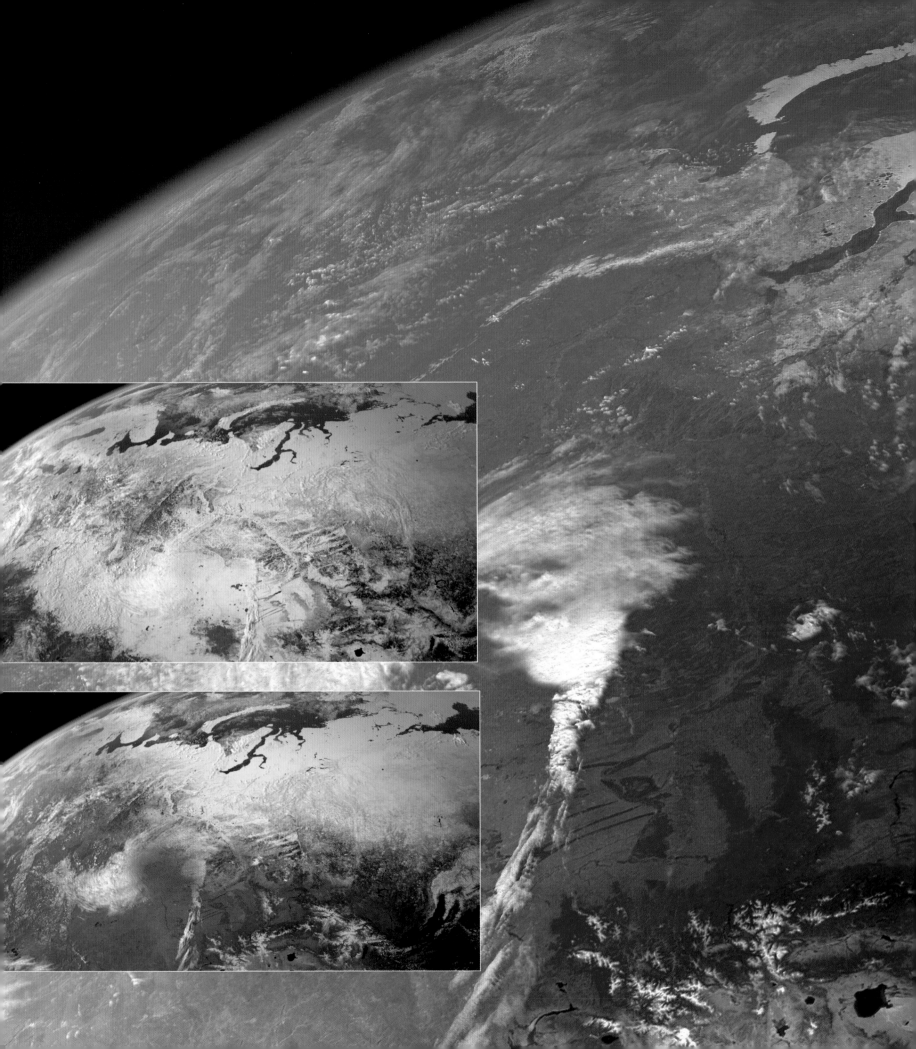

THE TEMPERATE LIFE

Conifers reign supreme between the latitudes of 70 and 55 degrees, but as you travel south, the summers lengthen and broadleaf trees such as birch, beech, aspen and maple begin to dominate. Broad leaves are far more efficient at trapping sunlight than needles but less resistant to freezing, and their large, thin surfaces lose far more water. Trees make up for this by dropping their leaves in winter. The costs of growing new ones in spring are more than offset by the gains from having more productive leaves during the longer growing season.

THE EDIBLE FOREST

The switch to disposable leaves brings great richness to the forest calendar: the ground-flowers of spring, the heavy green darkness of summer, the colours of autumn and the stillness of winter. But the greatest impact is on the animals. Deciduous leaves make excellent food, unlike conifer needles, which are virtually inedible. Shake the branch of an oak in summer, and lots of leaf-eating creatures will drop out, from sap-sucking aphids and the larvae of butterflies and moths to their predators – ladybirds, wasps, spiders and beetles. These small creatures will be collected by birds such as blue-tits and treecreepers – which as they flit from branch to branch, are in turn hunted by birds such as sparrowhawks.

This edibility extends beyond the living leaves. Under the tree you will find springtails, millipedes, centipedes, slugs, snails and many tinier creatures involved in leaf decomposition. By comparison, the sterile mat of dry needles beneath a conifer forest is virtually lifeless. Many broadleaves also defend their leaves with chemicals, but their priority is to grow quickly before the leaves of rival trees block out their light. A proportion of the sunlight trapped by leaves will therefore flow to other creatures, fuelling an elaborate web of life. In a conifer forest, much of that energy is locked away in giant columns of standing wood.

BROOD X

Few creatures illustrate the edible woodland better than the periodical cicada. If you had been in Indiana, USA, in May 2004, you would have been near the epicentre of a huge insect spectacle. In 1987, the adult cicadas of 'Brood X' laid their eggs on the leaves of deciduous trees, particularly those such as maples with a lot of sugar in their sap. The eggs hatched and tiny nymphs dropped to the ground, dug down and plugged their syringe-like mouthparts into the roots. For the next 17 years, they fed underground, unnoticed. In May, they began reversing their maiden journey, climbing from the soil and marching up towards the leafy branches. At 4cm (1.6 inches) long, they were a thousand times larger than when they first crawled underground. They climbed from the soil in their millions, marching like zombies towards anything upright and coating the bark of trees. Once high enough, the nymphs stopped moving. Underneath the crisp exoskeletons, their bodies were reorganizing. The adults that emerged were soft and white, but within two hours, they were dark, hard and able to make the deafening screech for which they are famous. After 17 years underground, the cicadas now had 10 days to find a mate and lay their eggs before dying.

Everywhere, other animals were exploiting the glut. But the cicadas' defence was

OPPOSITE TOP *Spring blooming of bluebells in an English wood. Most temperate woodland plants flower in the spring before the woodland canopy closes over.*

OPPOSITE MIDDLE *The opening of the beechwood canopy in late spring. By summer, very little light will reach the woodland floor.*

OPPOSITE BOTTOM *Autumn leaf-fall. Red and gold pigments are revealed as the chlorophyll that colours leaves green is withdrawn in advance of the leaves being discarded for the winter.*

PREVIOUS PAGE *The Russian part of the vast belt of taiga forest, August.*
INSET TOP *In midwinter, January.*
INSET BOTTOM *In spring, April.*

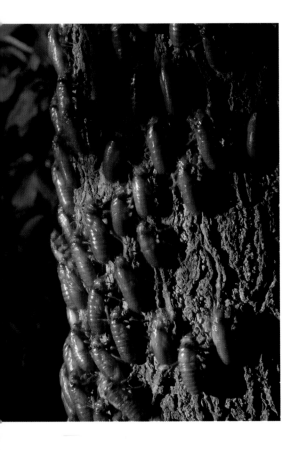

numbers. More than a trillion had emerged in just a few nights. There were birds too full to take off, and chipmunks gorged to the point of vomiting. This predator-swamping effect is presumably why cicadas synchronize their emergence. How do nymphs underground know when 17 years has passed? Perhaps they taste the surge of sugary sap or sense the drop of pressure in autumn when the trees lose their leaves and can somehow count the cycles.

The ecological significance of this event is written in the growth rings of the trees in the cicada belt. Once every 17 years – the exact years that Brood X emerges – the spacing between rings widens, representing a spurt in growth. Why? On an emergence year, all the nymphs stop sucking sap, releasing a massive burden on the trees. And in the aftermath, a trillion rotting adults release back into the soil all at once the nutrients accumulated over 17 years.

THE ICE-AGE LEGACY

The structure of temperate forests worldwide is quite similar. A few large tree species such as oaks and beeches form the canopy, while smaller trees such as maples, alders, dogwoods and hawthorns make up the understorey, which is more complex than in the tropics because of the extra light that penetrates to the forest floor. But the range of species that make up this structure varies with the history of the landmass. The ice ages had an enormous effect on tree diversity in the northern hemisphere. At the start of the last one, 80,000 years ago, when sheets of ice started creeping down from the north, trees in Europe were prevented from 'migrating' south to warmer climes by the west-east barrier of the Alps and the

Pyrenees. But in North America, where the mountain ranges all run north-south, trees were able to move south through the valleys. When the ice retreated, the American trees were able to recolonize, whereas many of the European trees died out. This may explain why there are 3000 species of deciduous trees in North America and only 1000 in Europe.

Broadleaf trees make excellent timber and, once felled, leave rich soils ideal for agriculture. Consequently, few northern hemisphere deciduous woodlands remain intact, and the area they cover has shrunk to less than a quarter of that of the past. In North America, there would have been a great swathe of forest, from the Gulf of Mexico up to the Great Lakes in the north. Through western and central Europe into Asia, there would have been an enormous forest belt, sandwiched between the Alps and the Pyrenees to the south and the boreal forest to the north, fading out at the Urals in western Russia and reappearing in the Amur region of eastern Russia and parts of China and Japan.

THE GREAT WILDWOOD

When the last ice age ended in Europe 10,000 years ago, the land was rapidly recolonized by broadleaf forests until 90 per cent of it was wooded. Around 5000 years ago, its rapid deforestation began. In England, the Domesday census of 1086 showed that there was already less forest than there is today. The situation was similar in France, and the rest of Europe was not far behind. To see what the middle of Europe would have looked like before this, you need to visit Bialowieza – a 1500-sq-km (580-square-mile) block of old-growth

OPPOSITE *Brood X cicadas climbing up a tree trunk to the point where they transform into adults – the end of a 17-year underground life feeding on the sugar-rich sap of the tree.*

BELOW *The wildwood of Bialowieza, a natural jumbled mass of trunks, fallen branches and rotting wood – fuel for a complex woodland society.*

forest on the border of Poland and Belarus. Only the very core of this forest is virgin – unlike anywhere else in Europe. There are large trees here, but they are hidden within a clutter of trees at every stage of growth – very different from the more familiar oak and beech forests, which are unnaturally full of large trees, either because these were all planted at the same time or because livestock grazing has prevented seedlings growing into an understorey. In most European woods, dying trees are felled for safety reasons, and fallen trees are removed for firewood. But in Bialowieza, there is wood at every stage of decay, from standing dead trees to fallen trunks so rotten that they blur the boundary between wood and soil.

The forest's final quality is only revealed to the visitor patient enough to sit quietly under a tree. After 15 minutes or so, forest life resumes. Birds flit past and the undergrowth rustles with small mammals. Stay longer and you may glimpse less common animals such as stoats or weasels, wild boar or even forest bison. This forest bustles with life. To a large extent this final quality is related to the first two. Some of the larger creatures such as wolves and bison survive here because they are protected from hunting, but most of the other 58 species of mammals and 200 species of birds thrive because it is a healthy forest that has a rich variety of tree species at every stage of growth and wood that is allowed to rot, fuelling food chains and completing the recycling of nutrients back to the trees.

FORESTS OF MANY SEASONS

A temperate deciduous woodland is so different in each of the seasons that you can only start to understand it by looking at all of its many faces. Spring in Europe starts in late February, as winter begins to relax its grip and resident songbirds start to stake out their territories. Soon after, blackbirds and thrushes begin building their nests. By the end of March the first migrant birds return – chiffchaffs from the Mediterranean and willow warblers from Africa. Snowdrops and primroses flower early, before the trees are in leaf and block out the light. By the time the beech and sycamore leaves open, spring is at full pace. Bluebells carpet the forest floor just before the canopy closes in late April, about the time the cuckoos arrive.

If spring is the season of change, summer is the time of productivity. There is warmth, plenty of sunlight and the soil is moist. Vegetation is growing rapidly, and animals are breeding at speed. Increasing numbers of insects are being eaten by small mammals and birds, which in turn are being eaten by stoats, weasels and owls. A new wave of flowers, from willowherbs to foxgloves, bloom on the forest floor, but growth in this layer is dropping off as the leaf-cover on the larger trees reaches its full extent and steals most of the light.

Autumn is when the days shorten and the air begins to cool. The roar of red deer can be heard echoing through the forest as males prepare for the annual rut. The migrant birds start to leave, and many resident creatures rush around making preparations for winter – hedgehogs and dormice store fat on their bodies before hibernation, squirrels and jays stock their larders. Trees begin to close down their leaves, withdrawing what nutrients they can. Sap stops flowing into the leaves, causing chemical changes that turn the forest a succession of spectacular colours. With dampness and decay come toadstools, the only visible sign of filamentous fungal networks that stretch through the forest.

An eerie silence descends. Most insects have died, leaving only eggs to continue their line when conditions improve. Next year's leaves are also in suspended animation, wrapped in

OPPOSITE *The colours that precede the first fall of autumn leaves, North America. Temperate trees have an inbuilt mechanism, perhaps triggered by decreasing daylight, that causes them to pull back nutrients from their leaves and break down the green chlorophyll in advance of the frosts that will destroy their cells. The pigments that show are the remaining yellow carotenoids and the newly formed red anthocyanines.*

BELOW *Fungi – here sulphur tuft – the great woodland recyclers, helping to decompose fallen plant material and also forming relationships, supplying trees with vital nutrients.*

protective waterproof buds in place since before autumn. Mammals such as badgers and weasels still move around; others such as dormice are in a deep sleep. Decomposition goes on, but slowly and at a speed dependent on the temperature. The leaves that fell will have vanished in two years, much of their mineral content reabsorbed by the trees.

BELOW *A marbled murrelet chick balancing on a redwood branch – the tree equivalent of a cliff ledge. Its parents are at sea fishing.*

OPPOSITE *Pacific-coast temperate rainforest trees, host to a community of epiphytes – plants that use them as a surface on which to grow, gaining moisture from the mists and heavy rain and nutrients from the accumulation of litter that gathers.*

RAIN GIANTS

On the Pacific coast of North America is the world's largest remaining temperate rainforest. This forest grows where you would expect broadleaves, but here are conifers – 50-million-year-old relics from a time when the planet was moister and moisture-adapted conifers could be found across Europe and into Asia (modern conifers are adapted for life in dry places, hot or cold). This forest is often described as 'cathedral-like', and it is easy to see why. Walking among groves of giant Douglas fir, hemlock, Sitka spruce and coastal redwood is a humbling experience.

Most of the forest is on the Olympic Peninsula straddling the US and Canada, an area that gets 381cm (150 inches) of rain a year – three times more than is needed to qualify as a rainforest. Heading south, the rains become more seasonal, and the summer months would be too dry were it not for the daily fogs that roll in from the Pacific and allow isolated stands of giant redwood to grow as far south as Big Sur in northern California. During the 'fog months', redwood needles are drenched in mist for half the day, and an extraordinary 'reverse transpiration' occurs: instead of water being collected by the roots and transported to the needles by rising sap, the moisture is collected by the needles and carried by the sap towards the roots. Mist also settles on needles and trickles down the tree to the soil, where it is soaked up by roots near the surface. A redwood receives up to 40 per cent of its water 'raked' from the air in this way. But being so reliant on water has limited the distribution of redwoods.

Unlike northern conifers, redwoods do not need to shed snow, and instead of a conical shape, they have the most complicated three-dimensional structure of any tree, with many canopy layers at different heights on the same tree. These form when horizontal side shoots from major limbs meet and fuse with others, forming giant platforms on which needles collect and other plants grow. These mist-watered aerial gardens receive far more light than ever reaches the forest floor and support high-living communities of plants and animals.

The biological mass of these forests can reach 2000 tons per hectare (810 per acre), more than a tropical rainforest, but it is made up almost entirely of standing wood from a handful of tree species. These are quiet places where the cackle of a jay or the hammering of a pileated woodpecker echo through the forest unmuddled by other sounds. One of the most curious creatures found here is the marbled murrelet. Murrelets are ocean-foraging seabirds, and so the lack of food among the conifers is of no consequence. They use the giant redwoods as other seabirds use cliff ledges. A single egg is laid on a narrow branch high above the forest floor. Once the chick hatches, the parents commute to the ocean to tend it, which means it spends most of its time alone, perched precariously on the branch. Just prior to fledging, the chick plucks out its remaining down, leaving only its flight feathers. After nightfall, it leaps from its branch and somehow finds its own way to the sea.

LEFT TO RIGHT *A bristlecone, at least 1000 years old and probably older, growing on California's White Mountains. Bristlecones grow in the rainshadow of the Sierra Nevada to the west, where less than 30cm (12 inches) of rain falls, mainly as snow in winter, and so growth is extremely slow. But that also means there is little competition with other trees and little fungal rot.*

Giant sequoia growing on the wet, eastern slopes of the Sierra Nevada. Trees older than 1000 years are still growing, and the soft, fibrous bark may be 60cm (2 feet) thick – ideal protection against cold, wind, snow and fire, though they rely on fire to thin out invasive firs and pines.

Preparations for climbing one of the tallest coastal redwoods in Jedediah Smith Redwoods State Park. The lowest branch is more than 60m (200 feet) up.

A redwood nearly 100m (330 feet) tall. The tallest of all and the tallest in the world is more than 112m (370 feet) high.

THE SOUTHERN MIRROR

As you head south from the equator, the length of the summer begins to shorten just as it does in the north, and the impact on the distribution of forest is similar. But the full extent of this parallel is never realized, as there is no land sufficiently far south to equate to the boreal forests that circle the Arctic. Altitude does, however, have a similar effect on the growing season, and for this reason there are areas in southern Chile and Argentina that have tree-line habitats populated by hardy conifers.

The most famous and beautiful of the conifers is the monkey-puzzle, or araucaria, which has a prehistoric appearance, with leaves like reptilian scales, and has existed since the time of the dinosaurs. It populates the snow-capped slopes of volcanoes in the Andean mountain range and completes a truly otherworldly scene. Like trees in the boreal north, the monkey-puzzle's horny leaves are well protected against moisture loss and are tough and inedible. Only the seeds are worth eating, and these are extracted from the cones by slender-billed parakeets – specialists at the job, much like the crossbills and nutcrackers of the north.

If you travel down the slopes – as though heading towards the equator in latitude – you reach a forest that parallels those on the Pacific coast of North America. The Valdivian coastal rainforest in Chile and Argentina is the world's second largest temperate rainforest after those of the American northwest. It is constantly drenched by rains generated by wet air from the Pacific rising against the foothills of the Andes. Even Charles Darwin, presumably a hardy, outdoor sort, was forced to complain about the 'gloom and ceaseless rain' of the place.

One tree type in particular towers from pristine areas of this forest. The alerce, or Patagonian cypress, can grow to more than 50m (165 feet) in height and live for 3500 years.

Like the redwood, it is highly valued for timber and, as a result, is now scarce. In Chile, it is protected in places such as Los Alerces National Park.

The Valdivian forest is peculiar – dripping wet, dense, tangled and, with the exception of the occasional alerce, low in stature. Clearings are often impassable due to the abundance of gunnera, a plant (familiar to gardeners) with enormous leaves and spiny stems that grows to a giant size in the wet conditions. Gunnera forms a low canopy that miniature animals pass beneath.

The pudu is the world's smallest deer, standing only about 30cm (12 inches) high, with antlers no more than 10cm (4 inches) long. It is a secretive and solitary creature and is hard to see, except when it stands on its hind legs to nibble vegetation out of its short reach. At night you have a reasonable chance of spotting another miniature, the monito del monte, or 'mountain monkey'. This is a South American marsupial (mammal with a pouch) about the size of a dormouse and the only surviving member of an ancient order. The monito will eat anything it can catch, from insects to frogs, and is an excellent climber, using its prehensile tail to help it clamber through the dense shrubbery.

Both the monito del monte and the pudu are more active at night and so need to beware of the kodkod, or guigna, a beautifully marked hunting cat no bigger than a domestic cat. It has been suggested that the kodkod is highly social, but as yet, comparatively little is known about its behaviour or about the behaviour of many of the specialist animals of this region.

BELOW *On the slopes of the Andes, towering above southern beech, are monkey-puzzle trees several hundred years old and virtually unchanged since they evolved some 200 million years ago.*

ABOVE *Mandarin ducks, familiar in European parks but originating in China, Japan and eastern Siberia. The camouflaged female (first picture) lays her eggs in a tree hole that can be high up. When all the ducklings have hatched, she calls to them from the ground, and one by one they leap out, free-falling to the forest floor and bounce-landing.*

OPPOSITE *A female Amur leopard – one of the most endangered races of large cats in the world. In the mixed deciduous forest of the remote Amur River valley, on the China-Russia border, no more than 40 or so leopards remain. Logging, poaching and hunting of the deer it preys on mean it is unlikely to survive much longer in the wild.*

Russia and China, the largest and fourth largest countries in the world respectively, have between them examples of all the world's major forest types, from boreal through to tropical. It is their temperate forests, though, that are particularly rich in tree species – evergreen and deciduous broadleaves as well as temperate pines – with large areas of forest containing a mixture of all three.

Southern China in particular is rich in broadleaf forests. Sichuan province in the southwest is dominated by mountain ranges, and the fluctuating altitude has led to tree species and forest types that change rapidly over relatively short distances. Adapted to roam between them is the golden snub-nosed monkey. This extraordinary-looking animal climbs to altitudes of 4500m (14,760 feet) or more, making it the highest-living monkey in the world. Its thick fur helps to keep out the cold, and its intestines have multiple sacs filled with special bacteria that allow it to digest almost anything, including cellulose. Unlike most monkeys, which are reliant on fruit and insects, golden snub-nosed monkeys can be less fussy and eat large quantities of lichens, conifer needles and even bark, depending on the time of year and the type of forest it is passing through. In winter, a shortage of food forces the monkeys to live in quite small groups of 20–30 individuals, but in the summer they form some of the biggest gatherings of any monkey – up to 600.

The mixed deciduous forest of Russia's Amur region can look passably similar to the broadleaf forests of Western Europe and North America. As well as familiar trees, there are an abundance of jays, chipmunks and deer. But the top predators are less familiar. Siberian tigers prowl these woodlands, feeding mainly on deer. So do Amur leopards, which hunt roe deer, badgers and racoon dogs. The Amur leopard is the rarest of the 30 or so races of leopard, with no more than about 40 individuals remaining in the wild. It grows a luxurious coat in winter, reminiscent of a snow leopard, but the fur is a deep orange colour with widely spaced rosette-like spots.

HOT FORESTS

Further south towards the equator, winters become milder, and the sun stays for more of the year, leading to hotter, drier summers. With no winter frosts to damage leaves, broadleaf tree species that keep their leaves all year round, such as magnolias and evergreen oaks, start to appear. The new priority is to save water, and these trees tend to have smaller, shinier leaves with waxy coatings. In the driest areas, conifer trees re-establish themselves. The waxy needles that allowed them to survive the water shortages in the frozen north give them an advantage again. Much of the Mediterranean would have been covered with vegetation of this type – evergreens such as cork oak and olive as well as conifers such as cypress – but a lot of this forest was lost to early agriculture and has been replaced by imported vegetation, including eucalyptus.

In the tropics, seasonality in day length has almost vanished, and the sun is overhead, delivering maximum energy. Where there is ample water, the conditions are ideal for steaming tropical jungle – the most productive forest on Earth. But the weather systems on our planet are complex, and even at the equator, rain can be entirely absent for much of the year. Where this happens, the extra intensity of the sun can lead to a pronounced dry season.

Look at a picture of an Indian teak forest in the dry season, and you might think it was a northern deciduous wood in midwinter. But a visit would quickly change your mind. The heat would be overpowering, and you would find the teak leaves that cover the ground tinder crisp and crackly, every bit of moisture having been withdrawn by the trees before the leaves were dropped. You might hear surprising bird calls – such as those of courting peacocks. If you were to wait by one of the few waterholes, you would see a procession of Hanuman langur monkeys and sambar deer coming to drink, perhaps even some wild dogs or a tiger.

The teak forest of southern India is the setting for Rudyard Kipling's *The Jungle Book*. The actual forest that inspired Kipling is Pench Reserve, 750 sq km (290 square miles) of deciduous teak and mixed forest in Madhya Pradesh. Pench is near the equator, but it is highly seasonal, with virtually all the rain falling in just a couple of months during the monsoon. When the forest is at its driest, many of the animals seek shade and do their best to conserve water, but Indian gaur – wild cattle – choose this time to rut. The huge bulls, with their exaggerated, angular shoulders, curl their lips into a strange grimace – behaviour known as flehmen, which seems to help them to focus on the smell of nearby females and assess their reproductive state. If there is no clear hierarchy between the largest males, they will fight to establish one. These fights are a last resort: gaur have such sharp horns that they can fatally wound one another, and besides, unnecessary exertion at this time of year is to be avoided. The forest is now bare, and much of the gaur's food and water comes from stripping bark from the teak. There is, however, a short respite in May, when a very unusual tree comes to the rescue. The mahua chooses the driest times to produce succulent flowers, which draw animals from all over the forest. At its peak, a mahua is filled with barbets, parakeets, squirrels and several species of monkey. Beneath it, gaur, sambar deer and chital pick up the fallen flowers, frequently joined at dusk by sloth bears. The spectacle is a reminder that every living thing in this forest is a slave to water and that while the amount of sun is critical to a forest's productivity, the availability of fresh water is every bit as important.

ABOVE *A bull gaur in Nagarahole National Park. The mixed deciduous forest includes canopy trees such as teak and rosewood, which drop their leaves in summer to avoid losing precious water. The gaur will strip bark for moisture as well as food.*

OPPOSITE *An Indian peafowl (peacock) displaying in the forest on an arena of dry leaves. He adds an acoustic embellishment to his display, deliberately agitating his quills to create a rustling clatter.*

4

the great plains

The great plains cover more than a quarter of

the land on Earth. These hugely productive,

vast open spaces are fuelled by grass

and support the greatest gatherings of wildlife

anywhere on the planet.

ABOVE *The great plains of Tibet, with a herd of yaks in the distance.*

OPPOSITE *African elephants and buffaloes trekking over the dusty, dry Botswana plains to reach water.*

PREVIOUS PAGE, TOP *North American bison.* BOTTOM *Migrating wildebeest.*

Great plains are found on every continent except Antarctica. They range from the baking savannahs of Africa to the frozen tundra of the Arctic, from the sweeping prairies of North America to the tall-grass pampas of South America, and from the lush, lowland floodplains of India to the harsh, high-altitude steppes of the Tibetan plateau. Together they cover a quarter of the Earth. The central Asian steppes alone stretch unbroken nearly a third of the way around the world. The great plains are also hugely productive. Nowhere else do you find such large concentrations of animals – 1.5 million wildebeest on the East African Serengeti savannah, up to 2 million gazelles roaming the Mongolian steppes and more than 3 million caribou on the North American tundra. Millions of grass-eaters in turn feed thousands of plains predators, from lions and hyenas in Africa to wolves and eagles in America and Asia. Though the names for plains may vary – steppe, savannah, prairie, pampas – these great oceans of grass have two things in common. First, they occur where rainfall is too low to support forests and too high for deserts to develop (250–750mm, 10–29 inches, per year). Second, they have a distinct growing season – when the tropical rains or the temperate summer arrives and grass dominates.

TUNDRA JOURNEYS

Travel north beyond the tree line and you emerge onto the Arctic tundra – a windswept wilderness larger than Australia that encircles the Arctic Ocean at the top of the world. Virtually unpopulated and devoid of life in the frozen, dark winter, the tundra undergoes a transformation in summer. When land temperatures rise above zero long enough for ice and snow to melt, light, warmth and moisture are suddenly available, and nutrients that have been locked in the frozen soil are released. As the ice recedes, the first grass shoots emerge, and within days there is a rich supply of food. This, together with few predators – the result of its remoteness – and 24-hour daylight in summer, makes the tundra the perfect place to raise offspring. Animals are drawn here in their millions, including birds and mammals that have overwintered far to the south.

THE WORLD'S BIGGEST BARNYARD

Migration can transform the barren tundra almost overnight. In early May, though much of the snow has melted, the Egg River on Banks Island in the far north of Canada seems like the emptiest place on Earth. Crushed and scoured flat over millennia by the abrasive powers of ice and wind, the plain ahead is featureless apart from patches of snow. The only sound is the wind. But all that is about to change, literally overnight.

One day at the end of May, an incredible noise fills the air – a honking and squawking that marks the arrival of hundreds of thousands of lesser snow geese. This is the end of a 12-week, 4000-km (2485-mile) journey from their wintering grounds along the Gulf of Mexico and the southern US. The plains around the Egg River are transformed instantly from vacant tundra into a huge barnyard – a breeding colony of half a million geese 20km (12.5 miles) long and 5km (3 miles) wide.

Male and female lesser snow geese pair for life and tend to return to the same breeding sites each year, forming the biggest and most dense nesting concentrations of waterfowl in the world. Nests in a colony are spread out over the tundra roughly 10m (33 feet) apart – far enough from each other to avoid conflict with the neighbours but close enough for protection against predators. From a distance, the pairs of geese appear like thousands upon thousands of golf balls scattered over the ground.

Snow geese usually lay four or five eggs, which are incubated by the female. She sits tight for the next month, during which time she may lose 25 per cent of her body weight. Her partner guards her and the nest from intruding geese and predators – gulls, which pick off unattended eggs, and the resident Arctic foxes. A pair of foxes will often den within the goose colony or just at the edge, though they have only a month to take advantage of the sudden bounty on their doorstep.

Taking an egg requires skill. As soon as an Arctic fox approaches a nesting pair, the alarm goes off and a ripple of activity sweeps through the colony as the fox runs a gauntlet of furious ganders, beating their wings and biting. When it has chosen a nest, the fox will dodge and weave around it, trying to draw the enraged geese away from their eggs. As the goose joins her partner in the attack, the fox darts forward, pinches an egg and flees, with the birds in panicked pursuit. Some eggs are eaten, some are fed to the cubs and the rest are buried for later in the year. Very occasionally, a fox will catch an adult goose and make a real killing.

Hatching is highly synchronized, and 23 days after nesting, the whole colony is suddenly awash with fluffy yellow goslings. Foxes gather up as many as they can steal from the protective parents and carry them back to the cubs at the den – in a good year, foxes can rear up to 15 young. But the foxes don't have long to feast.

Within 48 hours, most of the goslings have been led away by their parents to the safety of the lakes and rivers that pattern the tundra. As quickly as they arrived, the geese are gone, and once again the Egg River feels like the loneliest place on Earth. They disperse across the plain, where for the next two months, the goose families feed on insects and grass. Left behind, the Arctic foxes survive on what they managed to stash during the period of plenty, on their fat reserves, on the odd ptarmigan and lemming and by scavenging the carcasses of caribou and other animals.

ABOVE *An Arctic fox failing to steal a snow goose egg and being chased off by the gander, whose beak can deliver a damaging blow.*

OPPOSITE *The big barnyard of Egg River, with nests close enough for group defence against predators but spaced out enough to avoid squabbles.*

ABOVE *Arctic wolf. Those wolves that remain in the Arctic have a tough life. Cubs are left for long periods when the pack treks across the tundra on the hunt for caribou calves.*

TOP *Caribou on the move, fleeing mosquitoes rather than wolves.*

OPPOSITE *The great caribou march across the tundra to the calving grounds – in this case, the Porcupine Herd moving across the Arctic National Wildlife Refuge in Alaska.*

THE BIGGEST HERDS OF ALL

At the same time as the snow geese are heading north, 3 million caribou (North American reindeer) are embarking on the longest of all land migrations. Moving through snowy forests, crossing icy rivers and braving bears and wolves along the way, they head for the tundra across Alaska and northern Canada – a round journey of up to 3000km (1865 miles).

Like the snow geese, they migrate to the tundra to feed on the new growth and raise their young as far as possible from predators. Pregnant caribou lead the way, travelling as much as 50km (31 miles) a day. They reach their calving grounds by mid-June, returning to a broadly similar area, the exact location depending on weather, snow and the condition of the females. Some bears and wolves live far enough north to take advantage of the births. But the calves are well adapted: they can stand almost at birth and run within a day.

Caribou remain fairly spread out at the calving grounds for a week or two and then gather together in large herds to move off to new pastures. By now the calves are walking up to 14km (9 miles) a day, fording lakes and rivers with their mothers. But this time they are moving not just to find new grass but to escape the clouds of mosquitoes that engulf you wherever you walk. On windless, warm summer days, swarms are so dense that you find yourself breathing them in, and the only thing to do is to keep moving. The caribou herds walk into the wind or to higher ground where there is a breeze or seek out any remaining snow – anything to gain relief from irritating insects. This constant movement, missed feeding time and blood loss from insect bites cause caribou to lose weight during a time when they need to be storing fat. After calm summers with high insect harassment, calves do not grow as big, and fewer survive the winter.

Flies and mosquitoes can bite through thick cotton shirts, and so the only way to wait out on the tundra for the late-June caribou spectacle is to wear a mosquito net over your whole body. The Bathurst Herd in the Barrenlands of northern Canada move off the calving grounds in spectacular fashion. On calm days, groups of up to 60,000, packed tightly together to protect themselves from insect attack, flow across the landscape as one. Herds do not move in a straight line or follow a totally predictable route and are constantly on the move, and so even a substantial number of caribou can be surprisingly hard to locate on the vast tundra. But if you find one heading your way, sit perfectly still, and it may sweep either side of you, within touching distance, mothers and calves are always grunting to each other so as not to get separated, moving fast over the rough tundra in a rhythmic trot.

Wolf packs are a constant threat and, for some herds, may be responsible for up to 70 per cent of all calf deaths. Sometimes the caribou herd is so large that the individuals at the head are still grazing, oblivious to the mayhem behind them. Once a calf is singled out, the hunt becomes an endurance race. The wolf will chase the calf until one or other becomes exhausted and gives up, which can be up to 8km (5 miles) later.

As the brief Arctic summer ends, the caribou head back south to spend the winter sheltering and feeding in the forests. Soon the plains are empty once again. Walking across the Barrenlands, you occasionally meet a lone caribou calf lost and heading in the wrong direction. When it sees you, it runs over bleating eagerly, only to find that you are not its mother. During the migration, the river crossings and the wolf hunts, many caribou calves become separated and perish. Their carcasses will become food for the scavenging ravens, bears and Arctic foxes left behind.

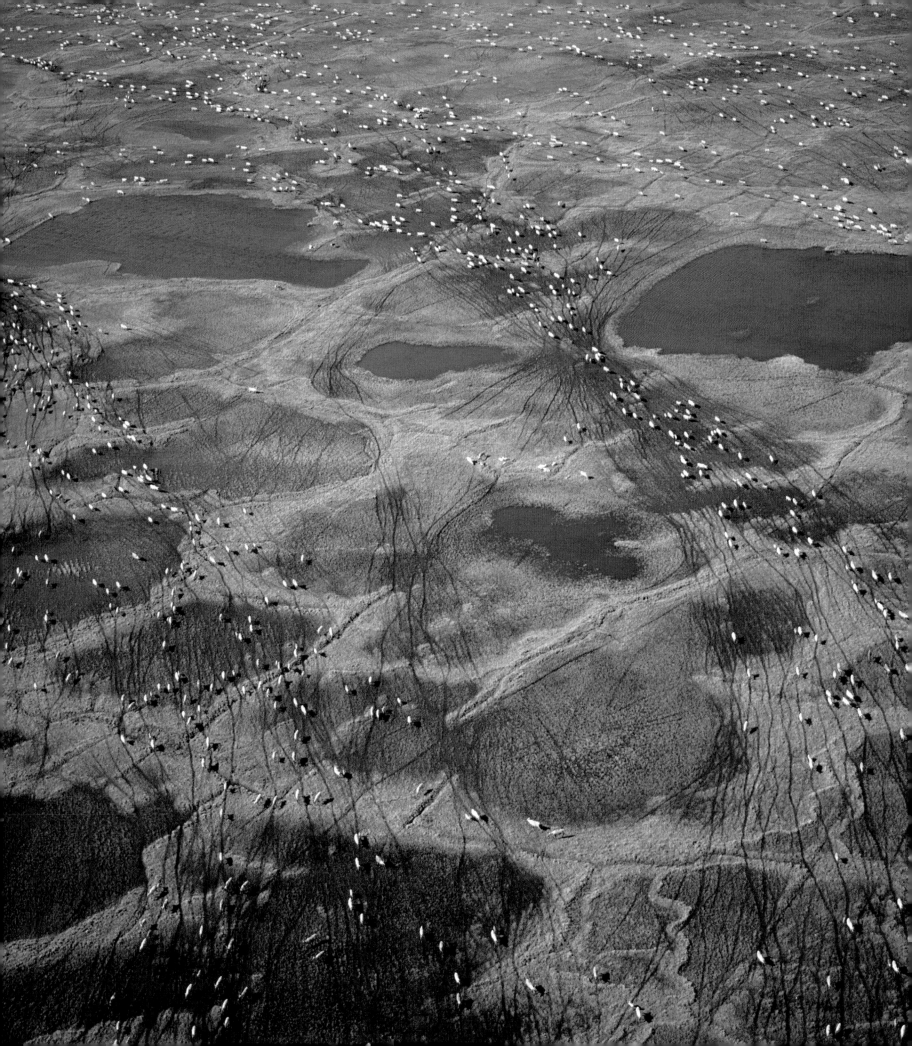

KEEPING ONE STEP AHEAD

ABOVE *Juvenile spotted hyenas at the den. Adult hyenas are forced to leave their pups for days when hunting the migrating wildebeest.*

OPPOSITE *An Arctic ground squirrel eating grass seeds in the brief summer.*

On the great plains of Africa, seasonal tropical rainfall means that grass and water are available in different places at different times. During the dry season in East Africa, more than 1.5 million wildebeest traverse the baking plains and cross crocodile-infested waters in search of food and water. In the wet season, they migrate to areas of fresh grass rich in phosphorous, needed to produce milk and promote healthy bone growth – vital for their newborn calves. By keeping on the move, they also stay one step ahead of many of the predators. Lions, cheetahs, jackals and leopards do not shadow the migration – they are tied to specific areas by the need to defend a territory and protect their young. Hyenas, however, commute between their cubs at the den and the migrating herds of wildebeest – a round trip of up to 140km (87 miles) – and mothers can be absent for as long as four days. It is a strategy that seems to be successful in the Serengeti, where spotted hyenas are the most abundant large carnivores.

On the tundra, caribou migrate as far away from the wolves as they can for calving. So the Arctic wolves, which also have young at this time, must leave their cubs alone at the den, just as the hyenas have to do, and commute to the caribou herds. Finding the herds on the vast tundra requires great endurance and can involve a round-trip of up to 200km (125 miles).

On the steppes of Mongolia, the last remaining great Asian migration takes place, with possibly up to 2 million Mongolian gazelles moving between their winter breeding grounds and their summer calving areas. Driving their migration is probably a combination of predator avoidance, insect harassment, the search for minerals and good grazing, and the extent of winter snow cover, though the exact reasons are still being researched.

SUPER GRASS

There are around 10,000 different species of grass. Covering the plains and feeding the great herds, this family of plants is the most widespread and abundant on Earth. They are also among the toughest. Able to withstand being burnt, frozen, drowned, parched, grazed or trampled, their secret is the fact that, unlike trees, bushes and other flowering plants, their leaves grow continuously from the base. So as they are being grazed or damaged from the top, they are regenerating from below.

Grasses are not only great survivors, they are also opportunists, capable of making use of the sun's energy and growing rapidly when conditions are good. On the tundra, when the short summer arrives and the snow melts, grasses use their reserves to produce a full complement of leaves in just a few weeks.

Some grasses can spread without setting seed by putting out runners along the surface, from which shoots and leaves can grow. During the winter, they do not die but simply stop growing and wait for the good times to come again. Many species retreat underground, remaining in a dormant state as rhizomes. The food stored in the rhizomes as starch allows them to take advantage of favourable situations when they arise. On the African plains, though, most grass species are annuals, setting seed as drought conditions return and surviving the dry season in this state. As soon as the rains come, the seeds germinate, producing new leaves within just a few days. Even a light shower can result in a green flush on the savannah.

Boom and bust

Many of the great migrations are now a shadow of their previous extent, and many of the species are threatened – due largely to human encroachment. A few hundred years ago, grassland would have covered almost twice its current area, but much of that land is now farmed or fenced.

Hunting is also to blame. The most famous example of overhunting on the great plains is that of the bison of North America, more than 60 million of which once roamed the prairies. Hunting nearly wiped the species out, and though last-ditch conservation has built the population back to 350,000, it is fragmented and restricted to refuges and national parks.

In southern Sudan, a million or so kob (large antelopes) are known to have migrated more than 1500km (930 miles) annually – a scene to rival that of the East African plains. Sudan's recent civil war is thought to have reduced numbers dramatically, though little information exists about the current situation.

In South Africa in the nineteenth century, 10 million or so springbok once trekked across the veldt. Today, springbok herds seldom number more than a few hundred, and many of their migration routes are blocked by fencing.

Chiru, or Tibetan antelope, still undertake a great migration across the plains of Tibet. Exactly why is not yet fully understood, and even the location of their remote calving grounds remained a mystery until a few years ago. Today, though, they number fewer than 75,000, down from possibly several million, having become victims of fashion. Hundreds of thousands have been killed for their fine wool, known as shahtoosh, which is woven into ornate shawls that can sell for up to $15,000 in New York and London. That trade has largely been stopped, and some parts of the Tibetan plateau are receiving protection, though poaching still continues.

The saiga saga
Perhaps the most drastic population crash of any large mammal in recent years has been that of the saiga antelope of the central Asian steppes. In the early 1990s, more than a million remained. Fifteen years later, fewer than 30,000 were left.

A saiga antelope is roughly the size and shape of a goat, but with a huge, bulbous, flexible snout – a comical nose with a serious function. Its generous nasal chambers have evolved to filter, moisten and warm the air before it enters the lungs, as the saiga antelope lives on the central Asian steppes of Russia, Mongolia and Kazakhstan, where the atmosphere is dry and dusty.

Each autumn, as the snow starts to fall on the steppes, saiga travel to less snowy areas

in the south of their range. Here they mate, and in the spring they head north again to give birth. For thousands of years they have made these journeys, and for thousands of years they have been hunted for their meat, skin and horns (used as an anti-inflammatory in traditional Chinese medicine).

With the arrival of vehicles and guns, hunting became excessive, and by 1920, the population came near to extinction. Following the Russian revolution, saiga hunting was banned, and by the 1950s, the antelopes had made a remarkable recovery, increasing to more than 2 million. Numbers bounced back because saiga are well adapted to their unpredictable environment. In drought years and times of high snowfall, many starve to death – up to 80 per cent of the population. In favourable years, saiga can reproduce rapidly. Females frequently have twins (rare among antelopes), and the young are

sexually mature at just eight months old – ready to mate when the winter rut starts.

Recently, saiga populations have taken another hit. In the early 1990s, in a bid to save rhinos, some conservationists encouraged the use of saiga horn as an alternative to rhino horn – also used in traditional Chinese medicine. More importantly, at this time the Soviet Union was collapsing. Regulation of trade in saiga horn ceased, and hunting reached new levels.

Conservationists hoping for another miraculous recovery have been alarmed by recent findings. Selective hunting for males – only males have horns – means that the population is now predominantly female and cannot reproduce well enough to bounce back. The likelihood is that the saiga antelope population in Mongolia will become extinct this year, and if poaching is not controlled, the other populations may follow suit.

LEFT TO RIGHT *A relict herd of North American bison, South Dakota. A century and a half ago, more than 60 million wandered the prairies.*

Sparring kob. In southern Sudan, a million or so of these antelopes migrate in search of new pastures, but civil strife may have decimated numbers.

Springbok on the move. The great springbok migration of Southern Africa is a spectacle of the past, as numbers have been greatly reduced and fences criss-cross the grasslands.

A saiga displaying its extraordinary nose. The story of the saiga in Asia rivals that of the bison, with hunting having reduced them to near-extinction levels.

THE HIGH PLAINS

ABOVE *A kiang stallion rounds up his harem of mares. Kiang – the largest of the wild asses and true grass grazers – are found on the vast steppes and alpine meadows of the Tibetan plateau, along with the endangered Tibetan antelope and the Tibetan gazelle.*

Forty million years ago, the Indian subcontinent collided with Asia, and over time, the land buckled upwards more than 8km (5 miles) into the sky to form Mount Everest and the rest of the Himalayan range. This range now divides two plains that are complete opposites. If you were to stand on the top of Everest on a cloudless day, you would see to the north the dry, desolate Tibetan plateau – the roof of the world – stretching far into the distance of Asia. To the south you would see a lush, fertile, low-lying green expanse spreading across India – the Gangetic Plains, one of the most densely populated regions of the world. Tibet is in the shadow of the mountains and receives little rain, while the Gangetic plains are soaked by the monsoon. The Tibetan plateau was once the floor of an ancient sea, and you can still find marine

fossils here at more than 4000m (13,120 feet) above sea level. Today, it is an immense plain nearly four times the size of France, most of it higher than Europe's highest peaks.

When you arrive here, the first thing you notice is your own heartbeat. You feel dizzy, and your head throbs as the blood pumps faster through your body to compensate for the lack of oxygen in the thin air. The second thing you notice is that there is no one here. You do meet the occasional nomad tending sheep, but vegetation is so scant and fresh water so sporadic that you are unlikely to find many livestock or people. The spartan plateau is incredibly dry, and a desiccating wind gives you a perpetual thirst. Camping out, you can go for day after cloudless day with nothing but deep blue sky between you and the rest of the universe.

Yet even in this barren landscape, grasses are able to grow. More than 70 per cent of the plateau is grassland, and there is enough plant life for hardy animals to eke out a living. From a distance, wild yak look like huge, hairy, black cows. They are exceptionally shy, but if you can crawl closer, you see what impressive beasts they are. With hair so long it nearly covers their feet, they look as if they have been draped with shaggy blankets. Females and young live in herds of up to 200, but the bulls are largely solitary. As they amble across the plains, their magnificent broad heads are slung low, their square muzzles are pressed close to the ground, nibbling at the meagre grass. If they do look up and spot you, they adopt a proud posture to show off their horns, before trotting away. Until the 1950s, more than a million wild yaks lived in Tibet. Hunting has reduced that number to fewer than 15,000.

On these high plains, cloudless nights are cold, but when the sun rises, temperatures can increase by as much as 27°C (49°F). Thin air and bright skies mean exposed skin burns easily. Black hair protects the yaks from intense solar radiation, though a few rare golden-coloured wild yaks do exist. Supremely adapted to the harsh, high-altitude conditions, yaks are the highest-living large mammals in the world. Compared with cows of the same size, wild yaks have larger lungs and hearts, and their blood is capable of transporting more oxygen. Their thick fleece, which is coated with frost in winter, keeps out the incessant Tibetan wind and freezing temperatures – as low as −40°C (−40°F).

Black-lipped pikas are equally hardy, living at the same altitude as yaks, at around 6000m (19,700 feet). Relatives of rabbits, these small grass-eaters look like a cross between a guinea pig and a mouse and are known locally as Himalayan mouse-hares. They live at incredibly high densities – up to 300 in an area the size of a football pitch – but spend much of their lives underground. If you sit quietly among the many holes that pepper the plateau, you will eventually see them emerge. Pikas stay close to their burrows, squatting with their fur fluffed up against the bitter cold. If you make a move, the ground seems to come alive as hundreds rush for safety. Pika families use their burrows to shelter from the elements and from predators, but unlike other small mammals in harsh environments, they do not hibernate but somehow manage to store enough food to remain active all year.

The robust pika is fundamental to life on the high plains. In this treeless environment their burrows provide homes for lizards and various nesting birds such as snow finches and Tibetan ground-tits. Predators on the plateau – wolves, snow leopards, buzzards and foxes – all feed on pikas. One of the most surprising pika predators is the Tibetan brown bear. Thought to be the inspiration behind the legendary Yeti, just a few remnant populations are scattered in the mountains around the plateau, and their habits remain a mystery.

Though Tibet itself is dry, its enormous presence and position exert a huge influence on the rainfall and rivers across Asia. In the summer, the sun warms the massive flat expanse of Tibet, and the plateau heats up like a giant hotplate. As the warm air rises, humid air is drawn in from the Indian Ocean to the south. Clouds build, and as they hit the Himalayas, monsoon rains fall over the foothills and the Gangetic Plains to the south. On exceptional occasions, the Tibetan plateau receives snow in the summer. If this happens the white blanket reflects the sun and the plateau takes longer to heat up, delaying the onset of the monsoon rains. And being the 'roof of the world', all the major Asian rivers – the Ganges, Brahamaputra, Yellow, Indus, Irrawaddy and Yangtze – begin their journeys in Tibet. Together they provide water for nearly half the world's population.

ABOVE *A black-lipped pika on alert. Being the main prey of most Tibetan predators, it needs to be. Its burrows also provide nest holes for birds and refuges for reptiles, making the pika one of the most important mammals on the plateau.*

OPPOSITE RIGHT *Autumn at the edge of the Kunlun Mountains. Pikas are abundant here, and yaks graze the sedges growing alongside the creeks.*

OPPOSITE LEFT, TOP TO BOTTOM
A wild yak with its tail raised in alarm. Wild yaks are now confined to remote areas on the Tibetan plateau and probably number fewer than 15,000.

A Tibetan brown bear, with its characteristic pale face, using its long, powerful claws to dig for pikas.

A Tibetan fox on the lookout for pikas. It hunts in the day, using the slightest depressions as cover, its ears laid flat as it stalks.

WHERE THE GRASS IS GREENER

Follow the Brahamaputra off the Tibetan plateau, and it will lead you out onto the plains of India. When the Tibetan plateau was formed on one side of the Himalayas, the Gangetic Plain was born on the other. It is a large depression that, over millions of years, has filled with sediment washed down from the mountains. In places it is thought to be 13km (8 miles) thick. Monsoon rains drench this region every year, making it lush and green and one of the most productive plains in the world.

Keep following the Brahamaputra, and you will eventually end up in northern India, in Kaziranga National Park in Assam. This is home to one of the highest concentrations of tigers in the world, possibly about 90, though you are unlikely to see them because the grass grows to more than 5m (16 feet) high in some places. The animals that you can sometimes see above the grass are the jumbo-sized herbivores – wild buffalo (1400), elephants (1000) and greater one-horned rhinos (1600), which look like armour-plated versions of their African cousins.

Just up the road from Kaziranga is Manas National Park. Like Kaziranga, Manas is dominated by luxuriant long grass and is home to a much smaller plains resident – the rarest and smallest wild pig in the world – the pygmy hog. It uses the long grass to construct a thatched nest, which keeps the rain off during the monsoon, provides shade on hot days and can be a nursery for up to ten piglets, each small enough to sit in your hand.

AFRICA'S GREAT SAVANNAH

East Africa is often portrayed as an endless plain filled with hordes of grazing animals. For once the cliché is true. The largest of all the great plains are found here. Starting at the southern limits of the Sahara, these tropical grasslands form a huge arc that spans from the Atlantic coast in the west to the Indian Ocean in the east. From here they sweep down to the southern tip of Africa, together covering a third of the continent. These vast savannahs are highly productive and support some of the greatest concentrations of large animals. During the annual migrations in East Africa, 200,000 zebras and 400,000 Thomson's gazelles trek across the plains along with more than 1.5 million wildebeest.

Africa's grasslands are not only highly productive, but they also support the greatest variety of wildlife of all the great plains, including around 100 species of grazers. The diversity is the result of a mosaic of habitats – from the treeless plains of the Serengeti to the acacia-wooded grassland of the Ngorongoro Crater. The unifying theme is grass – some as tall as an elephant, some that could only conceal an ant.

Drive across Africa through this remarkable patchwork and exactly which type of savannah scenery you can expect to see will depend on a history of complex interactions among the plants, the animals and the elements. Fire, soil type, rainfall and the contours of the landscape are all important in shaping the different savannah backdrops. Each habitat hosts a different set of characters, from the sinuous gerenuk in the wooded savannah to the lolloping topi on the open plains, each adapted to fill one of many niches.

ABOVE *Common zebras in the Serengeti. They are among the most water-dependent of the plains herd animals and will trek long distances daily to waterholes or rivers. In the dry season, they are forced to migrate, along with the wildebeest.*

OPPOSITE TOP *A pygmy hog in Manas National Park, Assam – the world's rarest and smallest pig (less than 65cm/26 inches, long). It lives only in the tall grass, foraging for roots and tubers and other items, and constructing its nests out of grass.*

OPPOSITE BOTTOM *A greater one-horned rhino grazing on the floodplains of Kaziranga National Park, in Assam, India – its last stronghold.*

RECYCLING ON THE SAVANNAH

With numerous animals come heaps of dung. But the savannah is a dynamic place, and nutrients are recycled rapidly. Even before the dung has cooled, male dung beetles may have flown in, worked the waste into manageable balls, rolled them away and presented them to the females to lay their eggs in. The beetles bury the balls as deep as a metre (three feet or so) underground, providing a ready meal for their larvae when they hatch out. In the Serengeti, three quarters of all animal dung is dispatched by beetles, which fertilize the soil in the process.

A brisk turnover on the savannah ensures that these great plains can continue to support large numbers of grazers year after year. The most numerous and perhaps the most influential grazers are largely unseen – the termites. There are literally billions of them in vast underground colonies, and it is thought that termites take more material from the plains of Africa than all the large grazers combined.

Grass may be readily available, but it is difficult to digest. Both termites and large grazers use microorganisms such as bacteria and fungi in their guts to break down the tough parts. Microbes within a termite colony, which include gardens of fungi nurtured in special air-conditioned 'rooms', are believed to equal the weight of the termites found there, which can amount to up to 7 million in a colony. Above ground, the larger grass-eating mammals in turn support meat-eaters such as lions, leopards and hyenas. And cleaning up after them are the scavengers, including jackals and vultures.

ABOVE *Baboons wading through the floodwater of the Okavango, which often means walking upright.*

OPPOSITE *Drought in Botswana. When the dry season arrives, even giraffes are forced to trek to faraway rivers and waterholes.*

PREVIOUS PAGE *The great Serengeti, famous for the enormous herds of plains animals it supports. Millions of wildebeest migrate across it, following the rains and the flush of grass.*

RAIN AND DROUGHT

Spanning the equator, the African plains do not have the temperature changes of the tundra, but seasonal variation is just as dramatic. Where the tundra and prairie have summer and winter, the African savannah has wet and dry seasons. For much of the year the savannah is baked hard. But after heavy rain, the parched earth becomes lush, green grassland in just days. Tropical sunshine and seasonal rains provide readily available and renewable food for millions upon millions of grazers, from the petite dik-dik antelope to the colossal elephant. Close on their heels comes an impressive array of plains predators, from lions and cheetahs to wild dogs and hyenas. African savannahs are fantastically prolific – able to support more than 200 times the mass of animal life compared to a rainforest of equivalent size. But the tropical lifestyle is also one of feast and famine.

The timing and quantity of rainfall is unpredictable, and drought is common. If it does rain, the annual supply may pour down within just a few weeks. Sometimes the ground is so baked or the rain falls so hard that most of the water pours off the surface. Intense tropical sunshine evaporates up to 80 per cent of the downpour, and what moisture does remain may have to sustain life on the plains for the rest of the year. Animal and plant life on the savannah must be able to react to the whims of the weather. Grass can remain dormant until favourable conditions return, but the animals reliant on grass must migrate. It is these annual cycles of wet and dry that drive the great African migrations.

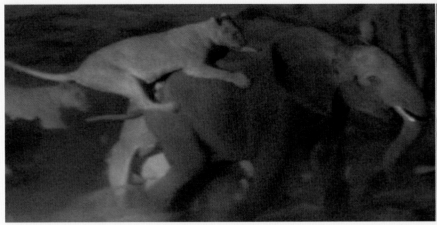

PREDATOR AND PREY

Sometimes, individual groups of animals adapt to very specific conditions. Across most of Africa, lions and elephants tend to steer clear of one another, but around a few waterholes in Chobe National Park in northern Botswana, circumstances are different. Under cover of night, lions hunt elephants.

During the dry season it may not rain for eight months, and temperatures reach a debilitating 50°C (122°F). By October, the plains are a dust bowl. Elephants can only go for a few days without a drink, and during the driest months, tens of thousands stream across the dry hinterland towards areas of permanent water such as the Chobe River and the Okavango swamps. Thousands of elephant convoys, up to a hundred strong, follow the same pathways – wave after wave. Repeated pounding of feet engrave deep furrows across the landscape – northern Botswana is home to 130,000 elephants, a quarter of the world's population. Through dust storms and stifling heat, 6-ton adults, tiny, week-old babies and all sizes between march up to 80km (50 miles) in a day on their way to water.

In one area of Chobe National Park there is a cluster of small waterholes that elephants frequent – a pit-stop on the way to distant rivers. As they arrive at the waterholes, they bump and jostle against each other to squeeze into a space where they can drink. On the fringe of this boisterous gathering sits a pride of lions. If they need a drink, they must run the gauntlet of the herds and creep around at the elephants' feet. Repeatedly the lions are chased off – adult elephants charge and kick up dust, scattering the pride with a wave of their trunks. Eventually the lions manage to take a drink. Finding food can be even more difficult – the wildebeest, zebra and buffalo that live here in the wet season left long ago.

Night falls, and a cool breeze diffuses the tension. All seems peaceful. As the elephants drink, you can hear their rhythmic sloshing and gurgling and the rasping sounds of them rubbing their thick, hairy skins against each other. They rumble greetings to the herds that continue to arrive at the water throughout darkness. In particular, breeding herds with young ones seem to prefer travelling during the cool of the night. After sunset, lions are more comfortable, more confident and more alert. The balance of power has changed.

ABOVE *Waterhole – a pit-stop for elephants but an ambush spot for lions.*

TOP *Death of an elephant. As a youngster runs away, one lioness leaps at its rear end. Once she has a hold, she drags herself up on top and rides the elephant as it crashes through the bushes. Four or five other lionesses cling to its hind legs, and as the youngster slows, more jump on until the sheer weight of lions brings the elephant to its knees. One lioness bites the end of its trunk, which may restrict its breathing and control a potentially dangerous weapon.*

OPPOSITE *Stand-off. In the daytime, elephants rule the waterholes in Chobe National Park, chasing away the lions, but at night, the tables are turned.*

ABOVE *An aardvark, a nocturnal African-plains animal that feeds mainly on termites. Powerful legs and long, chisel-like claws make it capable of digging long bolt-holes in the baked earth and tunnelling into termite mounds.*

OPPOSITE *American pronghorns, the fastest species on Earth over a sustained distance, capable of cruising at 67kph (42mph) for 1.6km (a mile). A pronghorn has powerful lower-torso muscles, lightweight legs and a long, airborne, galloping stride – ideal for racing across the plains. And its protruding eyes and binocular vision are perfect for spotting predators. Such adaptations may be the result of it once being the prey of a now-extinct super-predator, perhaps a cheetah with both stamina and speed.*

The pride here is uncommonly large. In Africa, lions usually live in groups of no more than about 10–12 adults. At this waterhole, the pride is at least 30 strong, and at times there can be as many as 50 individuals. In the darkness, they take up position, fanning out across the well-worn elephant trails between two of the small waterholes. They make no attempt to get out of the way of the elephant traffic. It looks like an ill-prepared ambush. Lying draped across the cool sand, two or three of the females scrutinize the procession of herds. Sitting quietly in a vehicle among the lions, you can feel the tension. You notice elephants stumbling into the pride by accident. In the dark, they seem clumsier, perhaps because their eyesight is not as good as the lions'. Big bull elephants and large breeding herds are ignored. They seem too strong and well defended to interest the lions.

Occasionally, one or two recently weaned individuals pass the lions. Not yet fully grown, they are 2–3m (6–10 feet) at the shoulder and are travelling separately from the other herds. As they wander close to the pride, all the lions jump up. Elephants trumpet in alarm. Lions roar excitedly. The African night erupts. As a young elephant runs away, a chaotic pursuit begins. Thirty big cats are on its heels. One lioness leaps at its rear end, biting and clawing. Others join in until the sheer number of lions overwhelms the elephant and brings it to its knees. It may take 20–30 minutes to die.

Lions normally hunt smaller prey such as wildebeest and zebra, though in some parts of Africa, they will take baby or injured elephants opportunistically. At this waterhole, though, in the absence of more normal prey, lions seem to have worked out a successful strategy for overpowering adolescent elephants. A large pride is necessary to undertake such risky attacks. Some lionesses are injured in the chase, and some elephants do manage to escape by wheeling around and throwing their pursuers off. Others are helped by their mothers. If nearby, a mother will try to thrash the lions off with her trunk and her tusks.

From observations over six weeks, about one in four attempts are successful. A large pride of lions can devour an elephant in less than two days. Sometimes they kill on consecutive nights, before they have even finished eating one animal, and through the dry season, they may kill as many as 30 or 40 elephants.

LIFE UNDER THE OPEN PLAINS

One of the greatest challenges to animals living on the open plains is the lack of shelter. With so few trees, there is little shade from the sun and wind and few places to hide from predators. Many mammals live below ground, and as a result, some plains can look devoid of life at first sight. Nowhere is this more evident than on the Mongolian steppes. You can drive for mile after empty mile and not see a single animal. But beneath the soil are numerous small burrowing mammals, including marmots, hamsters and gerbils and even a burrow-dwelling cat, Pallas's cat.

Burrowing beasts are common across all the great plains – pikas in Tibet, lemmings in the tundra, viscachas in South America and ground squirrels in America. The biggest burrows are those of the aardvark. An aardvark can dig a 10-m (33-foot) long burrow with an entrance hole almost large enough for a person to crawl in. Among the most extensive burrows are those of the prairie dogs on the North American plains. These rodents live in gigantic colonies – 'towns' – containing million of residents and extending over vast areas.

Sometimes disused prairie dog holes are taken over by burrowing owls. In the absence of trees on the prairie, they may choose to nest in burrows. The burrowing owl has another ingenious trick. In some areas, a male will place bison and cattle dung outside the burrow, which attracts dung beetles that they then eat.

STRENGTH IN SPEED AND NUMBERS

In these large, flat, open landscapes, running is a good strategy for both predators and prey, and so it is not surprising that plains animals are among the fastest in the world. In Africa, the cheetah has been recorded at 103kph (64mph) and the ostrich at 72kph (45mph). In America, the pronghorn antelope has been recorded running at up to 88.5kph (55mph) for 0.8km (half a mile) and can cruise at 67kph (42mph) for more than 1.6km (a mile).

Grazing animals that cannot escape underground tend to live in large herds for protection – up to 100,000 individuals, in the case of the Mongolian gazelle. More animals mean more eyes to look out for predators such as wolves. Female Mongolian gazelles, like the snow geese, caribou, wildebeest and many other plains animals, also have a highly synchronized calving season – they nearly all give birth during one week in June. If an area is swamped with calves for a few days, predators can kill only a fraction of the newborns before the rest are old enough to run away. From the Arctic tundra and the Tibetan plateau to the tropical savannahs of Africa, impressive herds gather on the great plains to raise their young. Together they form the greatest aggregations of wildlife on the planet.

5

the great sands

These are the last great land wildernesses –

the hottest, most arid regions of the world,

continually changing, scarred by the wind

and alternately baked and chilled. Only the hardiest

of plants and animals can survive there, each

with a special repertoire of tricks.

When astronauts return to Earth after circling the planet, they have a common view of what impressed them most from their privileged perspective in low-space orbit. Surprisingly, it is not the white of the polar ice caps, the intricate latticework of river deltas or even the massive scale of the Himalayas that leave the strongest images in their minds. Instead it is the world's deserts. They describe the extraordinary dark red colours of Australia's Great Sandy Desert, the beautiful patterns created by the giant sand dunes of the Namib – clearly visible from space – and more than anything else, the complete absence of any sign of humans. It is the sheer extent of the world's deserts that impresses them. Perhaps this is hardly surprising considering that deserts and semi-deserts make up the largest natural landscape on our planet. Deserts cover almost 50 million sq km (19.3 million square miles), just over a third of the total land surface, and are expanding every year.

Though only too easy to recognize from space, deserts are not so easy to define. The English word is derived from the Latin *desertum*, which means abandoned place. A botanist would characterize deserts as large areas without durable expanses of vegetation. A climatologist would say the key indicators are a lack of rainfall combined with high temperatures and subsequent evaporation. But it is not as simple as that. Temperatures in the Gobi Desert often fall as low as −40°C (−40°F), and the Kalahari has many trees and bushes. In Europe, we tend to think in terms of the endless sand seas of the Sahara, while in North America, any arid region without agriculture may be called a desert. The most useful and widely accepted definition for a true arid desert is a region receiving less than an average of 50mm (2 inches) of rain a year. This designation would encompass the polar regions, where at the South Pole, for instance, the annual average precipitation is only 20–50mm (0.8–2 inches).

GLOBAL BANDS OF SAND

There is a marvellous symmetry to the distribution of the world's deserts. Most of them lie in two globe-circling bands centred on the tropics of Cancer and Capricorn. In the north you find the deserts and semi-deserts of North America, the vast expanse of the Sahara – the largest desert in the world, covering about the same area as the US – the Arabian deserts and the Central Asian deserts. In the southern hemisphere, there is the Atacama in Chile and the semi-desert of Patagonia, the Namib and Kalahari in Africa, and the deserts of Australia – the driest of all the inhabited continents, with 80 per cent of its total area either arid or semi-arid.

All these deserts are found along the edges of the tropics, mainly because of the way the Earth's atmosphere circulates. The atmosphere operates as a kind of heat machine, kept in continuous motion by solar energy. At the equator, the sun is always vertically overhead, and so the regions around the equator absorb most of the solar radiation that reaches the Earth. The air above the land warms, expands and rises, carrying with it vast quantities of water vapour from the warm tropical oceans. As it rises, it cools, loses its buoyancy and spreads laterally north and south. Cooling reduces the air's ability to hold water, and the moisture condenses to produce the enormous deluges typical of the equatorial regions. The moisture-stripped air continues to travel north and south and starts to sink. As it sinks,

OPPOSITE TOP *Salt polygons stretching across the Salar de Uyuni – Bolivia's desert of salt, the evaporated remains of a high-altitude lake.*

OPPOSITE BOTTOM *The snowy wastes of the Gobi, a desert the size of Holland, with extreme heat and extreme cold.*

BELOW *A satellite view of the linear dunes of Australia's Simpson Desert – the longest dunes in the world.*

PREVIOUS PAGE *The specialized desert elephants of the Namib.*

the continuous flow of air starts to compress and warm up again. As a result, all along the tropics of Cancer and Capricorn, you find parched, warm, high-pressure air at the Earth's surface. This air and the winds associated with it are the principal reason why most of the world's deserts are distributed along these two symmetrical bands north and south.

RAIN BARRIERS

Other, more local factors can also create deserts. Mountains can force air to rise and drop its moisture, creating rain shadows on their leeward sides. The great mountain chains of the Rockies and Sierras influence most of the desert regions of North America. California's Mojave Desert, for example, lies in the rain shadow of the Sierra Nevada and San Bernardino Mountains, which block off the moist Pacific winds. As a result, the Mojave has the lowest rainfall of all of North America's deserts – just 40mm (1.6 inches) of rain a year in Death Valley, the hottest place on that continent. In South America, the long chain of the Andes also blocks out rain from the Pacific, creating the vast semi-desert of Patagonia. And the Himalayas keep back the Indian monsoon from large expanses of the Tibetan Plateau, creating desert. The sheer size of continental masses can also play a role. Vast areas of Central Asia are deserts simply because they are too far from the oceans to receive moist air.

Surprisingly, some of the driest places on Earth lie within sight of the oceans. The Atacama in South America, the Namib in southwest Africa and the Sonora on the peninsula of Baja California are all deserts created by a close proximity of cold ocean currents. They have all developed along the western coastlines of their continents, where the prevailing

winds tend to blow offshore, pushing surface water out to sea. This surface water is replaced with cold water drawn up from the depths, and any moist air crossing these stretches of frigid water is chilled. The moisture condenses out at sea as rain or forms dense banks of fog along the coast. Little or no rain ever makes it inland to the thirsty desert. This is why the Atacama, for example, is the driest desert on Earth. Over the course of time, the average rainfall has been 1–5mm (0.04–0.02 inches) a year, and in places, it has seen no rain for years. Considering that the long, thin strip of the Atacama starts in Peru just 400km (250 miles) south of the equator, in a region where you would expect permanent tropical moisture, it is clear how important a role local factors can play in desert creation.

THE HOTTEST LAND OF ALL

Deserts are the hottest environments on the planet. With so little cloud cover, the sun can regularly heat the deserts to a searing 40°C (104°F) and, in some cases, up to 50°C (122°F). But that's just the air temperature. On the sand and rocks, temperatures of up to 75°C (167°F) could burn your feet. Even people used to that kind of heat find it difficult to spend much time in the midday sun. The Tuareg people of the Sahara and the Bedouin of the Arabian deserts – all desert people – have long known that protective headwear is essential and choose to travel only in the relative cool of the early morning or late afternoon.

And the hottest place on Earth? There is dispute about the accuracy of recording methods, and some claim the record should go to Death Valley in California, where in July 1913, a temperature of 57°C (135°F) in the shade was measured. But the generally

ABOVE *Great waves of fog washing over the coastal edge of Africa's Namib Desert. This provides enough moisture for a community of specialist plants and animals to survive.*

OPPOSITE TOP *The driest desert on Earth – Atacama, running down the coast of Chile. Cold Pacific water at its edge provides a permanent rain barrier, and the only moisture reaching inland is fog.*

OPPOSITE BOTTOM *A Eulychnia cactus growing at the edge of the Atacama, covered in dew from the early morning fog sweeping off the sea.*

accepted record holder is El Azizia, in Libya, where an incredible 57.8°C (136°F) in the shade was recorded on 13 September 1922.

Taking deserts as a whole, the low-lying southern Sahara is the hottest desert on the planet, while the Gobi Desert is the coldest and is covered in snow for two months of the year. The Gobi's winter temperatures may drop as low as −40°C (−40°F) but reach more than 40°C (104°F) in the summer.

THE SCULPTING FORCES

ABOVE *The rippling Rose Dunes of Mali. Sand dunes cover just 20 per cent of the world's deserts.*

OPPOSITE *The barren hills of the semi-desert North American badlands. They have been eroded by ancient rivers and then by wind and infrequent but intense rainstorms.*

Water and wind work their erosive ways more violently in deserts than in any other environment, and their combined forces have created some of the world's most spectacular scenery. Without the protection of trees and bushes, erosion from the baking sun, cold nights and strong winds have laid bare the bones of the Earth. Generations of desert explorers have been unable to resist the call of these wild and pristine landscapes. Even today, when camels have been largely replaced by vehicles, desert travel remains a special experience.

Almost every week, a few ancient lorries leave Timbuktu in Mali and head north across the Sahara. They are carrying sheep to sell in the markets in southern Algeria. It is a gruelling five-day crossing, which they then repeat with a cargo of dates to sell in Timbuktu. Hitch a lift on one of these lorries, and you can experience the whole range of desert scenery. Soon after leaving Timbuktu, you cross a wide, flat pavement of small rocks that have been worn beautifully smooth by the wind. This is the reg desert characteristic of much of the southern Sahara. If you are lucky, you might then pass groups of tall, rock pillars that break up the monotony of the endless flat horizon. It is only after three or four days of hard driving that you finally reach the sand-dune scenery everyone expects to find in deserts. These massive dunes of southern Algeria's sand sea dwarf the lorry and are impossible to cross without the broad feet of a sure-footed camel.

SAND SEAS

Even in the driest deserts, tiny amounts of water are present in rock. Wildly fluctuating desert temperatures continually freeze and thaw this water. After being baked and frozen like this for thousands of years, even huge rocks break down into smaller and smaller fragments until they eventually blow across the desert as grains of sand. Blasted by the power of the wind, thrown against cliffs and rubbed against each other, grains become rounded and coated with a red polish of iron oxide. As the sand particles continue to flurry across the landscape, they gather in piles – sand dunes – which today cover up to 20 per cent of the world's deserts.

Sand dunes are surely the most evocative features of a desert landscape. Powerful winds blow the sand into some of nature's most beautiful fluid sculptures, ranging from small heaps to rolling mountains of sand more than 300m (984 feet) high and several kilometres (a mile or more) long. Large groups of them form the beautiful, undulating landscapes

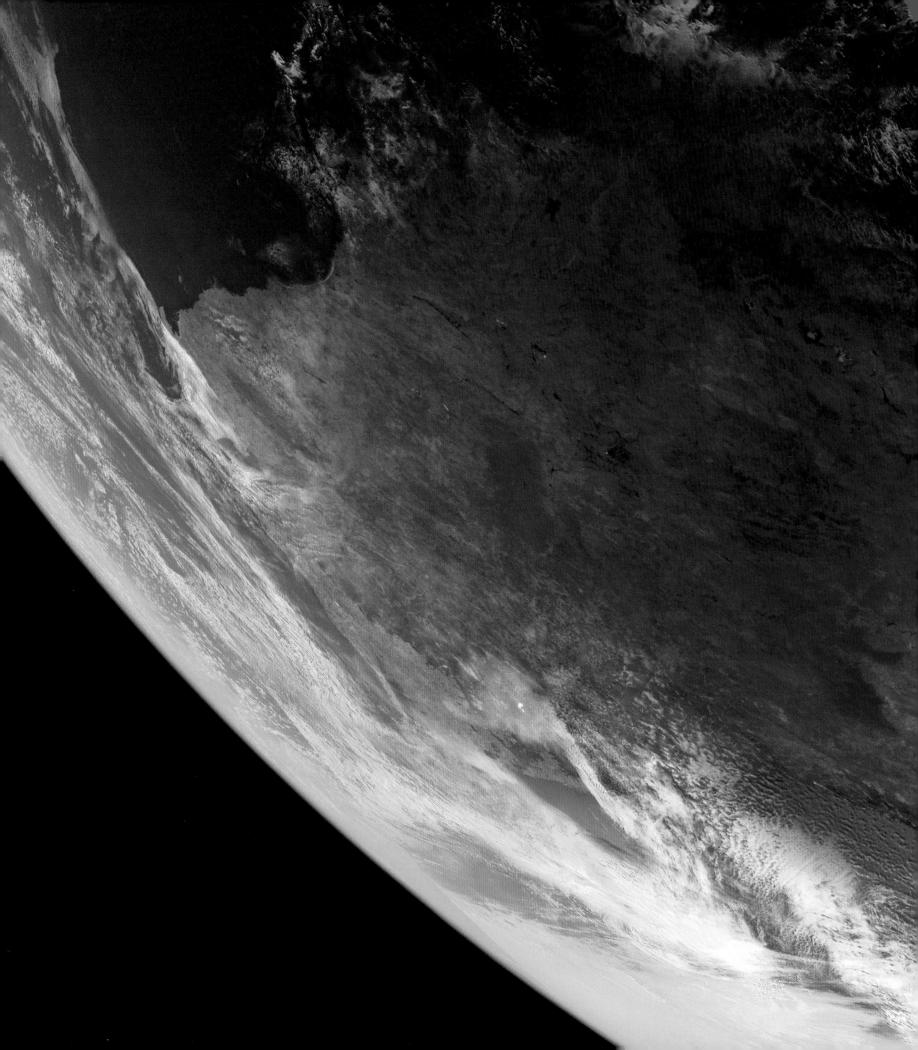

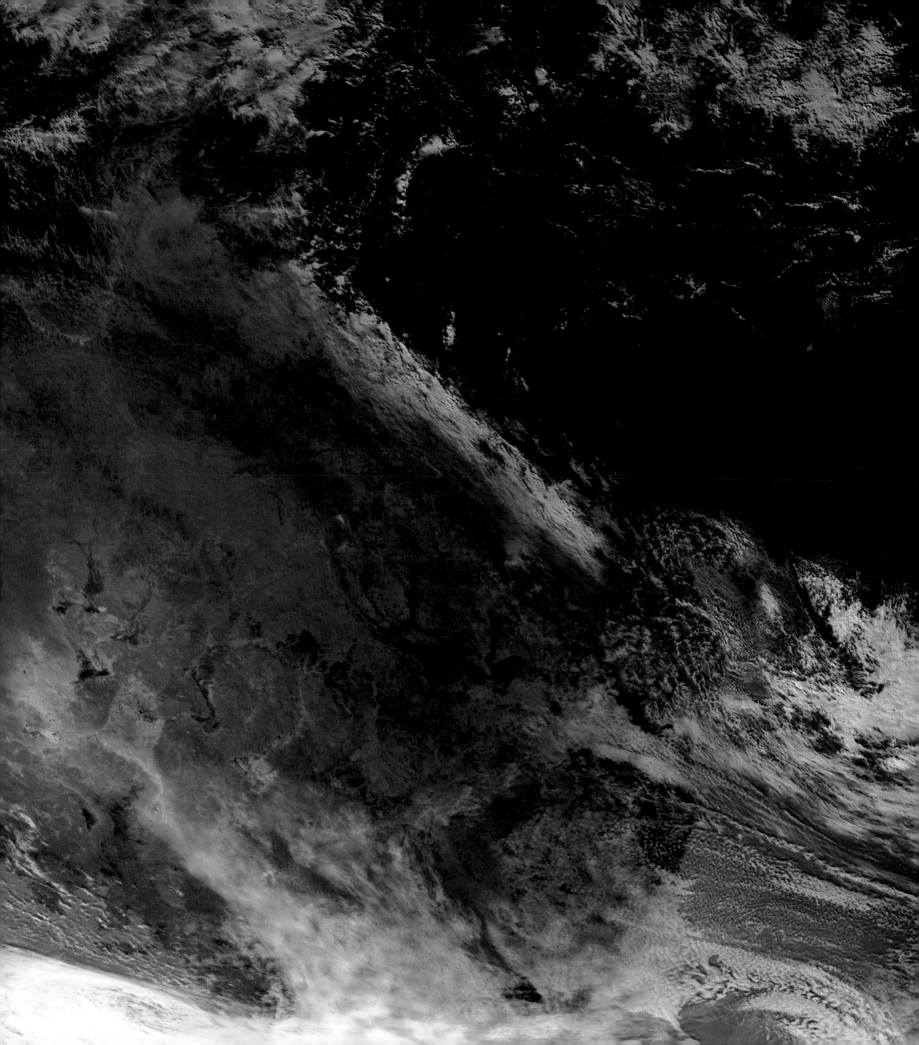

ABOVE *Chalk mushrooms – all that remains of an ancient seabed, now weathered and eroded into landmarks in Egypt's Western Desert.*

PREVIOUS PAGE *The great deserts of Australia, as seen from space.*

known as sand seas – vast expanses of sculpted sand rippling away to the horizon. The largest sand sea on the planet is the Rub' al-Khali, or Empty Quarter, on the Arabian Peninsula. It covers 560,000 sq km (216,220 square miles) – an area larger than France.

Differences in local wind patterns and the supply of sand produce various types of dune systems. The most common are the linear dunes that form in a series of parallel lines, like so many waves coming into the coast. Linear dunes are typical in Australian deserts and include the longest sand dunes in the world – the 300km (186-mile), parallel, red sand ridges of the extraordinarily beautiful Simpson Desert in South Australia – the continent's driest region. The majestic sand dunes of the Sossusvlei sea in the Namib Desert also stretch in long lines, but these ever-shifting folds of sand are much higher, forming some of the largest dunes in the world, up to 300m (985 feet) high. Moulded by wind, some of these fluid sculptures slowly creep across the Earth's surface – many by 10–20m (33–66 feet) a year and some by up to 50m (165 feet) a year.

WIND CRAFT

Wind is a powerful force, especially when carrying particles of sand, and in some places it has created almost alien landscapes. On a small scale, wind-blown sand erodes rocks into beautifully rounded and weathered shapes called ventifacts. On a larger scale, wind erosion can carve spectacular rocky pillars and create aerodynamically shaped hills – yardangs. Some of the most spectacular yardangs are found in Egypt's Western Desert, where a whole chalk seabed has been eaten away into a series of strange shapes. Many resemble giant, white mushrooms, the bottom of the rocky pillars abraded into streamlined, tapered forms. And in Iran's Dasht-e Lut Desert, the yardangs have been carved into building-like shapes, which the local Iranians call desert cities.

STORM POWER

Nothing transforms a desert landscape as quickly as a massive sandstorm. Seasonal winds pick up huge clouds of sand and dust, blowing them across the deserts, burying villages and blacking out the sky. The few animals that can cope in these conditions have special adaptations, such as a camel's extra-long eyelashes and long, hair-filled nostrils that can be individually closed. In the Sahara, walls of moving sand can reach more than 1.5km (a mile)

WATER POWER

Water has played a significant role in shaping desert landscapes. Millions of years ago, ancient river torrents scoured their way across plains of rock. These rivers have long since dried up, but their once powerful forces have sculpted dramatic landscapes. One of the most spectacular examples is in western North America, where soft rocks or weak clays have been eroded to create the desert badlands.

The extraordinary shaped mesas, buttes, knife-like ridges, pillars and columns of the badlands and canyons of the North American desert have all been shaped in this way. And in Utah's Bryce Canyon, (left) the pink towers are all that remain of a limestone plateau, the softer rock having been cut away by ancient rivers. Rain still plays a part in eating away the soft desert rock today. Sparse vegetation and thin soils, combined with short but intense rainstorms, mean that semi-desert regions suffer the highest rates of water erosion anywhere on Earth.

high and are clearly visible from space. The Sahara alone is thought to generate as much as 300 million tons of airborne sand each year, some of which travels as far as Greenland and South America. This is the world's largest source of dust and plays a vital role in the global ecology, creating storms in Florida, helping to produce plankton blooms in the Atlantic and even fertilizing the Amazon.

LIFE IN THE OVEN

For animals and plants trying to survive in the deserts, there are two key challenges: lack of water and extreme temperatures. Though they rarely occur in large numbers, a huge variety of different plants and animals – from almost every major group – have become highly adapted to cope with the demanding conditions.

Plants have little option but to stay where they are, and so it is hardly surprising that deserts are defined by their lack of vegetation. In the vast wastes of the Sahara – 9 million sq km (3.5 million square miles) – only 1400 different plant species have ever been identified. And the majority of the plants of the world's deserts have opted for just two basic strategies. They are either drought-resistors or drought-evaders. The resistors are perennials that are always there, fighting to survive. The evaders are ephemerals, only appearing when the conditions are right.

WATER RETENTION

To hold on to what little water there is and avoid drying up, the drought-resistors have developed a wide range of adaptations. They either specialize in storing water or reducing its chance of evaporation. Typically, they have small, simple leaves with impermeable coatings to minimize water loss or, in some cases, no leaves at all. Living stones, or lithops,

in the Namib Desert are an extreme example of this strategy. These plants look like a handful of small, grey pebbles. This conceals them from plant-eaters, but their round surfaces also expose just a small area so that they lose as little water as possible.

The roots of desert plants have three main designs: extensive, shallow, fibrous systems that make the best of sudden and unpredictable desert rainfall; bulbs that store water underground; and deep tap-roots. Most desert shrubs and trees are small or squat with extensive root systems, tapping into groundwater far below. For many years there was a solitary acacia tree in the Sahara that acted as a famous landmark for camel trains and travellers. When this lonely sentinel finally died, its roots were discovered to have reached a depth of 35m (115 feet). Other desert trees such as mesquite and tamarisk have even deeper roots, which may penetrate as far as 50m (165 feet).

The North American creosote bush has a root system that permeates the earth around it so effectively that the plant seems to be able to extract every available molecule of water in its vicinity. No other plant can survive nearby, and even its own seedlings can't compete for water, which makes reproduction something of a problem. The solution is to colonize nearby ground, not by setting seed but by sending out new stems from near its base on a slowly expanding network of roots. As the bush spreads outwards, the inner stems die away, with the effect that the creosote bush expands into a larger and larger ring, and goes on growing and expanding. One individual has been recorded as being more than 11,700 years old, making it among the oldest known individual organisms on Earth.

SPINY SOLUTIONS

Cacti, the archetypal desert plants, have a shallow, dense, network of fibrous roots that spread over a large area, close to the surface of the soil. These are designed for fast absorption of light rainfall that penetrates the soil only a short distance before evaporating.

BELOW *The making of a blinding sandstorm. Such storms travel at great speed and can appear within minutes. The whipped-up sand may land on the other side of the world – dust from the Sahara, for example, ends up fertilizing the Amazon.*

RIGHT *Perhaps the most famous cactus of all – the Sonora Desert's saguaro, which towers over all the other cacti.*

BELOW *A great horned owl uses a saguaro as the equivalent of a tree. Many animals make their homes in it and may also feed on its flowers and fruit, which offer vital refreshment for migrating birds and bats.*

Cacti have also attempted to solve their water problems by modifying their leaves into spines, greatly reducing water loss and at the same time discouraging grazing animals. Thirsty grazers are such a problem for desert plants that many are either poisonous or have developed thorns and spikes to protect themselves.

All of the 2000 or so species of ground-living cacti are found in the Americas, and their varied shapes and sizes are designed to produce the smallest surface area for any given volume, minimizing water evaporation. A plant's stomata (pores which plants use to take in carbon dioxide) also leak precious moisture, and so cacti have reduced their size and number. They keep them closed during the heat of the day and only open them at night to take in carbon dioxide. The gas is stored in solution as an organic acid, to be processed during the day, when sunlight makes photosynthesis possible once more. This clever technique of storing carbon dioxide has also been developed by many desert grasses.

Perhaps a cactus's greatest specialization is water storage. North America's Sonora Desert boasts the largest number and variety of cacti in the world. Of its 27 species, the most impressive and famous is the saguaro, with its candelabra of towering, column-like stems – the symbol of the Sonora. Its stems are made up of a series of pleat-like grooves and can grow for 75 years before the first side branches sprout. In its long lifetime – up to 200 years – a single saguaro may produce more than 40 million seeds, but only one seed is ever likely to reach maturity. This cactus can grow up to 15m (50 feet) tall, weigh more than 15 tons and have up to 50 separate branches. Its extensive root system stretches out as far as it is tall, and in a single day, it can take up a ton of water from a sudden rainstorm. After a succession of these rainstorms, 80 per cent of the plant's weight may be water. This majestic giant provides a welcome feeding station for all sorts of animals. At night it produces beautiful, large, white flowers that attract pollinating bats. Its flowers and fruit are also a valuable source of food for migrating animals such as hummingbirds and long-nosed bats. Without such feeding stations, many of these animals would not be able to cross the desert.

ABOVE *A Sonora barrel cactus with, behind it, an organ pipe and a saguaro. Arizona's Sonora Desert has the largest variety of cacti in the world. Here the scene is unusually lush, as an unexpected downpour has caused a desert flowering – the germination and flowering of dormant seeds, including Arizona poppies.*

ANIMAL TRICKS

Animals that survive in the desert are in many ways even more remarkable than the plants. Not only do they have to avoid drying out, but many also need to maintain their body temperatures at the same consistent level. Mammals in particular are vulnerable to extreme heat and extreme fluctuations in temperature, and their ability to survive freezing night temperatures can be just as crucial as their adaptations to the searing daytime heat.

Eternal life and resurrection

One the world's strangest plants is welwitschia, which grows in the Namib Desert and is designed to make the most of the early-morning fog that comes in from the Atlantic coast. Over millions of years, the plant has evolved into what is essentially a huge, swollen, turnip-like base, from which grow just two leaves. But these are monster leaves, which split into long ragged ribbons up to 9m (30 feet) long. This plant may live for more than 1500 years, throughout which time, its leaves continue to grow, fraying away at their tips as they are thrashed in the wind. Despite their ragged appearance, the leaves function as water gatherers. Covered in absorbent fibres that mop up water from the fog, the leaves absorb some water through their stomata and channel the rest of the condensation down towards the centre of the plant and its root system.

During extreme drought, some plants simply retreat from life above ground altogether. These geophytes, such as the fragrant, night-blooming cereus, survive below ground using bulbs, tubers, nodules or rhizomes. Grasses do it by developing large and complex root systems. When rain finally appears, these dormant plants are able to grow foliage within days.

One extraordinary plant in the Atacama Desert has no roots at all. The airplant *Tillandsia latifolia* just has stiff, springy leaves arranged in a ball and rolls across the desert whenever the wind blows. This structure is designed to capture moisture when the fogs roll in off the cold Pacific waters.

Deserts in bloom

The almost overnight transformation of a barren desert landscape into a sea of brightly coloured flowers is one of nature's greatest conjuring tricks. This is the show put on by plants that have opted for the ephemeral drought-evasion strategy. In effect, they are seeds that occasionally spend their lives as plants – but seeds designed to seize the moment and burst into life almost overnight should the desert be drenched by a storm. Ephemeral species such as poppies, rockroses and grasses are the grasshoppers of the plant world. Generally, there is only just enough seasonal rainfall for the plants to survive, but occasionally the rains are so good that the whole landscape is transformed. Seeds that might have lain dormant in the parched earth for 30 years suddenly germinate.

To make sure they don't blow their chances on a flash-in-the-pan downpour, the seeds have a special chemical inhibitor in their coats that must be dissolved by a good quantity of rain before they can germinate. Their big moment may not happen for years,

and so when it comes, they throw everything they have at it, producing large leaves and gaudy flowers.

Huge numbers of brightly coloured flowers can carpet a desert in days, but the whole show may be over in just a couple of weeks. The plants aim to be pollinated as fast as possible and therefore produce enormous quantities of seeds. These seeds can lie dormant for many years – those of one desert ephemeral that had been kept in a museum for 250 years were still able to germinate when given water.

The Lazarus effect

Good rains and a flush of vegetation can rejuvenate all sorts of life forms. In the Arizona Desert, heavy rain can seem to cause the ground itself to stir. Spadefoot toads that have lain buried and dormant in desiccated mud for as long as ten months kick-start their life-cycle in a matter of hours. As they emerge, they throw themselves into a frenzy of calling, for like the desert flowers, they have only a short time to reproduce before the baking sun will force their offspring back into hiding.

Insects such as desert locusts also use the dormancy strategy to survive long periods of drought. Their eggs can survive for 20 years until conditions are right for hatching. Then their numbers explode, producing swarms of biblical size. One recorded swarm covered more than 200 sq km (77 square miles) and was only one of several swarms in the area containing an estimated 500 billion locusts. An individual locust will consume its own weight in food every 24 hours, and so the swarms must keep continually on the move. Travelling at up to 130km (80 miles) a day, a locust swarm quickly exploits the flush of fresh green, and soon the desert returns to an arid wasteland.

LEFT TO RIGHT *Welwitschia mirabilis – the plant with the oldest leaves in the world. It lives in the Namib Desert, but near enough to the coast to make use of the fog that rolls in from the Atlantic at night, absorbing the moisture and channelling any excess down to its roots.*

The vlei lily, an amaryllis, flowering after summer rain in the Kalahari Desert. It copes with desert conditions by lying dormant as a bulb and then flowering fast when the rains arrive.

Sand verbena – a southern US annual that may spend much of its life in seed form. But as soon as enough rain falls, it can carpet a desert area with flowers in a matter of weeks. Hairs on its leaves and stems provide a moist buffer zone between the leaf and the hot air.

An agave succulent festooned with desert bluebells – a desert annual that undergoes a rapid life-to-death cycle brought on by heavy rain.

IN THE HEAT OF THE DAY

Roasting air temperatures and baking-hot surfaces mean that, for most animals, there is really very little choice except to avoid the day altogether. This is where it helps to be small. Even within a few hours of sunrise, most sandy surfaces are already burning hot. Yet burrow just a few centimetres into the sand, and it is surprisingly cool. Small desert animals such as insects, scorpions, reptiles and rodents know this and have learnt to survive below the surface or under rocks until darkness falls. Being small is such an advantage that a wide variety of small mammals have evolved to live in the desert. The Sahara, for instance, is home to around 40 species of rodent, including gerbils, mice and jerboas. Many of these have large hind legs so that, when they do venture out, they can run very quickly over the hot sand. The pocket mouse goes a stage further. In periods of extreme heat and drought, it takes refuge in its burrow and falls into a dormant state called aestivation.

If an animal's lifestyle forces it into the light, the only way to survive is to find shade and ways of losing heat. The African ground squirrel uses its bushy tail as a parasol, adjusting it to just the right angle to keep its body in shadow, the hairs on its tail spread to provide an ample canopy. Other mammals survive in the baking sun by turning parts of their body into radiators – the jackrabbit in America, the fennec fox in the Sahara and the bandicoots in Australia have all turned their ears into huge, efficient heat exchangers.

Sweating or panting also allows water to evaporate and cool the body. Some Australian marsupials begin to salivate freely as their temperature increases. They then use their tongues to spread the saliva over their bodies, and as it evaporates, the saliva cools them off. Kangaroos also have a special cooling area on their forearms – a network of capillaries near the surface – which they cover with saliva when the temperature rises.

Some large desert mammals have surprisingly thick coats. But dense, insulating fur works in both directions. As well as conserving warmth at night, a thick layer of hair is also

BELOW *Solifugids, relatives of spiders, with an extra-thick cuticle to reduce water loss. They scamper over the sand at night, using their huge jaws to kill scorpions, spiders and insects.*

BELOW RIGHT *The shovel-snouted lizard, hunting in the day. To stop its feet burning, it never has more than two on the hot sand at any one time.*

an effective heat shield. For instance, the outermost layer of a camel's shaggy coat may be up to 30°C (86°F) warmer than its body temperature.

Gazelles and antelopes do not have thick coats, and so the blazing sun quickly and dangerously heats them up. They could lose this heat by sweating and panting, but that would use up a great deal of water. So they allow their bodies to heat up to 46°C (115°F), a temperature that would cause brain damage in other mammals. The oryx, or gemsbok, manages to survive this by preferentially keeping its brain several degrees cooler than the rest of its body, using its nasal passages and an intricate system of blood vessels to cool the blood on its way to the brain.

NOT A DROP TO DRINK

Even at normal temperatures, animals need to balance the moisture they take with the moisture they lose through respiration and sweating. In the desert, this balance becomes crucial. The problem is particularly acute for smaller animals. Compared with the total volume of their bodies, they have relatively larger surface areas, and this makes them far more vulnerable to water loss through evaporation. By comparison, insects and arachnids

ABOVE *A wild Bactrian camel and her calf in search of water in the Gobi Desert. Bactrian camels are critically endangered, with just a few remnant populations in China and Mongolia. They are adapted to extreme heat and cold and to drought. In winter they grow thick coats (here, the mother is moulting hers) and obtain water by eating snow. In summer they allow their temperature to fluctuate to avoid sweating, and they also conserve water by producing dry faeces and tiny amounts of urine. Thick eyelashes and tightly closing nostrils keep out the dust, and splayed, padded feet enable them to walk on the hot sand.*

(spiders, scorpions and the like) are off to something of a head start. They are the most numerous of all the animals found in deserts and have the advantage of owning waterproof outer skeletons already designed to resist desiccation. Desert insects have even thicker waxy cuticles to further reduce water loss. But insects and arachnids are still vulnerable to desert extremes, and relatively few spend long periods on the surface during the day. Scorpions, for instance, have a very low rate of water loss and rarely drink, getting most of their liquid from food. But they spend their days under rocks or in burrows, emerging to hunt only at night.

WHEN IT PAYS TO BE THICK SKINNED

With their thin, water-permeable skins, amphibians find desert life particularly hard. Those that do survive tend to spend much of their lives underground. In the Australian deserts, there are at least 20 species of burrowing frogs, many of which have spade-like feet for

digging. They may also develop an external cocoon of dead skin that helps to keep them moist underground. When the rains finally come, the frogs emerge in enormous numbers to breed. Puddles of water are normally crucial for frog reproduction, but the tiny sandhill frog of Western Australia has got round the problem by laying its eggs in the moist conditions below the sand.

Among the vertebrates (animals with backbones), the most successful group in exploiting desert environments must be the reptiles. They are found in every one of the world's deserts, and in the Sahara alone there are nearly a hundred species. Their key advantage is their thick, impermeable skin, which helps retain water. They are cold-blooded and so do not need to rely on food intake to maintain their body temperature and can easily survive on the sparse supplies available in most deserts. Needing the heat of the sun to warm their bodies, many reptiles reverse the normal activity pattern of desert animals and hunt during the day. But even they have problems in extreme temperatures. The shovel-snouted lizard of the Namib Desert only ever keeps two of its legs on the ground at the same time – one in the front and one on the opposite side at the back. By reversing the two legs at regular intervals, the lizard ensures no two feet ever get too hot.

ABOVE *An Arizona spadefoot toad burrowing with its powerful legs. Underground, it protects itself from drying out with a cocoon of skin and will not emerge until rain comes again the following summer. It will then mate and lay its eggs in the temporary pools – eggs that can develop into tadpoles within two days.*

OPPOSITE *The oryx, one of the few large herbivores to be found in deserts. It makes use of any vegetation it can find, browsing, grazing or digging for roots and tubers (a source of moisture), and undertakes long treks in search of water.*

WATER ON THE WING

Birds do well in deserts as they have higher body temperatures than mammals and can tolerate temperatures as high as 45°C (113°F) for long periods. Most typical desert species are small, such as the larks and coursers, and many have opted to stay fairly inactive for much of the day. They also have the advantage of flight, which allows them to travel around the deserts looking for water. In Australian deserts, for instance, budgerigars travel in massive flocks – brightly coloured nomads following the unpredictable rains.

When adult birds are looking after their young, the problem of finding water can become even greater. Chicks get their water from the food they are given, and if this isn't juicy enough, they will need liquid from some other source. The chicks of the Namaqua sandgrouse have exactly this problem. Somehow the adults must bring them water, even though the nest may be up to 40km (25 miles) from the nearest source. The problem has been solved with a beautifully simple piece of design. The adult male sandgrouse's unique feathers across his chest and belly soak up water like a sponge. On arriving at the nearest standing water, he first satisfies his own thirst but then wades out until his chest feathers are saturated. As soon as he returns home, the chicks are upon him, jostling for a space to suck from the feathers.

In the deserts of Arizona and Mexico, roadrunners have found a different way to get water to their thirsty chicks. These birds nest in cactus or thorn bushes and rear two or three chicks, which are able to swallow and digest surprisingly large meals. Insects and even lizards are eagerly accepted from a very early age. But as a meal is handed from parent to chick, a strange dispute ensues. Neither seems to want to let go of the food. This apparent mealtime squabble is an essential feeding ritual. As long as the lizard or insect is held firmly in place, the adult can use it as a way to channel water from its mouth to that of its chick – water that has been produced during the adult's digestion especially for its brood. Only when the chick has finished drinking can it start to eat its meal.

ABOVE *A roadrunner giving water to its young by ingenious means. It allows a chick to grasp a food item but won't let go of it until enough water has trickled out of its beak, down the food and into the beak of the chick at the other end.*

OPPOSITE *A Peringuey's sidewinding adder, sidewinding its way rapidly across the sand. It is totally adapted to the shifting dunes of southwestern Africa's Namib Desert. In the heat of the day, it keeps cool by undulating its way below the surface of the sand, where it lies in wait for prey, with just its nostrils and eyes (placed almost on the top of its head) uncovered.*

MAKING YOUR OWN

Mammals whose diets are high in protein have a problem. Protein contains nitrogen and is metabolized into urea, which is highly poisonous if allowed to build up in the body. It must leave the body as urine, which means losing precious water. Some desert animals make up for this by producing metabolic water, made during normal metabolism within the body. For desert mammals such as kangaroo rats, the water budget is so tight that during the day they hide away in cool burrows, sealing up the openings to their nests with plugs of earth. But they still lose so much water through breathing and evaporation that their burrows are moist and their stocks of seeds can even become damp. The kangaroo rats live on a knife's edge trying to replace this water, and so production of metabolic water can be make or break.

WHY IT PAYS TO HAVE FAT

When green vegetation is available, camels can go for months without drinking. But during the Saharan summer, there is only dry food, and even that is very scarce. Camels can go for a week or more without water and up to ten days without food by burning up the fat stored in their famous humps. Metabolizing the fat with oxygen, they are able to release about 0.5kg (1 pound) of water for every 0.5kg of fat. When camels are finally able to drink again, they can imbibe up to 30 per cent of their body mass as water in a very short time – 50 litres (11 gallons) in just a few minutes – which they store in their stomachs. The fatty humps and their thick fur also help to insulate them so that they hardly sweat. This insulation is particularly important for the two-humped Bactrian camel, which lives in the deserts of China and Mongolia. Daily temperatures in the Gobi can vary by 32°C (58°F), and for two months of the year, this coldest of deserts can be covered in snow. Unfortunately for the camels, the air here is so dry that the snow never melts but just evaporates into the atmosphere. So the camels have no option but to eat the snow. To swallow large quantities would be dangerous, but with the snow on the ground for long periods, the camels do well, eating ten litres worth of water in snow each day.

DESERT GIANTS

You would not expect to find the world's largest herbivore in the desert, but there are two small populations of elephants that remain on the edges of the Sahara in Mali and in the Namib Desert along the coast of southwestern Africa. These animals are specially adapted for desert life, with smaller bodies and larger feet than other African elephants. The large feet help them cross the unstable sand on long journeys up to 64km (40 miles) a day in search of food and water. In the Namib, the elephants have learnt to dig away beneath the surface of the sand to find the roots of desert grass, which tends to provide the most nourishment. Unlike plains elephants, which need water every day, desert elephants can get away with drinking only once every five days.

Even more surprisingly, the Namib also has a small population of resident lions that survive by hunting oryx. They have adapted to the demanding conditions by having larger home ranges and smaller prides than lions living elsewhere in Africa. What is remarkable is that, in these low-density conditions, the desert lions manage to produce the largest litters and have the highest cub-survival rate of any African lions. For the moment at least, these mammals have joined the ranks of the incredible desert survivors.

BELOW *Namib lions, part of a remnant population of lions that survives in this desert by having large home ranges – larger than those of any other African lion pride. Their staple prey is the desert oryx.*

OPPOSITE *Namib elephants. They survive on meagre rations – often just the roots of desert grass – and have become smaller than normal plains elephants, with larger feet to help them walk on the sand in their search for food and precious water.*

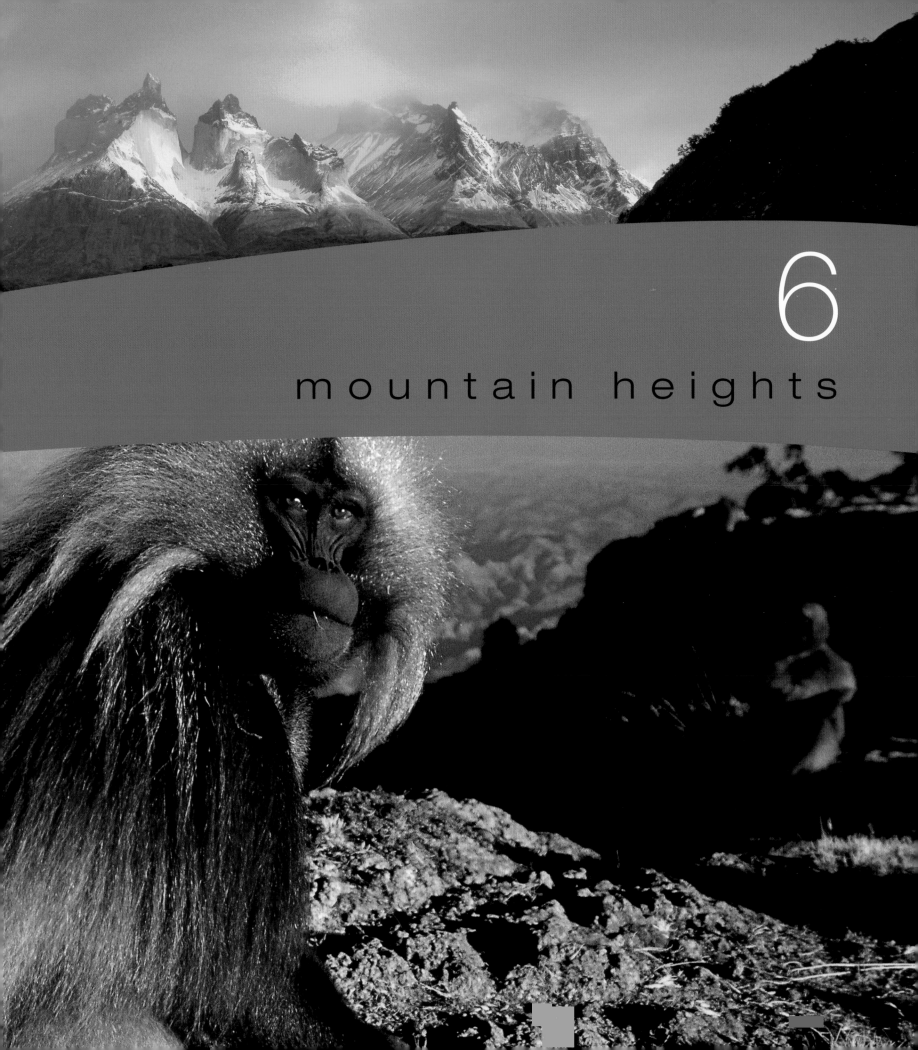

6

mountain heights

Mountains epitomize wilderness – remote high-altitude places, where only the hardiest of creatures can survive the cold. Yet at their inception they can also be dramatically hot, before mellowing with age, worn down by the ravages of water and ice.

Each mountain range has a distinctive personality, shaped by a unique life history. The high peaks of the Himalayas are young and crested with snow and ice – a frozen world that nothing can inhabit permanently. The Ethiopian Highlands of Africa are ancient, low and green to their summits, supporting a rich wildlife. The other great ranges fall between these two extremes, each a product of millennia of change to the surface of our planet.

What constitutes a mountain depends on the surrounding landscape and who is looking at it. The Watchung Mountains in New Jersey are a mere 120–150m (400–500 feet) high, whereas 3600-m (12,000-foot) protuberances in the Himalayas are shrugged off by Tibetans as mere foothills. As for a mountain's 'permanence', this depends on your view of time. That most rational and sceptical of men, the eighteenth-century philosopher Voltaire, regarded as preposterous the view held by a scientist friend of his, the Comte de Buffon, that even the small hills in France might not always have been there. Buffon had become fascinated by seashells he had discovered embedded in rocks on the hillsides of France. How, he wondered, had they got there? He became convinced that sea animals had lived in the places where the mountains now stood, suggesting that soft sediments had covered them and hardened into rocks in shallow seas and that, later, the rocks had been lifted high above sea level. Nonsense, said Voltaire – pilgrims from the seashore carried the shells to the mountaintop.

In Buffon's day, the science of geology was in its infancy, and the theory of evolution was still a hundred years away. Today, we know that a mountain does not endure forever. It is born and has a vigorous youth, a long maturity and an even longer old age until, finally, it is worn down into the earth and disappears.

MOUNTAIN BIRTH

Covering the Earth is a layer of rock which is broken into roughly seven ragged segments that fit together like a jigsaw puzzle. These segments, or tectonic plates, are thought to move extremely slowly (from 1–10cm, 0.5–4 inches, in a year) across the surface. When they move apart, new ocean floors may form in their wake; when they collide, there is no place for the rocks to go but upwards, and so they raise mountains. Flying over the Danakil Depression of Ethiopia is like looking out from a time machine at these titanic earth-

ABOVE *Acid pools and sulphur deposits on the bubbling volcanic crust of the Dallol Springs in the Danakil Desert, Ethiopia, which lies on the fault line of the Great Rift Valley.*

OPPOSITE *The Great Rift Valley, Kenya. Here, the violent activity that tore apart the Earth's crust caused huge chunks of it to sink between parallel fault lines and also forced up a chain of volcanoes.*

PREVIOUS PAGE, TOP *Torres del Paine, Chile – part of the Andes.* BOTTOM *Geladas in the Ethiopian Highlands.*

building processes in action. Textbook diagrams of tectonic plates come to life in the contorted landscape below you.

With its growing chain of newly emergent volcanoes and blackened lava fields snaking into the desert, the Danakil is one of the most geologically active places on Earth. From the air, Dallol Springs looks relatively unassuming, a circular area of desert that is a darker orange than its surroundings, but when the helicopter lands, you enter one of the most outlandish places on Earth.

What first hits you is a wall of heat so intense that every pore in your body screams for water – daytime temperatures here average 48°C (118°F), making it one of the hottest places on Earth. Burning-hot clouds of sulphurous fumes sting your eyes and leave you choking as you stagger into a landscape that would seem more appropriate on Mars. You are standing inside a crater nearly 50m (157 feet) below sea level in the Earth's lowest land volcano. One day its eruptions will reach the surface, the volcano will burst from the ground, and a mountain will be born.

The Danakil Depression is at the northern end of the Great Rift Valley, part of a huge set of cracks in the Earth's crust, which threatens to split Africa in two. It started to form 100 million years ago when underlying landmasses began to pull in opposite directions. As the crust stretched, volcanoes erupted, and today they dot the entire length of the rift. Eventually, the separation will be such that the salty waters of the Red Sea will spill across this desert, and the Horn of Africa will be separated from the rest of the continent and form an island.

THE ROOF OF AFRICA

The Ethiopian Highlands are the largest mountainous area in Africa, with one of the tallest mountains on the continent, Ras Dashen, rising to 4620m (15,158 feet). Two billion years ago, these highlands were as flat as the Danakil Depression, but over millennia, molten lava rising from the Earth's core forced up a huge dome 1000km (620 miles) across – the 'Roof of Africa'. In the north lie the Simien Mountains. These were glaciated as recently as 10,000 years ago, and ice and rain have carved a dramatic landscape of canyons and spires.

At about 4km (2.5 miles) up live walia ibex – invaders from Europe during recent ice ages, when the two continents were joined by tundra. These rare goats survive only on the remotest pinnacles, mountaineering across precipitous rock-faces on rubbery hooves to nibble on grass and herbs. They share the high plateaus with troops of geladas, which also navigate the death-defying crags with ease, possessing the strongest fingers for their size of any primate.

The geladas feed almost exclusively on grass, specifically the protein-rich alpine grasses found only at these heights. Keeping warm and finding ways to conserve energy is critically important up here. Geladas are coated with thick manes of fur, and they do all their feeding seated, shuffling on their bottoms from one clump of grass to another. Primates very often use their genitals as sexual indicators, but because female geladas have to spend so long sitting down, they have replaced colourful bottoms with bare skin on their chests, which swells and turns pink when they are sexually receptive.

Fossils show that geladas were once widespread in Africa – there was even a giant species

BELOW *The rare and endangered Ethiopian wolf, confined to isolated pockets of alpine grassland and heathland in the Ethiopian Highlands. It probably had a Eurasian wolf-like ancestor, but it behaves more like a coyote, feeding mainly on small rodents.*

OPPOSITE *The gelada, another species confined to the 'Roof of Africa'. Here it is relatively safe from predators and free of competition for the alpine grasses it depends on. The cliffs provide a refuge at night and a sunning place in the early morning.*

as big as a gorilla. It is thought that geladas were forced into isolation in the highlands from the hot African plains below by heavy predator pressure and competition with other primates, particularly humans. The Simiens have been an ideal refuge, with abundant grass, few competing grazers and good access to safe resting places on the nearby cliffs. Geladas are, though, still nervous of potential danger and frequently graze in mixed herds alongside walia ibex. The ibex are taller and, in long grass, may spot predators more easily. In turn, the ibex benefit from the eyes and ears of a gelada troop, which can number up to 800 towards the end of the wet season – possibly the largest monkey groups on the planet.

In the past, the Ethiopian wolf, also found only in these highlands, may have been a significant threat to the young of walia ibex and geladas. Today, only about 500 wolves remain, making it Africa's rarest large predator. It has become a specialist rat-catcher, normally hunting alone, with sensitive ears, slender muzzle and sharp, outward-pointing front teeth for detecting fleet-footed rats and snatching them from their burrows.

As the climate warmed after the last ice age, the broad belt of subalpine vegetation that these animals depend on contracted to higher altitudes. But these cold mountaintops receive three times more rain than the lowlands only 35km (22 miles) away and so provide a refuge from the rest of barren and arid Ethiopia. But as Africa's climate continues to dry out, the narrow band of alpine grassland and the animals that live there are being forced even higher, marooning them on the Roof of Africa.

BELOW *The sun rising over Lago Pehoe and Cuernos del Paine in Torres del Paine National Park, Patagonia, Chile. The peaks are part of the great Andean mountain chain that stretches down the western edge of South America. Continued volcanic activity results from the Pacific Ocean crust pushing against and sliding under the continent.*

THE LONGEST MOUNTAIN CHAIN ON EARTH

The highest active volcanoes in the world are in the Andes: Tupungato at 6550m (21,485 feet) in Chile and Cotopaxi at 5897m (19,342 feet) in Ecuador. The volcanic activity is evidence that the processes which built the Andes are continuing today. As the denser oceanic crust of the Pacific Ocean slips beneath the western edge of South America, causing it to buckle and fold, it melts and is forced back to the surface in violent volcanic eruptions.

The Andes also form the longest mountain chain on the planet, running down through 67 degrees of latitude. This modifies the effects of altitude, and as you travel down the Andes, you notice a dramatic effect: the tree line moves lower down the slopes the further south you go. Trees in the tropical Bolivian Andes grow as high up as 4000m (13,120 feet), but the tree line at subpolar Tierra del Fuego is almost at sea level.

Locals advise that if you want to see Patagonia just stand still and it will blow past you. Wind is certainly the first thing that hits you when you reach the southernmost tip of the Andes, with freezing blasts reaching more than 160kph (100mph). Three huge ice-sheets dominate the region. Covering more than 18,130 sq km (7000 square miles), they are the largest expanse of ice outside the poles, so vast that they generate their own weather.

Almost nothing lives on the ice-sheet itself, and surviving on its edge requires great stamina. The three famous mountain towers of Torres del Paine project from this ice edge. Living in their lee are more than 40 mammal species, which endure the most unstable mountain weather on the planet. Storms build on the ice-cap and funnel down between the towers, and even in the height of summer, temperatures can plummet, plunging the animals into subzero blizzard conditions. The guanaco, in the camel family and ancestor of the domestic llama, is particularly well adapted for such dramatic shifts in climate, with its dense, woolly coat, and is numerous in the Torres del Paine National Park. Absent, though, are the normal mountain inhabitants of North America and other regions of the world — wild goats and sheep — which did not make it south after the gap between the two Americas was bridged.

LIONS OF THE ANDES

The Inca word for mountain lion is puma, meaning powerful — a perfect description of the Patagonian puma. Pumas range more widely in the Americas than any other terrestrial mammal and are found from the Canadian Yukon south to the Strait of Magellan. There are more than 25 races, and by far the biggest is the Patagonian one — its large size helping it to conserve heat in the bitter winters. Pumas in the Torres del Paine park are generally solitary, the largest social group being a mother with her cubs, which stay with her for 18 months. To find enough food here, a female needs 100 sq km (38 square miles), and a male

even more, and the sheep ranches that surround the park provide an irresistible temptation for a hungry cat. Despite legal protection throughout Chile, pumas are ruthlessly persecuted, with ranch owners offering bounties and sometimes even employing lion-hunters. There are estimated to be 25 pumas in Torres del Paine, though this figure is debatable due to their elusive nature. But numbers could be increasing in response to the recovering population of guanacos, their main prey — now totalling more than 3000.

LEFT *Four adolescent puma cubs in the Torres del Paine National Park, feasting on a guanaco killed by their mother — a rarely witnessed scene.*

OPPOSITE *A bachelor herd of guanacos, grazing below the three towers of Torres del Paine. These 'mountain camels' are supremely adapted to cope with the extreme temperature fluctuations and poor forage of the high Andes.*

PREVIOUS PAGE *The great Andean backbone of South America, beginning at the equator and ending 7000km (4350 miles) south at Tierra del Fuego, just 1125km (700 miles) from Antarctica.*

THE NORTH AMERICAN SPINE

From space, the main mountain system, or cordillera, of the Americas extends like a spine down the western edge of both continents. Beginning in Alaska near the Arctic Circle, it stretches in an almost unbroken series of mountain chains. At one time, it is thought that the Rockies and the Andes formed a continuous active mountain belt. But unlike the Andes, which continue to grow as the oceanic crust slips beneath the western edge of South America, the Rockies are effectively dead and in decline. The plate that moved underneath North America was entirely consumed, and the active mountain-building which folded and faulted the rocks of the Rockies to such an extent that they look like rolling waves on a sea has effectively been switched off.

WINTER REFUGES

In winter, the Rockies are shrouded with snow – in places, nearly 60m (200 feet) falls every year. Slopes between 35 degrees and 45 degrees are particularly prone to avalanches, the most dangerous angle being 38 degrees. The precise angle of slope is also thought to be key to how one mountain animal survives the winters. Grizzly bears prefer to dig their dens into slopes with an incline of 30 degrees – thought to be just steep enough to make a roof overhead that won't collapse in winter but at an angle that allows the opening to be covered by a heavy, insulating blanket of snow.

A grizzly enters its den in October or November, and during the next six months, it will live off its accumulated fat reserves. It enters a form of hibernation where it takes just one breath a minute and its heart rate drops to ten beats a minute. A female will have mated in late spring, but an embryo won't develop inside her until she has gone into hibernation. If she has not accumulated enough fat to sustain both herself and any offspring over the winter, no embryos will implant. Cubs are born in January but don't emerge until they are three to four months old. While the steep slopes around their den may be challenging for novice climbers, they make it difficult for adult males – twice the size of females – to reach the nursery and eat the cubs. But since there is little food for the mother at these heights, she is forced to lead the cubs away from the safety of the nursery slopes after just a couple of weeks. More than half of grizzly cubs die in their first year, from predation, infanticide, accidents, starvation and disease.

In summer, the peaks are stripped of snow, revealing the true nature of the Rockies. Now the upper reaches can be reclaimed by mountaineers such as the American mountain goat – not a goat but a 'goat antelope', more closely related to the musk ox. It is the best equipped of all the North American large mammals for survival in these craggy peaks: a double coat provides superb insulation, and hooves have both flexible rubbery cores to grip smooth rocks and hard, sharp keratin rims to catch onto the smallest of footholds.

By now, most grizzly bears are on the lower slopes fattening up for the winter, but not all. Some climb to the summits in search of a surprising feast – moths, by the million. Each summer, army cutworm moths migrate to mountain regions to feed at night on the nectar of alpine flowers. During the day, the moths roost in the scree, which is where the bears root them out. Though moths may appear to be a meagre meal for a bear, when eaten in massive numbers, they are as nutritious as egg-laden salmon.

BELOW *A grizzly mother with her two cubs newly emerged from their winter birth den. She must lead them from the high, snow-covered nursery slopes to feeding areas lower down.*

ABOVE Part of the great Rockies (here in Alberta, Canada) – a series of mountain chains stretching the length of North America. Unlike the Andes of South America, these are 'dead' mountains.

LEFT The American mountain goat, built for mountaineering, with a deep chest and massive shoulder muscles, relatively short legs and special traction pads on its hooves. Its long, thick coat enables it to withstand the severest of winters.

THE MOUNTAIN DESTROYERS

Rivers are the great levellers. They carve deep V-shaped valleys in mountainous regions, carrying away the eroded mountain material, which they finally deposit in the sea. The main rivers of the Himalayas – the Indus and the Ganges – carry between them a billion tons of sediment per year. If trucks were to be loaded up with this material, the line of vehicles would stretch more than 40 times around the planet. This creates the largest body of sediment in the world: the Bengal 'fan' covers 56,980 sq km (22,000 square miles).

As snow accumulates high in the mountains, the excess is released in the form of great waterfalls of snow – avalanches. Travelling at speeds of up to 400kph (248mph), they are immensely destructive. Since these releases follow the most efficient route, they normally follow the same path year after year, creating distinctive chutes on the slope. If snowfall is heavy, the chute may widen, while in other years, less avalanche activity may allow tree growth slowly to reclaim the path.

RIVERS OF ICE

When snow accumulates in depressions or cirques, it turns into ice under its own weight, creating a glacier. Seven per cent of the world's fresh water is stored in glaciers, which cover 10 per cent of land (during the last ice age, they covered 32 per cent). If all this ice melted, it is estimated that the sea level would rise by approximately 70m (230 feet).

The Baltoro Glacier in Pakistan is part of the largest mountain glacier system on Earth. It is 60km (37 miles) long and in places up to 6km (4 miles) wide and is fed by more than 30 tributary glaciers. As it moves down the slope, the surface ice cracks and forms deep crevasses. Debris that falls from the surrounding terrain builds up on the sides as lateral moraines or becomes engulfed in the glacier and spat out at the other end as a terminal moraine (the dark stripe that you may see in the middle of a glacier is formed by the joining of the lateral moraines when two glaciers meet). Over time, when air has been forced out between the crystals, the ice turns blue. The Kutiah Glacier, part of the same system, holds the record for the fastest glacial surge: in 1953, it travelled more than 12km (7.5 miles) in three months, averaging about 112m (365 feet) per day.

As they move, glaciers erode the mountains by freezing to rocks and plucking them from the valleys and by grinding down the bedrock. They are the most powerful erosive forces on our planet. When melt-water streams plunge down inside a glacier, vertical shafts form. Called moulins, these have provided glaciologists with windows into the internal workings of a glacier. Movement is by no means uniform inside – the influence of drag means that the flow in the centre of a glacier is more rapid than that along the 'shore', much as in a river. And the deeper you go, the slower the movement. Since rates of movement can now be precisely calculated, a ghoulish kind of arithmetic has emerged: when will the body of an entombed man reappear at the melting face of a glacier? In the summer of 1956, a glacier at the foot of the Swiss Weisshorn ejected the preserved body of a 19-year-old German climber, Georges Winkler, who had fallen from the peak in 1888. It had taken 68 years for the ice to carry the corpse a mile or so from the upper glacier to its terminus.

Swiss scientists were the first in the world to study the habits of glaciers and to conclude

BELOW *Pakistan's Baltoro Glacier, grinding away the valley as it slowly descends. The 'tracks' are medial moraines – ridges of mountain material from the edges of glaciers that have converged into a giant ice river, 6km (4 miles) across in places.*

OPPOSITE *A powder-snow avalanche down Gasherbrum in the Karakoram Mountains, the high, jagged range that separates Pakistan from China. More people have died on these slopes than on any other mountains.*

ABOVE *Everest – the highest mountain in the world – emerging above the other Himalayan mountains. By the time the monsoon winds ride up into the Himalayas and reach Everest's summit at 8850m (29,035 feet), there is little rain left, and so the top of the enormous pyramid remains relatively snow-free. The total lack of food and deadly cold winds mean that nothing can live here permanently.*

OPPOSITE *A satellite view of the Himalayas, showing Everest as the largest triangular peak in the centre. This range stretches one sixth of the circumference of the planet. It was pushed up in the past 50 million years, and the sharp ridges – yet to be worn smooth by the elements – are evidence of its relative youth.*

that the Swiss glaciers are actually remains of giant ice-sheets that covered northern Europe as recently as 12,000 years ago. Present estimates indicate that the glacial cap in the Alps may have been as much as a mile deep. The country was drowned under millions of tons of solid ice, and only the tops of the highest mountains projected above it. In the past century, they shrank fairly steadily, in tandem with almost all the world's glaciers. In recent decades, glaciers in some parts of the world have begun to grow again as a result of increased precipitation, but most are melting faster than ever before.

THE GREATEST PHYSICAL FEATURE ON EARTH

The Himalayas demand superlatives: the highest mountain, the highest pass, the deepest gorge, the highest-living plants and animals. Other mountain ranges are penetrated by roads and railways, but no railways and few roads cross the Himalayas. These mountains are so large that they can be flown over but never tunnelled into, climbed but never conquered, mapped but seldom inhabited. They are – as Kenneth Mason, formerly a Superintendent of the Survey of India, called them – 'the greatest physical feature on Earth'.

Back when dinosaurs still dominated the planet, India floated freely as a continent in the southern hemisphere. Seventy million years ago, it crossed the equator and eventually collided with the continental plate of Asia. As the Indian plate continued to push northwards, the edges of the two continents squashed and thickened. The result was the Himalayas, a buckled and jumbled mixture of ancient rocks from the two plates, mixed with more recent sedimentary rocks from the floor of the ancient Tethys Ocean that once separated India and Asia. The relentless move northward continues today, which is why the Himalayas are still growing and why there are so many earthquakes in the region.

Look at a relief map of the world, and you will notice that the Himalayas do not make a clean arc like the Alps or a firm line like the Andes. Instead, they twist and turn as they cut across Afghanistan, Pakistan, India, Nepal, Bhutan and China. They also include a number of ranges: the Hindu Kush in the west and the Karakorams, which span across northern Pakistan and the territories of Jammu and Kashmir. Both these ranges have been referred to as Trans-Himalayan, and a debate still rages as to whether they are part of the Himalayas. The Himalayan mountains themselves span the northern frontiers of India, Nepal and Bhutan. One thing that is definite is that this gigantic mountain system has created one of the most formidable barriers to climate, and therefore to life, that the Earth has ever seen.

THE GREAT WIND

The Himalayas are so vast that they have shaped the world's climate. When the continents collided, India shunted Asia upwards, creating the Tibetan plateau – a flat land half the size of the US. At 5km (3 miles) above sea level, the plateau acts as a 'hot brick', soaking up the sun and drawing in the sea air from the Indian Ocean. This creates the monsoon, a gigantic weather system that brings welcome respite to India after the annual drought. Scientists now believe that the monsoon strengthened greatly about 20 million years ago, possibly when the Himalayas reached 2–3km (1–2 miles) in height, increasing significantly the temperature difference between the Tibetan plateau and the sea.

You can stand in the foothills of the Himalayas and be dripping with sweat, in temperatures of 30°C (86°F), surrounded by Indian jungle. But vertically above you is an ice world, lashed by 160kph (100mph) winds that take the temperature as low as –70°C (–94°F). If you make the 8km (5-mile) climb, you will pass through a range of climates and habitats that otherwise you would need to travel from the equator to one of the poles to experience. In no place on Earth is there so great a vertical rise in so short a distance.

There is another axis along which the Himalayas have created diversity. If you stand on the southern slopes at the eastern end of the range, you will be immersed in cloud forest, dripping with orchids and crammed with oriental species. Switch to the northern slopes at the western end, and you will find yourself in a desolate desert. This marked contrast results from the interaction of the range with the monsoon that it has created.

The monsoon is not a rain but a wind that carries rain. Between April and October, when this wind rides up the slopes of the Himalayas, it expands and cools, vapour condenses, and rain pours in torrents on the southern slopes. Above 6000m (20,000 feet), little moisture remains to fall, which is one reason why Everest's summit is snow-free – a pyramid of black rock. As it moves westwards, the monsoon's load decreases, and by the time it reaches the Hindu Kush and Karakoram ranges of Pakistan, it is a spent force.

DEATH IN THE KARAKORAMS

The Karakoram range forms an arc across northern Pakistan, separating it from China. The name means black-gravel mountains, which describes their desert-like nature but in no way prepares you for their scale. While the mountains of the Everest region fill you with awe, these bleak peaks fill you with fear – it is not surprising to learn that more people have died on their slopes than on any other mountain range.

This is the home of K2 – at 8611m (28,245 feet), second in height only to Everest. K2 is one of a cluster of giant peaks that include 10 of the world's 30 highest. While the mountains of the Everest region appear majestic, the peaks that surround K2 are savage. This is a jagged, unstable landscape of sheer rock walls and sharp spires, a truly vertical world where no rock looks as if it has a permanent home. Indeed, the collision between the Indian and Asian plates continues to shape the lives of both the mountains and its inhabitants.

In 1841, an earthquake triggered a huge landslide north of Nanga Parbat. The entire side of the valley fell into the Indus, blocking its flow completely, and a lake 32km (20 miles) long built up behind the obstruction. Eventually, the dam burst, drowning an entire Sikh army camped 480km (300 miles) downstream.

OPPOSITE *K2's peak – just 239m (784 feet) lower than Everest – rising high above the other jagged spires in northern Pakistan's bleak Karakorams.*

PREVIOUS PAGE *Satellite views of rain clouds being carried by the monsoon winds across India.*
MAIN PICTURE *When the vast Tibetan plateau to the north (top) heats up in summer, it draws in moisture-laden sea air from the Indian Ocean (right). The resulting cloud mass moves from the east across the subcontinent.*
INSETS *The monsoon reaches west to Pakistan but is prevented moving north by the mountain barrier of the Himalayas. This leaves the Tibetan plateau perpetually parched.*

The 2005 Kashmir earthquake hit at 8.50am on 8 October. The 7.6 magnitude quake struck close to Muzaffarabad in Pakistan-administered Kashmir. This is comparable in intensity to the 2001 Gujarat earthquake and the 1906 San Francisco earthquake. Some estimate that the death toll may have been more than 100,000. The majority of the casualties were in the mountainous regions, where at least 3 million people were made homeless.

HIGH PEAKS AND SNOW CATS

The national park of Chitral Gol lies within the Northwest Frontier province of Pakistan, just 50km (31 miles) or so from its border with Afghanistan. It is a dry, desolate place, the near-vertical slopes dotted with the odd holly oak and juniper tree. These mountains are beyond the range of the main monsoon, and so most moisture comes from heavy winter snowfall. The snow isolates the valleys from people but turns them into havens for wildlife.

It is a tough walk to get to the heart of the reserve, picking your way across steep scree slopes while dodging the rockfalls. On entering the park, you might come across the bizarre sight of a tribe of large goats feeding high up in a holly oak. These are markhor, possibly the largest concentration anywhere, though numbering only a few hundred. In winter, groups of up to 70 gather on the lower slopes to browse on the sparse vegetation. This lures in predators and presents an opportunity to glimpse a snow leopard, the highest-living land predator on the planet.

Snow leopards tend to give birth in caves, which they line with their fur. Until the cubs are able to catch their own prey, the mother is forced to go out hunting every few days to feed them. Though it is said that a snow leopard can kill and drag an animal up to three times its own body-weight (30–45kg/66–100 pounds), it will normally choose more manageable prey – a young markhor or, in summer, marmots and hares. Only a metre tall (just over 3 feet) at the shoulder, a snow leopard is smaller than a common leopard but looks larger due to its long fur and extremely thick, long tail – almost the same length again as its body. A long tail probably helps with balance and also provides an extra layer of warmth when wrapped around the body. Other adaptations include dense, woolly belly fur as long as 12cm (5 inches), large paws for walking on snow and gripping rocks, an enlarged nasal cavity and chest capacity to help it breathe more easily in the thin air at altitude, and powerful chest muscles for extra strength when climbing. Short front legs provide a low centre of gravity – useful for steep slopes – and long back legs help it leap onto prey.

Though the snow leopard has a wide distribution throughout the high mountains of central Asia, mostly above the tree line, ranging as high as 6000m (19,680 feet), the population is probably just 4000–7000. It faces increasing pressure from poachers for its pelt and bones (used in Chinese medicine) and the enmity of local herders, who continue to resist the need to guard their livestock against occasional predation. The snow leopard's wild prey are increasingly replaced by domestic livestock as humans encroach further into its habitat. In the Chitral region, the drug trade has also played a part. The border between Pakistan and Afghanistan used to be a major trade route for heroin smugglers, who discovered that smearing snow leopard fat onto the drugs made them undetectable by dogs. In the past decade, a dramatic decline has taken place, which raises the likelihood that the snow leopard may soon be as endangered as the Indian tiger.

BELOW *A male markhor, in Chitral Gol National Park. This large Himalayan goat has horns that can reach 2m (6.5 feet) in length. It lives in alpine areas, grazing on grasses and browsing on leaves and twigs. Though its young fall prey to snow leopards, the greatest dangers it faces are hunting by humans, loss of habitat, disturbance and disease passed on by domestic animals.*

GATEWAY TO THE ORIENT

At the eastern end of the Himalayas the great collision of continents has created a gateway through which many varieties of plants and animals have passed from the Orient. In spring, the slopes are ablaze with colour as great forests of rhododendrons come into bloom, from the tiny dwarf carpeter to the 18-m (59-foot) tall tree rhododendron – the national flower of Nepal – staining the mountainsides red. Rhododendrons are prevalent in Western gardens today thanks to the botanists who transplanted them to Europe in the nineteenth century.

Even the gnarly understorey of these forests is full of colour in spring, as the male oriental pheasants flash their impressive plumage to their females. The most flamboyant is the satyr tragopan who, at the peak of his splendid courtship display, unfurls an electric blue wattle on his throat and erects a pair of fleshy horns on his head. The male Himalayan monal's striking iridescent plumage is revealed fully only when startled – a blue, red and gold blur sailing past you at hundreds of metres in seconds. Once he lands, however, he is forced to walk back up the slope, because his wings are not strong enough for full flight. The male blood pheasant is streaked with flashes of crimson in contrast to his extremely drab mate. This species is said to inhabit the highest pheasant habitat in the world and is particularly hardy. Even in winter, it does not descend below 2000m (6560 feet), and in summer, it goes well beyond the tree line.

ABOVE *A snow leopard and her year-old cub at their cave refuge. The mother is on a couple of days' break from hunting. While she is away, usually for three or so days at a time, the cub remains behind, sleeping in or in front of the cave or amusing itself by taunting the magpies that hang around. When she returns, the cub greets her with a nose-rub and 'mews'.*

THE SPECIALISTS

ABOVE *Yunnan snub-nosed monkeys – the world's highest-living non-human primates. Found only in the Yunling Mountains in southwestern China and one area of Tibet, these endangered monkeys are, like pandas, specialist feeders, whose diet consists almost entirely of lichens growing on the bark of pine trees.*

OPPOSITE TOP *A wild female panda with her three-month-old cub, in Quinling, Shanxi province, China.*

OPPOSITE BOTTOM *A wild red panda eating bamboo on the forest floor in the eastern Himalayas. It is solitary, secretive, arboreal (tree-living) and nocturnal, and therefore rarely seen.*

Among the most appealing mammals of the eastern Himalayan forests are the two pandas. 'Panda' comes from the Nepalese *nigalya ponya*, meaning 'eater of bamboo', and bamboo makes up 99 per cent of a giant panda's diet, though the red panda is a little more catholic in its tastes, supplementing its diet with eggs, insects and the odd rodent. Both pandas have meat-eater guts, which are hopelessly inefficient at extracting nutrients from plants, and so both must consume vast quantities of bamboo to survive – the giant panda, nearly a fifth of its body weight, and the red panda up to 45 per cent of its body weight (approximately 200,000 bamboo leaves daily).

The red panda is now classified as a small mountain bear, in a family of its own. It has scent glands on its feet to attract mates and thick fur on the soles to protect them from the cold. Females give birth to one to four young in large tree-holes, where they stay for three months, being cared for by both parents. Though the red panda ranges throughout the Himalayan mountains and the forests of China, its numbers are rapidly decreasing. An estimated 10,000 red pandas die every year – 7000 as a result of deforestation and others for fur coats and hats.

Recent DNA analysis indicates that the giant panda is also related to bears. Though close in size and weight to an American black bear, it does not hibernate and cannot walk on its hind legs. It also produces the smallest baby of any mammal other than marsupials

(relative to body size) – almost a thousandth of its mother's weight. Though a female will give birth to one or two cubs, only one usually survives, born naked, blind and toothless, in a cave or hollow at the base of a tree. The mother cradles her cub continuously for three weeks, suckling it up to 12 times a day. Growth is extremely slow, as milk from bamboo is particularly poor, but though tiny, a newborn panda has a voice out of proportion to its feeble body. By the end of the third week, it looks like a miniature adult, but its eyes don't open until it is four to eight weeks old, and only by the fifth month is it fully mobile.

There are probably fewer than 1000 giant pandas left in the wild. Up until the last century, they were found in eight provinces in southern China, and fossil evidence shows an earlier range that stretched from Beijing to Burma and northern Vietnam. But now agriculture has destroyed virtually all of the ancient bamboo and coniferous forests except for some very high, steep and hard-to-reach pockets on the eastern flank of the Himalayas, mainly in the mountains of central China. The fact that it is such a picky eater also makes the giant panda extremely vulnerable. Bamboo has a highly unusual life-cycle: every 60–120 years, all the bamboos of a single species flower simultaneously, set seed and then die. This is disastrous now that human encroachment has disrupted ancient corridors of bamboo forest, for if one stand of bamboo dies off, the pandas have nowhere else to go and face starvation. Having become so specialized, the giant panda is now held captive by its diet, trapped in its diminishing mountain habitat.

CROSSING THE ROOF OF THE WORLD

From the air, the mountains of the Everest region are an overlapping confusion of peaks. As you climb, they separate into distinct peaks with personalities. At 8000m (26,240 feet), you are still surrounded by summits until, at 8850m (29,036 feet), nearly 20 times the height of the Empire State Building, you have just one summit before you – the highest on the planet, Mount Everest. The great tradition of mountain-climbing began in the eighteenth century in the Alps. Techniques evolved, a literature was created, and when the major Alpine peaks had been climbed, men looked farther afield. The Himalayas became their target. But only after the Second World War were any of the world's 13 highest mountains finally climbed, and only in 1953 did Sir Edmund Hillary and Tenzing Norgay climb Everest. Today, Everest still kills one in ten who try to climb it.

Tenzing Norgay once said that sherpas describe Everest as 'a mountain so high no bird can fly above it'. Each year, more than 50,000 demoiselle cranes begin one of the most challenging migrations on earth – a 3000-km (1860-mile) journey from their breeding sites in central Asia to their overwintering grounds in India. Unable to fly over Everest, the cranes are forced to find a way around it using an ancient route passed down through generations – the Kali Gandaki valley, said to be the deepest gorge in the world. This gorge was carved by the great Kali Gandaki River, which cut down through the soft rocks, once at the bottom of the Sea of Tethys, as fast as they were forced up by the collision of India with Tibet. It separates the mountains of Dhaulagiri and Annapurna, their summits above the snow line at 7850m (25,750 feet). The widest part of the gorge is 22km (nearly 14 miles), and at its central point, the bed of the river that flows between the peaks is 5600m (18,370 feet) below. For centuries, the people of Nepal and Tibet have used this valley as a highway, one of the few that cuts through the almost impenetrable barrier of the Himalayas. The valley is more than just a conduit for water and birds – it has been a thoroughfare for centuries. Salt traders from Tibet have used it to access trade centres in India, while Hindu and Buddhist pilgrims have migrated in the opposite direction, to visit one of the holiest shrines in the region at Muktinath, where it is believed that Guru Rimpoche, the father of Tibetan Buddhism, stopped on his way to Tibet.

For many of the birds, this will be their first journey across the Himalayas, but for some, it will be their last. In late morning, 145kph (90mph) winds start to roar up the gorge, forcing the cranes to gain height to clear them. They soon hit turbulence, which disrupts their flying formations and forces them to turn back for an unplanned stopover. Unfortunately, the local villagers are waiting for them. It is extremely challenging to make a living at these altitudes, and villagers are reluctant to share what little crops they have with the passing cranes.

When they take to the air again, using thermals or rising columns of warm air to help them gain height, golden eagles are waiting. With such a bird bonanza, the eagles take to working in pairs. They disorientate a young crane and separate it from the flock. If the crane escapes the clutches of one eagle, it will get caught by the other. The flock battles on, as the cranes must cross the 8000-m (26,240-foot) peaks before the weather deteriorates. In the final ascent, every wing-beat becomes a monumental struggle as each lungful of air contains a quarter of the oxygen it would at sea level. Eventually, the birds reach the summit, but like all visitors to the world of the high mountains, they dare not linger.

OPPOSITE A V-shaped formation of demoiselle cranes on their great journey from central Asia over the Himalayas to their wintering grounds in the Thar Desert, India. To get there, the cranes must risk starvation and run the gauntlet of extreme weather and attack by eagles.

7

the underworld

There can be no greater challenge for an explorer

than caves. They are the least known environments

on land, are home to some of the strangest animals

and offer extraordinary landscapes

and thrilling experiences.

ABOVE *A forest of sharp limestone pinnacles – the 'tsingy formations' of Tsingy de Bemaraha Strict Nature Reserve, Madagascar – a World Heritage Site, riddled with caves.*

OPPOSITE *The dramatic limestone mountain towers of Ha Long Bay, in northeast Vietnam, another World Heritage Site with spectacular caves.*

PREVIOUS PAGE, TOP *Carlsbad Caverns.* BOTTOM *Hundreds of thousands of wrinkle-lipped free-tailed bats exiting at dusk from a limestone cave in Thailand to feed in the rainforest.*

Most people are blissfully unaware of the hidden world lying beneath their feet – a world of often frightening mystery, yet breathtaking beauty. It is staggering in scale, with a huge network of underground shafts, passages, chambers and caverns, otherwise known as caves. Nobody knows the full extent of caves. There are thought to be about 80,000km (50,000 miles) of explored passages – equivalent of going twice around the world – but this may represent only 10 per cent of what is actually under our feet.

The standard definition of a cave is a natural underground space that people can enter. In other words, a cave is not officially a cave until somebody has been in it. This, of course, begs a question: if a cave has not been discovered, how do we know there is one there? We don't, but we do know where caves are likely to be found, and since a huge percentage of these suitable areas have yet to be explored for caves, experts have reasonably concluded that there are an awful lot of underground spaces waiting to be discovered.

Caves can be found in a variety of locations, from ice and sandstone to granite and volcanic lava. But overwhelmingly they are formed in one type of rock – limestone. This is found on every continent, including Antarctica, and covers nearly 10 per cent of the world's surface, making it one of the most common rocks on Earth – particularly in China, which has more limestone than the rest of the world put together. It is a sedimentary rock – deposited under water and built up in layers – but the key to its importance for caves is its composition. Limestone is made largely of calcium carbonate – a mineral extracted from seawater by shellfish and corals and used as the basis for skeletons and shells. As generation after generation has died and settled on the seabed, this mineral has been compacted into beds of rock, which geological activity has later caused to be exposed on land.

Despite its abundance, most of us would not recognise a piece of limestone if we stubbed our toe on it. But around the world there are some very visible examples. The most dramatic are the otherworldly limestone towers of China's Guillin and Vietnam's Ha Long Bay. Almost as striking are the limestone pavements of the Yorkshire Dales and the huge, dagger-like limestone pinnacles of Borneo and Madagascar. These sculpted formations provide one of the best clues to why caves are so common in limestone.

Limestone is mostly very hard, but it has a crucial weakness: the calcium carbonate in the rock can be dissolved surprisingly easily by carbonic acid, which is nothing more than a

combination of rainwater and carbon dioxide. As rainwater falls and percolates through the air and ground, it absorbs carbon dioxide, making it mildly acidic. Carbonic acid has little more power than a fizzy drink, but enough to dissolve the calcium in limestone.

Initially, the water flows down the rock's tiny fractures and fissures, caused by uplift and movement of continental plates. But over millions of years, the corrosive water widens these tiny gaps into tunnels and passages, and a cave is born. The force of friction further widens the openings, as water carries sand, rocks and boulders through the cave, scouring the walls and carrying off yet more limestone. The process is painstakingly slow, but the speed of erosion varies enormously. In the tropics, it can be 20 times greater than in colder climates, speeded up by plentiful rain and greater quantities of vegetation producing more carbon dioxide and organic acids for the rain to absorb.

Though most cave systems are relatively small, seldom exceeding 1km (half a mile) in length and 100m (328 feet) in depth, others almost defy belief, with labyrinths of shafts, passages, chambers and caverns. The Sarawak Chamber, in Mulu National Park, Borneo, is big enough to hold 40 Boeing 747s; the opening, bell-shaped shaft in Mexico's Cave of Swallows is deep enough to engulf the Empire State Building; and the longest cave in the world, Mammoth Cave in Kentucky, stretches over 563km (350 miles) – the distance between London and Edinburgh.

LIFE WITHOUT LIGHT

If you have never experienced the utter blackness of a cave when you turn out your torch, then it is difficult to fully appreciate quite how *black* black can be. You would probably have to go deep into space to get even vaguely close. But for a cheaper alternative, wait till it gets dark, close your curtains, turn out the light, put on one of those airline eye masks and sit in your bedroom cupboard with the door closed. You will not be quite there, but this is not a bad simulation. When you are in the dark zone of a cave you cannot even see your finger in front of your eye, let alone which direction you need to go in. (It is a sobering thought that if you found yourself in a cave without torchlight, the chances of finding your way out would be virtually nil, no matter how many times you had been in the cave before.)

Caves are one of the few habitats not directly powered by the sun's energy. Just a short distance from an entrance, photosynthesis becomes impossible. So in the absence of plants, food chains depend on nutrients being brought or washed into the cave. The most obvious way this happens is through the part-time cave dwellers, such as bats, which occupy some caves in huge numbers. Deer Cave in Sarawak, Borneo, is the daytime retreat of possibly 3 million wrinkle-lipped bats. Each evening the bats fly out over the forest, where they eat literally tons of insects. When they return in the early morning, their droppings are deposited on the cave floor. This guano forms the base of a complex food chain. Surviving on the nutrient-rich soup of bat dung are mites, springtails, beetles, crabs and cockroaches. These, in turn, are eaten by giant centipedes, cave crickets, spiders and other insectivores.

The vast mounds of guano in tropical caves are unforgettable. In torchlight everything shimmers with hundreds of thousands of dung-eating creatures, industriously picking their way through the stream of fresh nutrients from above. It is a 24/7 operation, since while the bats are out hunting, more droppings are being deposited by roosting cave swiftlets. But

ABOVE *Fantastic Pit – a 176-m (586-foot) deep sheer drop in Ellison's Cave, Georgia – lit by roped cavers.*

OPPOSITE *A base-jumper (with a parachute on his back) plunging into one of the deepest caves in the world – the Cave of Swallows, Mexico – a 376-m (1100-foot) deep limestone sink-hole.*

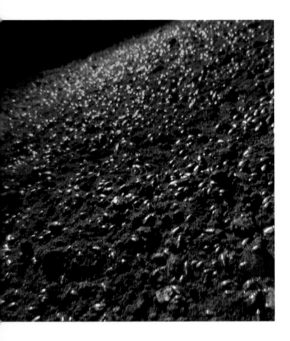

ABOVE *Hundreds of thousands of cockroaches swarm over bat guano – the droppings of 3 million or so bats that rain down in Deer Cave in Sarawak, Borneo.*

OPPOSITE *The evening emergence of millions of wrinkle-lipped free-tailed bats from their daytime cave roost in Thailand. Such caves are vital for the bats' survival. One bat can eat up to 3000 insects in a night, which means a huge colony such as this one may consume many tons of insects, including pests such as mosquitoes.*

do the guano-eaters show any gratitude to those that support their lifestyle? Not a bit. If a bat or swiftlet falls onto the mound, the ravenous hordes will happily consume it.

Bats are an important part of the other end of the food chain, too. Caves such as Deer Cave offer a great deal of protection from predators. But there are specialized hunters that can reach their roosts, such as the highly agile cave racer – a snake with the ability to climb up near-vertical cave walls. In Bracken Cave, Texas, home to the world's largest colony of bats – 20 million Mexican free-tailed bats – some very un-cave-like animals prey on them during their breeding season.

CAVE SKUNKS AND BAT-SNACKS

Skunks and racoons descend to the bottom of the cave and, in complete darkness, feel their way around the floor searching for fallen baby bats. The atmosphere is thick with near-suffocating levels of ammonia from the guano, but this appears to have little effect on the hunters (humans, on the other hand, must use respirators, which filter out the ammonia and also protect the wearers from histoplasmosis – a potentially fatal fungal infection associated with bat guano). When a baby is found, the skunk or racoon rolls it vigorously backwards and forwards to subdue it – a wise policy, as eating something with sharp teeth is risky when you can't see which end you are at.

How exactly the skunks and racoons find the bats is a mystery. Their sense of smell must be overwhelmed by the ammonia, and the sound of a squeaking bat, struggling across the cave floor would be drowned out by the noise of millions of roosting bats. The answer may simply be a combination of luck and perseverance – the skunks and racoons seemingly locate the bats by bumping into them. But the bats' real problems begin when they leave the cave. With thousands of bats leaving at once, the sight obviously attracts attention.

In Deer Cave, the bats begin to leave their roosts at around 5pm (though their timing depends on weather – if it is raining, they may not come out at all). At first, the flow is relatively modest, but like rush-hour in the city, the numbers build quickly. Within half an hour, there is a stream of bats 20m (66 feet) wide and several metres deep. Seen from the ground, the stream is sometimes so thick that it almost obscures the sky above. The bat 'fly out' from Deer Cave is, without doubt, one of the world's great natural-history spectacles.

Outside the 90-m (295-foot) high entrance to Deer Cave, the bats often form huge doughnut-shaped rings that twist and turn for minutes at a time. Why they do this is not clear, but it could be an attempt to confuse birds of prey. Certainly rufous-bellied eagles seem overwhelmed by the wheeling bats. When the numbers in the ring get to a certain density, groups peel off, either to make another ring or to fly out across the forest. Watched from below, the spiralling bats look like performers in a gigantic aerial ballet – with a million individuals seeming to move as one giant organism.

For the bats there is some safety in numbers. Individuals are, however, vulnerable to specialized predators such as bat hawks – the bird world's jet-fighters, which pluck bats out of the air with ease. But good hunting for hawks lasts only until the light fades, and so they fold the bats into little packages and eat them on the wing – then fly back for more. Yet no matter how many bat hawks turn up, the onslaught has virtually no effect on bat numbers. By morning, the vast majority of bats will be back in the comparative safety of the cave.

ABOVE *An Australian green treefrog with a mouthful of bat – a young one caught on its way out of Bat Cleft Cave, the centrepiece of Mount Etna Caves National Park. The limestone cave holds the largest known maternity colony of the little bent-winged bat. When the adults are out hunting, the naked young are kept warm by air trapped in the domes or closed shafts in the cave ceiling.*

At Bat Cleft Cave in Queensland, Australia, the exiting little bent-winged bats face another common enemy. Pythons and brown tree snakes wait just inside the cave entrance and try to pick them off as they funnel out of the cave. Despite the dense concentrations of bats, hunting is a hit-and-miss affair, with the snakes appearing to strike more in hope than expectation. Clearly, trying to catch the fast-moving, jinking bats in virtual blackness is a tricky business, but the snakes are armed with a secret weapon. Receptors in their heads pick up the heat given off by the flying bats, and this gives them targets to aim at.

Also lurking in wait on the limestone rocks are the most unusual bat predators of all. Large treefrogs wait for fledgling bats to be blown against the wall by wind buffeting against the cave entrance. Then, while the disorientated bat is trying to get airborne again, one of the frogs will jump over and grab it. Bats are well-known consumers of frogs, but to see the tables turned is an almost surreal experience.

Not all caves have bats or have them in enough quantities to support such a dense community of insects as Deer Cave. For many cave dwellers, finding enough food to survive is the ultimate challenge – made all the more difficult by having to do it in the dark. To help get around some of these problems, many cave invertebrates such as cave crickets have unusually long antennae, all the better to feel things with. But there's one animal that has evolved a particularly ingenious solution to life in this low-nutrient world.

PEARLS OF DEATH

Walk into Mangawhatikau Cave in New Zealand's North Island and you'd be excused for wondering whether you had entered a cave at all. The roof and some of the walls are bejewelled with thousands of little lights, making you feel that you're walking under a wonderfully starry sky. The sight is one of the most incredible you will see inside a cave. The lights are cave glow-worms, the larvae of a tiny gnat. Being luminous is clearly useful in the dark, but that's only half their story. The little larvae hang from the ceiling of the cave and spin a series of silken threads 5–20cm (2–9 inches) long that dangle from the rock. The silk – similar to that made by spiders – comes from glands in the glow-worm's mouth and is then weighed down by balls of mucus. These strings of pearls have a sinister function. They are fishing lines, and settled in its mucous hammock, the glow-worm waits by them like any patient angler. It is now that the larva's glowing ability really pays dividends. The light literally shines out of its backside, the result of a chemical reaction taking place inside a special capsule in the glow-worm's tail. Insects are irresistibly drawn towards the light and then get trapped by the sticky threads. Then it is just a matter of reeling in the lines and consuming the hapless victims – alive. Glow-worms, like spiders, suck their catches dry.

The glow-worm larvae survive partly on prey blown into their caves. But by positioning themselves above streams running through the cave, they also benefit from insects that hatch out of the water, such as mayflies. A mayfly's life is famously short, but in Mangawhatikau Cave, an adult lifespan may not exceed 20 minutes – just enough time to dry its wings and then investigate those interesting little lights above its head. Also there is a good chance that flying adult glow-worms mating and laying eggs in among the larvae will get caught in the snares. And as cave glow-worms are not very loyal offspring, they will eat their relatives, bringing about a strangely productive end to an otherwise short adult life.

THE TROGLOBITES

Not to be confused with troglodytes – people that live in caves – troglobites are non-human animals that live in caves. What separates them from other cave dwellers – troglophiles, which happily live both in and out of caves, and trogloxenes, which breed at the surface but sometimes go into caves – is that these animals never, ever leave their cave environment. Many caves are like islands, not just cut off from the outside world but from other caves too. This has resulted in the evolution of some weird-looking creatures, some without either eyes or pigment. And since it can take thousands (or even hundreds of thousands) of years for eyes to be lost, these animals have clearly been isolated for a very long time.

ABOVE *The glow-worms' beacons of death, attracting insects and even their relatives to a sticky end in Mangawhatikau Cave, New Zealand.*

TOP *The traps – strings of silk weighed down by blobs of sticky mucus that hang from the cave roof.*

BLIND EATING THE BLIND

ABOVE LEFT *A cave angel – a blind fish from Thailand, which lives in fast-moving underground streams and waterfalls, feeding on bacteria. Its flattened wing-like fins have microscopic hooks underneath them that enable it to grip onto sheer rock and climb.*

ABOVE RIGHT *Another troglobite – the Texas blind cave salamander, found only in caves in the San Marcos area. It keeps its larval gills and spends its entire life under water.*

One of the most remarkable troglobites is the cave angel, known from just two small caves in northern Thailand. With an estimated population of only 100, these 10-cm (3.9-inch) long fish have the classic troglobite characteristics: they are eyeless and pink. Nobody knows very much about their behaviour, but they live only in waterfalls inside caves – a fact which has led some experts to dub them one of the most adaptive creatures on Earth.

In the fast-moving water, the fish hang onto the rock using microscopic hooks on the underside of their flattened wing-like fins (which is what gives them their 'angel' appearance) and feed on bacteria in the oxygenated water. Their ability to grip tight to rock also allows them to crawl out of the water and up damp, vertical walls (a trick that presumably helps them to move from one waterfall to another). They don't appear to have any predators, which is just as well since they are oblivious to the approach of something even as large as a human. However, to be fair to the fish, the din of the waterfalls is so great that a human wouldn't be able to hear even the cave roof falling in.

On the other side of the world, there is another troglobite that has had to adapt to a very different set of conditions. The Texas blind cave salamander is completely aquatic and lives in totally still pools. Being an amphibian, it can breathe through its skin. But to enable a full-time underwater existence in poorly oxygenated water, external gills sprout out of its ears. Like the cave angel, the blind salamander has no eyes or pigment and is found in just a couple of caves and in a similar population size (though nobody knows for sure). But unlike the fish, receptors in its skin can detect the minutest movements in the water – vibrations that might be made by crustaceans. Such prey is in very short supply, and the salamander can't afford to miss it. By remaining motionless for long periods, this strange amphibian can, however, go without food for as long as six years.

THE SNOTTITES

Of all the unusual things that can be seen in caves, the snottites of Villa Luz Cave, in Mexico, must surely be the most bizarre. Snottite is the official term for what looks very much like a mucous stalactite. Just like ordinary stalactites, snottites also drip liquid from their ends. But that is where the comparison ends. The drops are sulphuric acid, strong enough to burn skin, and the structures are vast colonies of bacteria, capable of growing a centimetre a day.

What is equally incredible is that these bacteria manage to thrive in a cave whose atmosphere is thick with toxic gases. Not for nothing is Villa Luz known as the poisonous cave. Cavers entering it must wear full-face respirators and monitors, since poisonous gases can rise to fatal levels so quickly that an early-warning device is essential.

The source of all the toxic fumes comes from deep below the cave. Hydrogen sulphide bubbles up from oil deposits in the Earth's crust and leaks into the cave, rendering the air more or less unbreathable for two-legged intruders. The bacteria, on the other hand, get all their energy from the hydrogen sulphide (in much the same way as plants get energy from sunlight), and the sulphuric acid that drips from their ends is the by-product of this process.

The ability of these bacteria to survive in such extreme conditions has given them the name extremophiles. Since their discovery, different extremophiles have been found in a number of other caves – such as the ones in Lechuguilla Cave, which survive on a diet of rock. It is a field of science that has helped change our view of what life needs to exist. Indeed, some experts believe that extremophiles are evidence that surface life might even have evolved underground, rather than the other way around.

ABOVE *Snottites – structures formed from huge communities of bacteria in the poisonous cave of Villa Luz, Mexico. These bacteria feed on hydrogen sulphide and excrete drops of sulphuric acid.*

CAVE RICHES

In Southeast Asia are caves that harbour possibly the most expensive food item in the world. Forget beluga caviar (the eggs of beluga sturgeon) or black truffles (fungi) – the saliva nests of the white-nest cave swiftlet are worth, gram for gram, a lot more.

They are the principal ingredient of bird's-nest soup – a delicacy that's more or less tasteless until sweetened or spiced. But while it may not be famous for its raw flavour, to many Chinese, bird's-nest soup is thought to have remarkable health-giving properties, second only to ginseng. There are even claims that the soup could help sufferers of cancer and Aids. Chemical analysis of its properties has, however, shown the nests to have virtually no nutritional value. Nevertheless, men are willing to risk life and limb to collect the tiny nests.

The techniques used by nest collectors vary from cave to cave but invariably involve clambering to dizzying heights. In Gomantong Cave, Sabah, on the island of Borneo, the collectors must climb up 60-m (200-foot) ladders made from forest vines and then up onto bamboo pole gantries, which are manoeuvred into place by a ground team pulling on ropes. The collectors balance on the tip of the gantry to pick the nests off the wall. If the nests are still out of reach, the men use poles with trident-like spikes on the end to ease them off the wall. Either way, it's a hazardous business: with no safety equipment, a fall from this height is usually fatal.

In Gomantong Cave, the business is so valuable that key sites are guarded from poachers

around the clock – even when the birds are not nesting. Descending into Gomantong's Upper Cave is an extraordinary experience. On the floor of the cave, just above the thick layer of bird and bat guano, are small wooden houses raised on stilts – their corrugated iron roofs providing cover from the continual rain of droppings from above. Here, under artificial light, the guards eat, sleep and play, and at harvest time, literally dozens of people live in the cave. To the first-time visitor, it feels like a scene from a science-fiction film.

There is evidence that the trade in spit nests has been going on for up to a thousand years. And given that the birds start rebuilding as soon as their nests have been removed, it might even be regarded as one of the oldest sustainable uses of wildlife in the world. Recently, however, things have started to change. In Sabah, Borneo, new rules on the allocation of nest sites have actually encouraged overharvesting. Now, instead of two harvests a year, the Mafia-style gangs that run the businesses make as many as four. When combined with increasing demand for birds' nests, the current rate of harvest could result in the complete collapse of the cave swiftlet population. Indeed, one expert has argued that it might lead to the extinction of the white-nest cave swiftlet in just five to ten years.

OPPOSITE Gathering cave-swiftlet nests in the Upper Cave of Gomantong, Borneo. The job is a hazardous one, though there are big profits for the middlemen. The removal of the nests is now threatening to cause the extinction of the white-nest cave swiftlet.

PARENTING IN THE DARK

White-nest cave swiftlets are remarkable birds for two principal reasons. First, they build their nests entirely from threads of saliva, and second, they are somehow able to find them again in the utter darkness of a cave chamber. In human terms, it's rather like playing 'pin the tail on the donkey' in a room the size of a gymnasium – without knowing which wall the picture is on or how high up it is.

The cave swiftlet is one of only two species of bird able to echolocate (the other is the oilbird of Venezuela). As it flies through the inky blackness, the swiftlet utters a series of audible clicks. It is thought that, by listening to the echoes of these clicks, the bird is able to make a 3-D map of the chamber. Yet exactly how it finds a nest just a few centimetres wide, among hundreds of others, nobody really knows. For cave swiftlets, raising a family is an unconventional business. The lack of light means that, while in the nest, a chick never actually sees its parents. Then, on its maiden flight, the youngster must reach the cave entrance, often by flying through a maze of pitch-black passages. If it hits a wall or crash-lands on the ground (which many do), then it's very unlikely to get airborne again. The creatures of the guano pile will see to that.

Nature's decorations

When it comes to caves, the most often asked question is usually 'which hangs down: stalactites or stalagmites?' The answer, of course, is stalactites – because 'stalactites stick *tight* to the ceiling and stalagmites grow *mightily* from the ground.' But to make things easier still, cavers often refer to stalactites and stalagmites collectively as 'stals'.

Stals are what turn a black hole into a place of mystery and atmosphere. But they are just some of the formations (also known as cave decorations, or speleothems) that you can find in caves. Others include flowstones, columns, draperies, curtains, straws, cave balloons, moonmilk, popcorn and helictites, not to mention cave pearls, flowers and crystals. Like the stals, almost all are made from the mineral calcite, which builds up when acidic water loaded with dissolved limestone leaks into a cave passage or chamber.

The science behind the growth of these formations is actually quite simple. Basically, it's a reversal of the chemical process that dissolved the limestone in the first place. When the acidic water enters the air-filled cavity, it releases some of the carbon dioxide that it picked up on the way down. Without so much carbon dioxide, the water can't hold as much dissolved calcium and the surplus is deposited on the cave roof as calcite. Most 'tites' start life as straws, with drips flowing down the middle of the hollow tube. This continues until the tube becomes blocked, thereby forcing the water to flow down the outside, as on the typical stalactite. If, however, the water flows through the cave ceiling quickly, then the calcite builds up on the floor of the cave instead and forms stalagmites.

Most cave formations are created by the same process, but the variations in the way that they look depends on the rate of water

entering the cave. Helictites, for example, are thin, twisted fibrous formations (rather like the roots of a potato plant gone mad) that are thought to form when water seeps into the cave through pores so small that the flow is controlled more by capillary action than gravity. As a result, the water moves more randomly, which allows the calcite to be deposited against the force of gravity. Cave pearls, on the other hand, form when a piece of sand becomes evenly coated in calcite through being constantly agitated in a water-filled depression (not dissimilar to the way real pearls are formed).

The speed at which cave formations grow varies enormously, depending on the volume of water and its acidity. Generally, it is a very slow process, but the results can be spectacular. The largest stalactite in the world, in Brazil, is 28m (92 feet) long, and the largest stalagmite is a staggering 67m (220 feet) tall.

LEFT TO RIGHT The world's largest natural cave crystals, in the Naica mine in Chihuahua, Mexico. Composed of selenite (a form of gypsum), the largest crystals are more than 8m (26 feet) long.

The world's largest stalagmite at 67.2m (220 feet) in the cave of Cueva San Martin Infierno, Cuba. A caver in red stands to the left of its huge base to give the scale.

The calcite stalactites and stalagmites of Grand Cenote, one of the flooded caves of Yucatán, Mexico. They formed thousands of years before the cave was flooded with fresh water at the end of the last ice age. A guide-rope runs 1km (more than half a mile) from the entrance so divers can find their way out before their tanks run empty.

A cricket-ball-sized pom-pom in Ogof Ffynnon Ddu, South Wales, UK. It has formed over many years as calcite has crystallized around a straw stalactite touching the surface of the pool. If the water level drops, the stalactite will break.

THE UNEXPLORED

For most people, the idea of going inside a cave without a big entrance, concrete walkways and electric light is likely to bring on claustrophobia. But for those who can overcome this basic fear, caves offer fantastic opportunities for exploration. With perhaps 90 per cent of the world's limestone remaining to be explored for caves, it might justifiably be regarded as one of our planet's last frontiers. Even on a heavily populated island such as Britain, there are caves waiting to be discovered. After all, the biggest cave passage in the UK was discovered in 1998 and the longest vertical drop in 2003.

So, if exploring places where no human has set foot before is your thing (and you can't afford your own spacecraft or deep-sea submersible), then look no further than caves. Indeed, one of the greatest living explorers is a caver. Andy Eavis, from Hull, has arguably discovered more unknown places – including, among others, the three largest cave chambers in the world – than anyone else alive. In *The Oxford Book of Exploration*, his name appears alongside those of astronauts such as Neil Armstrong and Buzz Aldrin.

Nevertheless, it has to be said, hardened cavers are a strange breed. Tim and Pam Fogg, from Northern Ireland, are a case in point. They spend their spare weekends digging their way through a hillside in the hope of eventually reaching a fresh section of cave, which they are convinced lies somewhere ahead. While one of them is lying flat in the tiny, damp tunnel digging out the rocks and earth, either by hand or by using small explosive charges, the other is pulling the debris out on a tray attached to a piece of string. It's like tunnelling into prison. So far, in 18 months, they have gone just 10m (33 feet).

While exploring virgin caves, cavers often find themselves having to pull their way through long sections of passageway just big enough for the depths of their bodies, or worse, similar-sized passages half filled with water. (It helps being small, but being the smallest caver on a team will inevitably mean you'll be the one being pushed through the most ludicrously sized openings.) Narrow passages are appropriately known as squeezes. For the novice caver they mark either a period of extreme panic or exhilaration, or both – and not necessarily in that order. Unsurprisingly, squeezes are where you are most likely to get stuck, and the part of you most likely to get stuck is your shoulders. If this happens, and all the possibilities in the pushing and pulling department have been exhausted, the only thing left to do, one is told, is to break the clamped caver's collarbone.

If you can negotiate the squeezes without losing control of your bodily functions, there are the abseils into unknown blackness. If you're lucky, the rope may run down one of the chamber walls, but just as likely, you will end up dangling in space a long way from the comparative security of a limestone wall. Then there's the combination of being cold and wet for hours – especially if you're caving in temperate climates. Finally, when you are regretting the whole exercise and just want the sky above your head, there is the realization that you have to make the whole journey in reverse – though, of course, this time it is all uphill. Caving invariably tests both mental and physical resolve. Moving around underground, you use practically every muscle in your body while pushing and pulling, hauling, scrambling and sliding. Caving is the ultimate workout. But none of this should put you off. The author of this chapter was nervous about being in lifts but ended up spending a happy six days underground in one of the world's most demanding caves.

TOP, LEFT TO RIGHT *A selection of spectacular and rare cave formations from around the world.*

Egg-sized calcite balls in Lechuguilla, New Mexico, USA, formed when the tips of straw stalactites have been immersed in mineral-rich water (showing three different pool levels).

The world's only nickel-coloured green stalactites, in a secret location in France. A water drop gives scale.

A gypsum crystal flower, Lechuguilla.

MIDDLE, LEFT TO RIGHT *Unique, electric-blue aragonite needle sprays, about 13cm (5 inches) across, in a secret French location. Aragonite is made of calcium carbonate, but its crystalline structure differs from calcite and it usually occurs where evaporation has concentrated magnesium in seeping water.*

Triangular, hollow, crystalline calcite 'cave cups', about 10cm (4 inches) high, in the Bellamar system, Cuba.

A stalactite covered with a hedgehog formation of crystalline helictites, in the caverns of Sonora, Texas, USA.

BOTTOM, LEFT TO RIGHT *A large, 3.5-cm (1.4-inch) diameter cave pearl from southern France. 'Pearls' usually form in groups in shallow cave pools, when dripping water precipitates calcite that then collects around a grain of something such as sand.*

A very delicate, fractal, branching form of calcite, 6cm (2.5 inches) tall, found only in one cave in Cuba.

Unique blue-tipped helictites at the top of a more normal helictite, composed of individual crystals, from a secret location in France.

JOURNEY TO THE CENTRE OF THE EARTH

In October 2004, an important milestone was reached in cave exploration. For the first time, cavers broke through the 2000-m (6560-foot) mark – or, to put it another way, a point 2km (1.2 miles) down from the surface. The feat has given Krubera Cave in the Arabika massif, Abkhazia, in the Western Caucasus on the edge of the Black Sea, the accolade of being the deepest cave in the world. In achieving their goal, the team had to negotiate huge vertical drops and freezing torrents of water and to blast rubble from passages blocked by boulder falls, while carrying five tons of equipment. The cavers christened the final chamber, at 2080m (6822 feet), Game Over, assuming that this was as far as they could possibly go. Now they are not sure – believing that the cave could go deeper still. And that is the beauty of cave exploration. We know the exact measurements of the tallest mountain in the world, the length of the longest river and the depth of the deepest sea. None of these records are likely to change from one millennium to the next, but when it comes to caves we just have the current results. The records for the longest and deepest caves may literally change from year to year – and it is not just about extending the boundaries of the existing ones. Next year, a whole new cave system might be discovered that could completely change all present records.

ABOVE *One of an international team of caving explorers squeezing through a narrow passage – The Way to the Dream, at 1647m (5400 feet) – on the four-week journey down to the near-bottom of Krubera Cave, the deepest cave in the world.*

OPPOSITE *Lechuguilla's spectacular Chandelier Ballroom. The fragile 'snow crystal' chandeliers, many more than 6m (20 feet) long, that hang from the ceiling and walls are made of selenite (colourless gypsum) and have grown when water bearing dissolved gypsum has leaked through the rock and evaporated.*

THE MOST BEAUTIFUL CAVE IN THE WORLD

In 1986, cavers in New Mexico, USA, finally broke through several metres of rubble and into a large cave system. It was the culmination of several years of digging by a small group of cavers in their spare time. In caving terms, it has become one of the finds of the twentieth century. Today, Lechuguilla Cave is widely considered to be the most beautiful cave in the world – not to mention one of the longest and deepest – and the Holy Grail for any serious caver.

Unfortunately for the world's cavers, Lechuguilla's fragile beauty has made it one of the most restricted of caves – open only to scientists and those mapping its ever-increasing length – currently 193km (120 miles). Even its entrance remains secret. All who enter must sign a declaration saying they will not divulge its exact whereabouts – which, in fact, would be quite difficult to do, since it is at the bottom of a small, 20m-deep (66-foot) crevice in a lonely stretch of the Chihuahuan Desert. But if you are lucky enough to get permission to enter, a truly otherworldly experience awaits you.

Prior to its discovery, Lechuguilla had been completely cut off from the outside world. To maintain those same conditions deep inside, two airtight doors have been installed at the threshold of the cave. Were you to hold open both doors at once, you would be buffeted by 130kph (80mph) winds coming out of the cave – a force that could easily damage the delicate formations below. Once past the doors, you descend a large metal tube that makes you feel you're about to enter a giant grain silo, and for the next 30 minutes of the journey, it is all a bit underwhelming. Then you hit Boulder Falls. This is an adrenalin-fired abseil into what seems, on first impressions, to be a bottomless pit. From there onwards, Lechuguilla produces one surprise after another.

The first is Glacier Bay Cavern, with a floor that looks as if it was formed from huge chunks of calved ice. This is quickly followed by other chambers whose names neatly sum

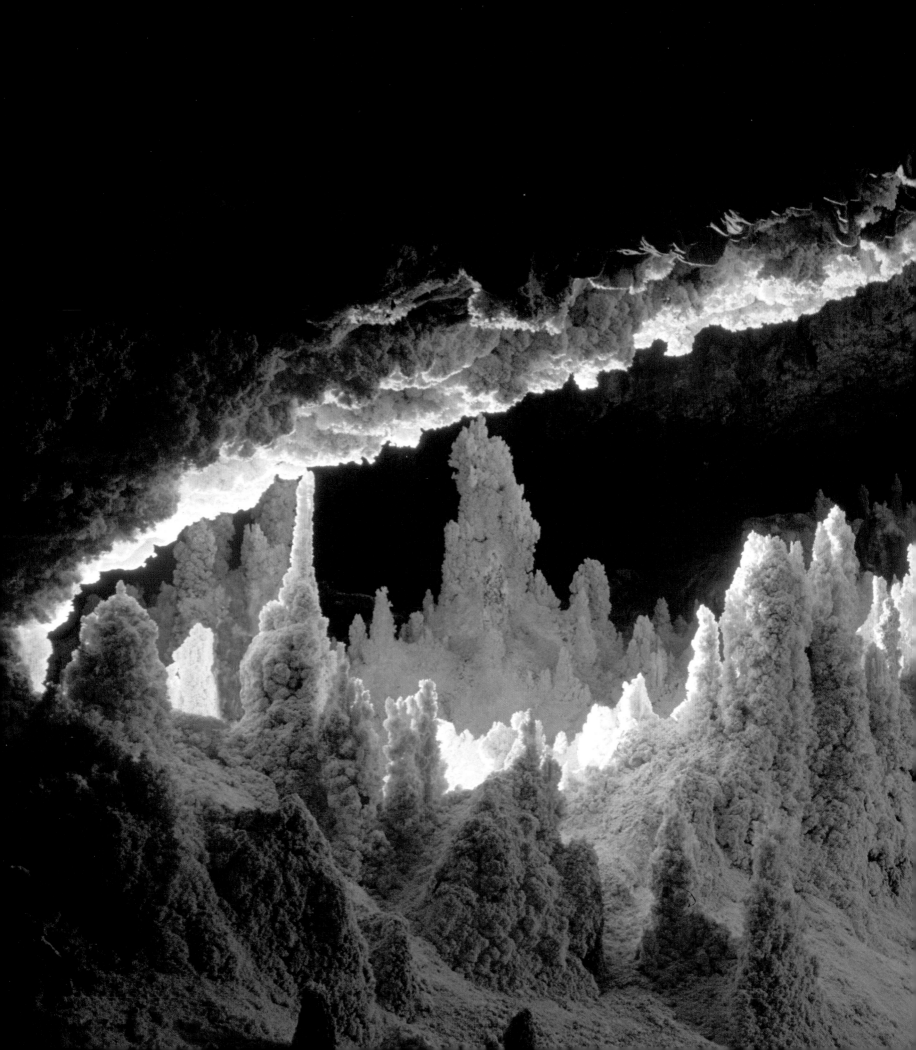

ABOVE *Lechuguilla's Hudson Bay Cavern, covered with pure white calcite. The rounded formations are referred to as mammaries, and in the foreground are aragonite 'bushes'.*

OPPOSITE *Lechuguilla's Pearlsian Gulf, named after the many shallow pools and the hundreds of cave pearls in them. The crystal-covered floor is so fragile that those cavers allowed to enter the cave must wear new 'dive' socks to protect the surface and are forbidden to touch the pure water.*

PREVIOUS PAGE *Lechuguilla's Hoodoo Hall, containing the most spectacular examples of 'raft cones'. These were formed when the cave was filled almost to the surface with very still water. Thin rafts of calcium carbonate crystals formed on the surface. Occasionally, water drops would fall and cause flakes to sink to the bottom. Over hundreds and thousands of years, these flakes built up into the delicate giant cones that fill the cave.*

up the feelings of the first explorers – Snow White's Passage, Tinseltown, Land of Awes, Prickly Ice Cube Room. For some reason, they never got around to choosing names like Santa's Grotto or Winter Wonderland, but these would have been equally applicable. Many of the walls are completely encrusted with the most delicate frost-like crystals, and if you'd been beamed in *Star-Trek*-style and didn't know where you were, you would swear you were looking at snow. Hoodoo Hall actually looks like one of *Star Trek*'s sets. This large cavern is filled with strange-looking cones, some more than 5m (16 feet) tall, all coated with incredibly fragile aragonite crystals. They could be frosted pine trees from another planet. The way they were formed is no less remarkable. In a previous era, the chamber was half-filled with water, and each cone was built up by tiny, wafer-thin rafts of calcite floating on the water's surface. Drops from the ceiling would occasionally land on these bits of calcite, forcing them to sink to the bottom, and their build-up created the cones. It is a process that must have taken literally thousands and thousands of years.

At least a dozen of Lechuguilla's chambers would have made the cave an important discovery, but there is one that is so astonishing that nothing quite prepares you. After around six hours, which takes you 2km (1.2 miles) from the entrance, you finally reach the Chandelier Ballroom. Here, 6-m (20-foot) long collections of hand-sized crystals hang from the ceiling. The sight is so otherworldly that comparing the experience to something familiar is almost impossible. Some liken them to grotesque witches' fingers. To others, the experience is rather like walking around a giant, empty freezer compartment.

Many of the crystals found in Lechuguilla are made of gypsum, a mineral that comes from limestone. The presence of gypsum deposits in such quantities made speleologists (cave scientists) question how the cave was formed. What they discovered was that it was not carved out by carbonic acid – like most other limestone caves – but by sulphuric acid. The discovery has helped change the way we think about the origin of caves. The sulphuric acid was formed by hydrogen sulphide from oil deposits deep in the Earth's crust bubbling through fissures in the rock and mixing with oxygen in the water table. It dissolves limestone five times faster on average than carbonic acid and leaves behind gypsum, the basis for Lechuguilla's remarkable formations. But the discoveries did not end here.

Originally, Lechuguilla was regarded as a dead cave – no longer expanding and containing no signs of life and virtually no nutrients. But several years ago, scientists discovered a unique bacteria on the cave walls feeding on minerals such as iron and manganese. The ability of these microbes to survive in such extreme conditions makes them truly extremophile. Their presence is another reason why access to Lechuguilla is so tightly controlled. If you want to go into the cave today, you have to be prepared to eat all your food on plastic sheets to prevent crumbs being left on the cave floor and put your bodily waste in bags (known euphemistically as burrito bags). In a cave with as few nutrients as Lechuguilla, even half a biscuit could provide a fertile feeding ground for the other bacteria that humans inevitably bring with them, upsetting the delicate ecosystem.

But despite all the regulations, conservation in Lechuguilla is an ongoing struggle. Since the cave's discovery, bacteria linked to people, such as *E. coli*, have been found in it. A cave may not be a cave until a human has entered it, but in Lechuguilla, every person who makes a trip into its depths inadvertently helps to make it a slightly different place – at least on a microscopic level.

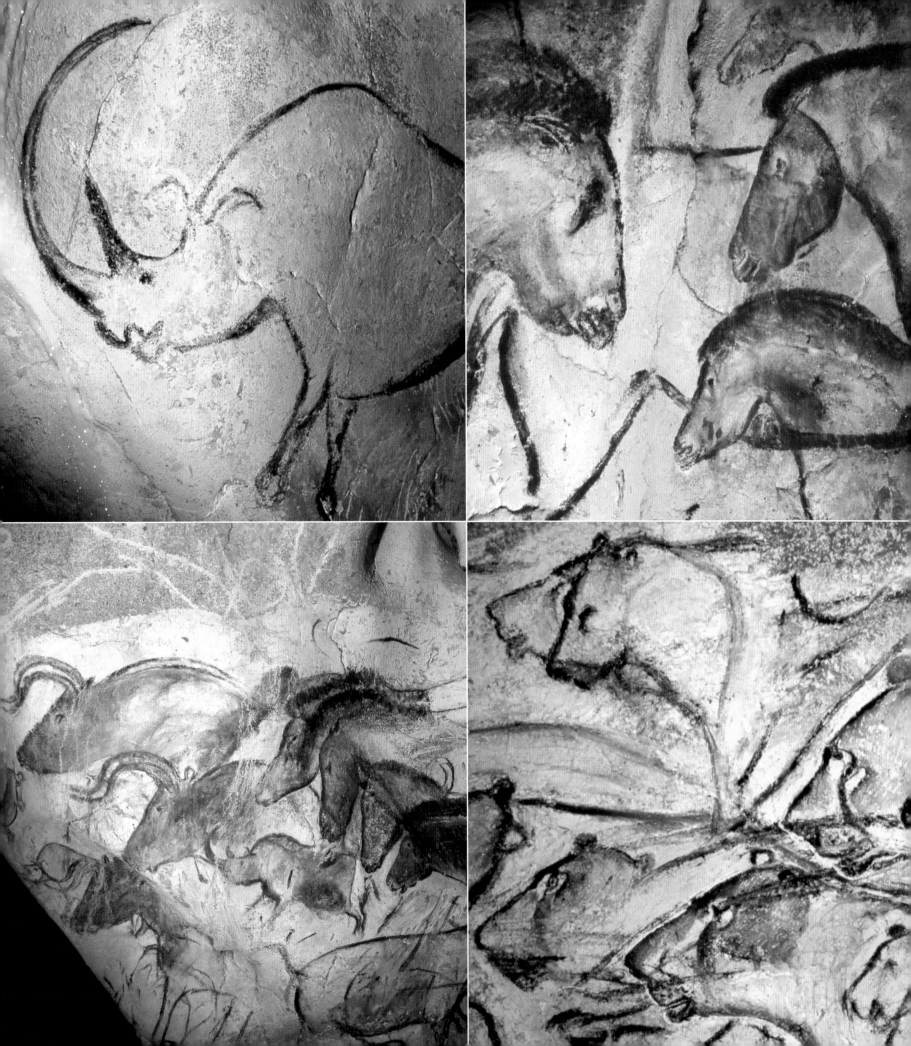

CAVEMEN

Our fear of caves might seem odd when you consider that, to our ancestors, they were the first places that could be called 'home'. Without them, the early Europeans – the Cro-Magnons and the Neanderthals – would have struggled to survive the storms of the ice ages. In fact, some European caves may have been continually occupied by humans for thousands of years. But they did not have them all to themselves.

Caves were also important refuges for the cave bear – twice the size of grizzly bears and terrifying opponents. Imagine entering a pitch-black cave chamber only to discover that it was already occupied by a family of cave bears, some possibly 5m (16 feet) long and weighing 400kg (885 pounds) – and you are armed only with a spear. It is tempting to imagine this is where our modern fear of caves comes from. Caves were, though, such a vital sanctuary for the Cro-Magnons that they had no choice but to fight it out with these giant beasts wherever they encountered them. Indeed, there is plenty of evidence to suggest that the Cro-Magnons were responsible for wiping out cave bears by the end of the last ice age – probably in the competition for safe, cosy caves.

They left plenty of evidence of their cave life, such as bones, hearths and weapons. But in some caves, our ancestors left something else, just as lasting and even more intriguing. In 1994, French caver Jean-Marie Chauvet, together with Eliette Brunel and Christian Hillaire, broke through loose rubble at the base of a cliff in southern France and made one of the greatest archaeological discoveries of all time (proving once again that we have probably only scratched the surface of cave exploration).

Inside the cave that now bears Chauvet's name was the most incredible gallery of prehistoric art. No fewer than 14 species of animal were depicted on the walls, including the only known cave paintings of a prehistoric panther and an owl, as well as images of hyenas, mountain goats, buffaloes, lions, mammoths, deer, bears and a woolly rhino. The scale of the artwork dwarfed that of the world-renowned Lascaux Cave, discovered 50 years earlier. But what was even more remarkable about the murals in Chauvet was their age. Radiocarbon dating techniques have now confirmed that these paintings are around 30,000 years old – 15,000 years older than the ones in Lascaux. And they are not just old: the use of perspective and subtle shading were so sophisticated that their discovery has forced experts to reconsider what they knew about the origins of art.

The discoveries in Chauvet have shown how important caves are as historical records. Cut off from the outside world, conditions inside many caves remain virtually unchanged from one millennium to another – a complete contrast to life at the surface which, over the same period, has undergone some astonishing changes. It seems incredible to think that, at one time, lions, panthers, bears, rhinos and mammoths roamed around southern France while our ancestors were scratching a living, but the proof is indelibly printed on the walls of Chauvet.

BELOW *The cave bear 'altar'. The skull appears to have been carefully placed on the rock in the deep chamber of Chauvet Cave. The floor is littered with many other bear skulls.*

OPPOSITE, CLOCKWISE *A rhinoceros, wild horses, lions hunting aurochs (wild cattle, now extinct), wild horses with aurochs – masterpieces of stone-age art from Chauvet Cave, using techniques of perspective and shading that have put the origins of art back 30,000 years. Evidence exists that these cave murals were visited by people over many thousands of years.*

fresh water

All life on land is dependent on fresh water. Though in short supply, its influence is enormous. Not only does it shape the landscape, but where it collects, it harbours communities of unique and surprising life-forms. It is quite simply the most precious resource on Earth.

Fresh water is rare. Just 3 per cent of the planet's water is fresh, the rest is seawater. And of that tiny amount, around 70 per cent is locked up as ice and snow, mainly at the poles. In Antarctica, the giant ice sheets nearly 5km (3 miles) thick in places are virtually incapable of supporting life within their frozen depths. Another 30 per cent of fresh water is stored within rocks and in soil as ground water – only 0.3 per cent flows on the surface as rivers and lakes. Yet rivers and lakes provide some of the richest habitats on Earth. Venture below their surface, and you will discover a world teeming with life of every size and shape. Forty per cent of all fish species live in fresh water, and most amphibians, countless insects, reptiles, plants, birds and mammals live in or on it. Science is slowly unlocking the secrets of this mysterious world, and finding new forms of life. The River Amazon alone – home to 3300 species of fish, more than in the Atlantic – is predicted to yield at least another 1700 new to science.

RUNNING WATER

The journey begins high in the mountains. Humble streams flow down to join mighty rivers that travel hundreds of miles to their ultimate destination – the sea. Here the cycle begins again, as water evaporates, precipitates over the land and eventually returns to the sea through rivers. This is the global hydrological cycle.

One of the most remote and isolated mountain plateaus, or tepuis, provides an insight into this rite of passage. Hidden in permanent cloud, the ancient tepuis of southern Venezuela rise 1000m (3280 feet) above the rainforest. This imposing landscape was the inspiration for Arthur Conan Doyle's *The Lost World* – an imagined prehistoric terrain cut off from the jungle below. The first explorer to fly over these plateaus, in the 1930s, was Jimmie Angel, an American aviator who set out in a small plane to look for signs of gold. He diced with death, and one journey ended dramatically when he crashed on top of the most famous tepuis, Auyan, or Devil's Mountain. He escaped with his life, but even today, flying over this tepuis is an unnerving experience. Fierce winds buffet the helicopter, and thick blankets of clouds close in, obscuring the way ahead. Though the shattered shards of Jimmie Angel's plane have long ago been moved to a museum, the wreckage of other aircraft is strewn across the rocks as a chilling reminder of the dangers of venturing over this high plateau.

ABOVE *The top of the unworldly Kukenon tepuis. Huge sandstone towers reach up into the clouds, the backdrop for a rain-bog filled with a community of insect-eating plants.*

OPPOSITE *The summit of the famous Auyan tepuis, or Devil's Mountain. From it pours Angel Falls, the world's highest waterfall, tumbling down from a height twice that of the world's tallest building and feeding into Venezuela's great Orinoco River.*

PREVIOUS PAGE *The predatory dorado, or river tiger, among piraputanga fish in the flood waters of the Pantanal.*

ABOVE *Torrent ducks are found only above 1500m (4920 feet) in the Andes. Slender, streamlined birds, they are powerful swimmers, built to swim and dive in white-water rapids.*

OPPOSITE TOP *A Japanese giant salamander sleeping in its daytime cave retreat. Giant salamanders are the world's largest amphibians, which can grow to almost 2m (6.5 feet) and live to be up to 80 years old.*

OPPOSITE BOTTOM *A nocturnal snatch. At night, these enormous predators emerge from their daytime sleeping dens to hunt for fish.*

The rewards of exploring this area, though, are enormous. Touching down on top of the Kukenon tepuis, you enter a strange world. Through the mist, weird forms appear – towers of sandstone, sculpted over the millennia by wind and torrential rain into shapes that eerily resemble figures. Underfoot in the bog is one of the greatest collections of insectivorous plants, the majority of which grow only here – pitcher plants and sundews that live on insects blown up from the jungle below. They thrive in the wet conditions created by an almost daily tropical downpour and an average annual rainfall of 400cm (155 inches).

The source of this rain is moisture rising as water vapour from the sea, blown inland and forced up on reaching the mountains. As it cools, it condenses into cloud and finally rain. Sheets of water pour over the rocks and flow down gullies into streams that are channelled into small rivers. By helicopter, you can chart the courses of the golden streams that delineate the top of Devil's Mountain until the water suddenly hurtles over a precipice – and your stomach falls into your feet. On a clear day, the full 979m (3211-foot) drop of the longest continuous waterfall in the world can be seen. The descent creates a force so great that, long before the chute of water reaches its base in the Devil's Canyon, it is blown by the wind into a fine mist. This waterfall – which eventually feeds into the Orinoco, South America's second largest river system – is called Angel Falls after who else but the man who discovered it back in 1933, Jimmie Angel.

LIFE IN THE FAST STREAM

Each spring, as temperatures start to rise, the melting ice and snow produce a surge of fresh water. These melt-water streams are full of energy as they cascade down the mountains, building pace and power as they go. As any canoeist hooked on the adrenalin of shooting rapids and plunging down waterfalls will testify, it is in these upper reaches that a river is at its most dramatic. Mountain water is cold and low in nutrients but high in oxygen. Here invertebrates dominate, but to survive in the torrent requires adaptations. The predatory North American hellgrammite nymph has a flattened profile to reduce drag and a series of grappling hooks to prevent it being swept away. Black-fly larvae anchor themselves with a ring of hooks on their abdomens and deploy silken safety lines if they come unstuck. Caddisfly larvae build cases of stone, sand and sticks to protect themselves against both predators and being bashed against the rocks. Specialized fish, including the Tibetan stone loach, the world's highest-altitude fish, feed by scraping the algae off rocks and hold on with enlarged mouth suckers.

It may be a harsh existence, but there are advantages to life in the fast stream. In particular, predators are few. But there are, of course, the specialists. Torrent ducks, found high in the Andes of South America, and harlequin ducks, found from Alaska across to Siberia, have streamlined bodies and powerful webbed feet to battle against the river currents as they feed on aquatic invertebrates. The only large predators in the remote mountain rivers of China and Japan are the world's largest amphibians, giant salamanders. These monstrous creatures, which can grow almost 2m (6.5 feet) long and live up to 80 years, have exceptionally slow metabolisms – ideal for a cold environment. By day, they rest in communal underwater caves, but at night, they emerge to hunt fish such as trout. A giant salamander has poor eyesight, but sensory nodes on its body detect the slightest change in water pressure. It lies in ambush, and as prey nears, it strikes with astonishing speed. Free from competition, it dines alone.

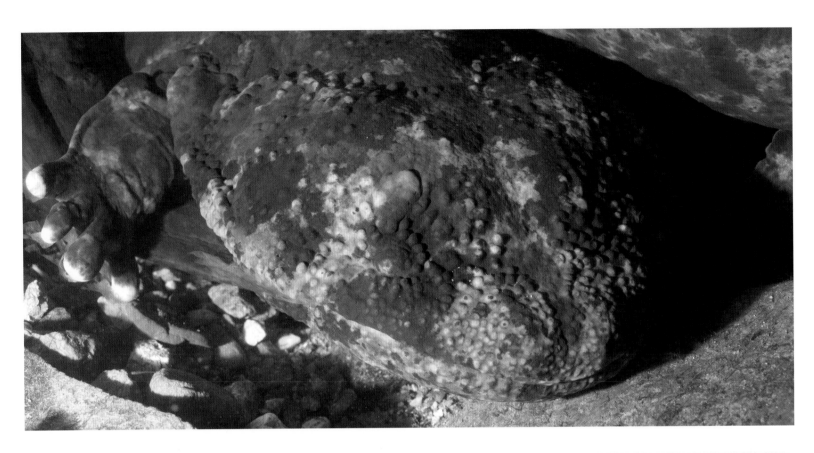

THE GREAT SALMON RUN

New life reaches the high, cool temperate rivers of the northern hemisphere in the form of the world's greatest freshwater fish migration. Each spring, at least 2 million Atlantic salmon invade around 2000 river mouths along the coasts of North America and Europe and battle upstream to their spawning grounds. It is a gruelling journey, in some cases more than 1600km (990 miles). Six species of Pacific salmon – sockeye (red), pink, chum, coho (silver), steelhead and king (Chinook) – pile into northern rivers from California to Korea. In the northwest Pacific alone, around 142–287 million salmon are thought to be on the move. Before commercial fisheries and habitat destruction took their toll, the amount was estimated to be up to 350 million salmon.

A salmon may spend several years at sea, feeding and growing. It needs all its strength to embark on the last and most demanding journey of its life – to its birthplace high upriver. These fast-swimming and streamlined fish can swim up large rapids and even leap up waterfalls on their titanic endeavour. On the Canadian west coast, sockeyes break their journey in resting pools, where they conserve their energy while waiting for the next pulse of floodwater to raise the river level and aid their upstream journey. Hazards are everywhere, but at this stage, it is the grizzly bear that poses the greatest threat. For the bears, it is a time of plenty. Capable swimmers, some have even learnt to dive after salmon, pinning them to the riverbed with their massive clawed paws. Cubs also join in the fishing sorties, but catching salmon in deep water is not easy, and for much of the time, they rely on handouts from their mothers. On average, an adult bear will consume more than a ton of salmon over the six-week spawning period, and for the growing cubs, the amount of salmon eaten may make the difference between life and death in their first winter.

The vast majority of salmon, though, escape to complete the final stage of their arduous journey. Their extraordinary homing and navigational systems guide them back to the streams where they were spawned years before. The physical transformation that began when they entered fresh water has now finished. They have changed from silver to bright red, and the males have hunched up and developed a kipe, an upturned lower jaw, which they use for jousting to secure a female's favour. Fertilized eggs are deposited in gravel scrapes, where they can develop bathed in highly oxygenated, relatively predator-free waters.

Once Pacific salmon have spawned, they die. The riverbeds become mass graveyards. Even in death, salmon play a vital ecological role, with more than 137 species – from caddisfly larvae to armies of crayfish, from bald eagles to wolf cubs – feeding on their carcasses. It is a massive injection of energy into these high rivers, and even the neighbouring forests benefit, growing taller in soils fertilized by carcasses scattered by predators.

But the future for salmon is looking bleak. In the North Atlantic, the number returning from the oceans has halved, possibly due to rising sea temperatures and a disruption in the food chain. Those that make it back to the rivers face another threat – escaped farmed salmon. In 2005, an estimated one million farmed fish found their way into the waters of Norway and Scotland alone. The escapees spread disease and mate with wild fish to create hybrids, which scientists fear will threaten the wild diversity and lead to genetic weakness and a drop in survival. Plans to farm transgenic or genetically modified salmon could pose more problems for the future.

OPPOSITE *Brown bears – grizzlies – fishing for salmon in Alaska. A bear can eat more than a ton of fish over the six-week salmon-spawning period.*

BELOW *Male sockeyes in fresh water. They turn bright red, hunch up and develop hooked and upturned jaws.*

BOTTOM *Eggs in a gravel scrape being fertilized. They will develop in the highly oxygenated upstream waters.*

ABOVE *A view from space of the 1600-km (1000-mile) scar and network of canyons eroded by the Colorado River in Arizona, USA.*

High-altitude rivers, fed by rain and melt water, continue to build in volume as they merge. Main tributaries, still powered by gravity, become the most erosive forces on the planet. They shape the land, carving out V-shaped river valleys, gorges and canyons. The deepest canyons are in the Himalayas – the world's highest mountain range and subject to massive river erosion – with the Yarlung Tsangpo Gorge, in a remote region of Tibet, being the deepest of them all (only recognized as such in 1994). Up to 5.9km (3.7 miles) deep and 45km (28 miles) wide in places, it was created by the mighty Brahmaputra River. Other giant canyons in the Himalayan plateau include the 4.3-km (2.7-mile) deep Kali Gandaki Canyon in Nepal, and the 3.6-km (2.3-mile) deep Tiger Leaping Gorge in China.

In the Americas, the deepest canyons include Colca in the Peruvian Andes at 3.6km (2.3 miles), the Copper Canyon in Mexico at 1.7km (5770 feet) and perhaps the most famous of them all, the Grand Canyon in Arizona, USA. The Grand Canyon is just one part of the world's longest canyon system – a 1600-km (1000-mile) scar, clearly visible from space – created over 5 million years as Arizona's Colorado River has eroded the sandstone.

Today, the mighty Colorado River has been tamed by the Hoover Dam, but its canyon legacy is testament to the land-shaping power of mighty rivers. At 355km (220 miles) long and more than 1.6km (a mile) deep and 27km (17 miles) across at its widest, the Grand Canyon draws enormous crowds to marvel at its colossal size and grandeur.

RIVER DRAMAS

As rivers wind their way down from the mountains, they start to slow down and gradually warm up, becoming richer in life as they do so. In southern India, the Cauvery River is laden with nutrients as it flows down from the Western Ghats. As its waters warm, they teem with fish, including 45-kg (100-pound) mahseer, prized by fishermen. Mahseer are food for mugger crocodiles – 4m (13 feet) or more long – which can be seen basking on the sandbanks. At dawn, great splashes reveal underwater dramas as the mahseers attempt to escape the muggers' jaws. The rich waters provide enough food to support family groups up to 17-strong of smooth-coated otters – the most sociable of all otters. In the dry season, before the monsoons arrive, when the water level falls and the boulder-strewn river divides into numerous channels and islands, it is possible to glimpse otters moving from one hunting pond to another. They leave their riverbank holts before dawn to begin their sorties across their huge, 10-km (6.2-mile) wide territories. When it comes to fishing, there is real strength in numbers. They often work together to drive and corral fish. Even the cubs may help, starting to learn to catch fish at about four months old, but only the adults have the necessary speed and agility to land prey. They can remain under water for up to three minutes at a time and catch, on average, an eighth of their body weight in fish a day.

The otters share the water with the mighty muggers, but the advantage the otters have is safety in numbers. Once in a while, there is an outburst of shrieking and primeval hissing as a crocodile appears to attack an otter. But watch closely and you will discover that it is the otters who are the aggressors, ganging together to hound the crocodiles off the sandbanks.

BELOW *Smooth-coated otters – the most sociable of all the otters – playing in the Cauvery River.*

BOTTOM *A mugger crocodile. It can grow to more than 4m (13 feet) long, mainly on a diet of fish but including the occasional otter or other mammal that strays too close.*

Crocodiles are cold-blooded, and all 22 species usually live in lower-altitude subtropical and tropical rivers and estuaries. Large concentrations of giant Nile crocodiles live in the rivers that snake across East Africa's Serengeti. These rivers are dangerous obstacles but also vital sources of water for thirsty herds of grazing animals crossing the parched grasslands in search of fresh green pastures. Once a year, a drama unfolds as 2 million wildebeest march across the plain. The crocodiles know the wildebeest are coming and gather in anticipation of their annual feast.

As the thirsty wildebeest file warily down the riverbank of the Grumeti, the crocodiles slide silently into the murky waters. Adapted to hunt in low visibility, they rely on stealth, crawling along the riverbed, homing in on the vibrations from the drinking wildebeest. Flattening themselves to remain hidden in only 30cm (12 inches) of water, they inch closer and closer until their snouts are almost touching those of the wildebeest above.

For a film crew, the tension can be unbearable. The nervous wildebeest edge ever closer to the water. It can take hours – one step forward, one step back. Then suddenly, the edgy calm is shattered by an eruption as a crocodile launches out of the water. Chaos breaks out as wildebeest jump back and topple over each other in panic. Zebras alarm-call in terror. Only a state-of-the art camera can slow down time enough to reveal the narrow line separating life from death. Once a crocodile has a hold, it never lets go. A titanic tug-of-war can develop between a bull wildebeest and a crocodile, lasting more than an hour before the crocodile manages to pull the bull into water deep enough to drown it in.

BELOW *A Nile crocodile striking with lightning speed. It normally eats fish, which comprise 70 per cent of its diet, but an annual feast of mammal meat arrives with the migrating wildebeest and zebras.*

GIANT LAKES

Most rivers drain into the sea, but the Grumeti flows inland from Africa's east coast into the world's second-largest freshwater lake, Victoria. Lakes hold most of the Earth's fresh water – at least 20 times more than the rivers. From space they appear as immense patches of silvery blue, large enough to be mistaken for seas. Some are so wide and deep that they have created their own weather systems. Others contain marine-like communities of seals, jellyfish and sponges. Each supports large numbers of species found nowhere else.

The world's largest lake is the Caspian Sea in southwest Asia, covering 370,000 sq km (143,000 square miles). Its waters are saline, giving it characteristics of a marine environment. The largest freshwater lake is Lake Superior, part of the Great Lakes of North America, which form the biggest continuous mass of fresh water on Earth, covering an expanse larger than the UK. But the mother of all lakes is Lake Baikal, in eastern Siberia, a huge chasm more than 1.6km (a mile) deep, which holds a fifth of all the world's surface fresh water.

For centuries, the deepest lakes have fuelled imagination, inspiring tales of prehistoric creatures surviving in bottomless, underwater worlds. Yet few lakes exceed 500m (1640 feet) in depth – Scotland's Loch Ness, famous for its 'monster', is just 230m (755 feet) deep – and only Lake Baikal sustains life beyond depths of 200m (655 feet). But one lake revered for its monsters does deserve its reputation. Lake Nicaragua in Central America is home to the dangerous bull shark, which grows to more than 3m (10 feet) in length. So numerous

ABOVE *A winter's view of frozen Lake Baikal in eastern Siberia, Russia. This lake holds more fresh water than any other – a fifth of all the fresh water found in the planet's lakes and rivers.*

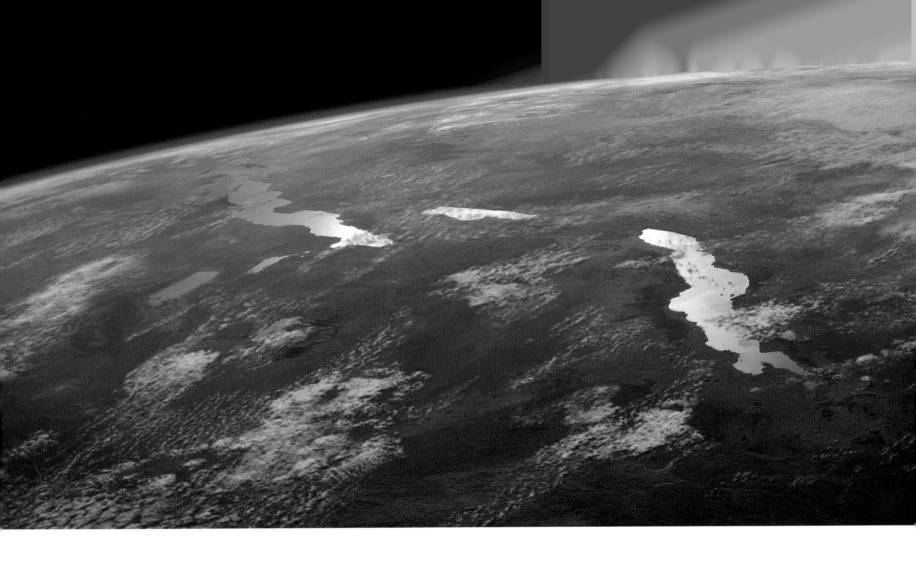

were its numbers that a shark-fishing industry operated until the 1970s, decimating the population. Bull sharks are now known to make their way up and down the connecting San Juan River, which drains into the Caribbean Sea. They are one of the few shark species that can tolerate the salinity change between salt and fresh water.

LITTLE CICHLIDS AND BIG SWARMS

East Africa's Great Rift Valley, running south from the end of the Red Sea to Tanzania, is a great split in the Earth's crust. In this trench are some of the world's largest, deepest and most fascinating lakes. Lake Victoria covers 70,000 sq km (27,000 square miles) but is relatively shallow and swampy. Scientists have so far identified more than 350 species of fish unique to the lake, mostly in the eye-catching cichlid family. Lakes Tanganyika and Malawi, though smaller in area than Victoria – 33,000 sq km and 30,000 sq km (12,700 and 11,580 square miles) respectively – have even more fish diversity. Set against breathtaking mountainous backdrops, these tropical waters provide a freshwater diving experience as close as it gets to a coral-reef one, their crystal-clear rocky shallows displaying schools of colourful cichlids. But the most fish of any lake – 850 species of cichlid alone – are found in Lake Malawi, the smallest of the three lakes but still bigger than the country of Wales. Some have evolved into algal scrapers, others into sediment feeders and some into predators of the fry of others. Almost all the cichlids protect their young using mouth-brooding – at the first sign of a predator, the parent signals its fry to swim into its cavernous mouth – and it will continue to guard its babies until they grow too large to fit in. At night, though, cichlids are prey to the mormyrid, an electric fish that emerges from its lair to sweep the rocks for fish, detecting them by distortions in the electric fields around their bodies.

Away from the shallow shore, the lake-bed plummets into an abyss without light, warmth or oxygen. Both Lake Malawi and Lake Tanganyika have a thermocline – a 200-m (655-foot) permanent barrier that seals off the upper warm waters from the colder waters below, preventing any mixing of nutrients and oxygen and creating a bottom dead zone. In Lake Tanganyika, the second deepest lake in the world at 1500m (4920 feet), 90 per cent of its water is uninhabited. In Lake Malawi, little survives in the dead zone apart from the larvae of the lake fly, or phantom midge. During the day, these larvae appear to seek refuge from predators in the oxygen-starved depths. At night, they balloon up to the surface to feed on plankton. Come the rainy season, they undergo a transformation. At dawn the first adult midges appear on the surface. Soon millions upon millions of newly hatched lake flies are taking flight – spiralling orange tornadoes of mating insects rising high in the air and at times so dense that fishermen are rumoured to have choked to death in the swarms. The spellbinding display lasts just a few hours. Once the flies have mated, they drop to the water surface, release their eggs and die. By the afternoon, all that is left is the orange stain of millions of dead insects on the water surface – soon cleared by the cichlids.

BELOW *Baby cichlids flocking into their parent's cavernous mouth. All except one species of Lake Malawi's cichlids mouth-brood in this way.*

BOTTOM *Some of the 850 or so cichlids in Lake Malawi. All of them evolved from just one ancestor isolated here thousands of years ago.*

The oldest lake in the world

Lake Baikal, which means sacred sea, holds a fifth of the planet's surface fresh water, and at 25–30 million years old, is the oldest lake in the world. Like Lake Tanganyika, Baikal owes its origin to movements of the tectonic plates that make up the Earth's crust, and is contained within a long, steep-sided trough, 650km (400 miles) long and nearly 2km (more than a mile) deep.

Life in eastern Siberia is harsh. Winter temperatures average –20°C (–4°F), and the lake is frozen shut for more than five months of the year by an ice sheet 1.2m (nearly 4 feet) thick – strong enough to support the 2-ton trucks that use it as a highway from one side to the other. Yet if you saw through the ice

and dive into the world below, you will find yourself in a winter wonderland.

Below the ice, the landscape is one of strange, translucent ice sculptures, and there is life in profusion. In its isolation, this ancient lake has undergone an evolutionary explosion and now holds more than 1200 species of animals and 1000 species of plant, 80 per cent of which are found nowhere else.

Many resemble marine creatures, such as the sponges that carpet the lake's shallows. There are 147 species of snails and 255 species of amphipods – shrimp-like crustaceans, some as large as mice.

Baikal holds 40 per cent of the world's amphipods, which play a vital role scavenging

on the dead. Amphipods can do the job in the dark, cold depths, where temperatures are not high enough for even decomposition bacteria to function properly.

Baikal is home to the world's only freshwater seal, the nerpa, which is thought to have migrated to the lake 22 million years ago from the Arctic Ocean, along rivers that have long since disappeared.

About 50,000 nerpa may live here. Smaller than most seals, they grow to just 1.2–1.4m (4–4.6 feet) in length. The females give birth during the winter in ice lairs. They maintain breathing holes in the ice by scraping the edges with their sharp claws or by gnawing. As spring progresses and the ice starts to

melt, the lairs become exposed and the pups become vulnerable to wandering bears or even crows.

As adults, nerpa can dive down to 300m (985 feet) and remain under water for more than 70 minutes at a time. Here they feed mainly on the translucent golomyanka, or oil fish, also found only in Lake Baikal. Golomyanka contain 35 per cent oil and are the commonest fish in the lake. They can cope with the crushing water pressure 1400m (4590 feet) down, but if they are taken out of the lake, they literally melt.

Extraordinary discoveries have been made by deep-water submersibles. The water is constantly well mixed, and so oxygen is

always plentiful, right to the very bottom, 1637m (5370 feet) down – which enables animals to live at any depth.

At a depth of 400m (1312 feet), scientists were amazed to find hydrothermal vents, previously only thought to exist in the deep oceans. Thriving around these superheated vents are unique communities of sponges, bacterial mats, snails, fish and transparent shrimps. Descending to depths of more than 1km onto the abyssal plain of the lake, which itself lies on top of a 7-km (4.3-mile) thick layer of sediment, they have found a giant deep-water flatworm that can grow to 40cm (16 inches) and preys on fish – just one of 80 species of flatworm in Baikal.

LEFT TO RIGHT *Forests of sponge lining the shallows of Lake Baikal. These slow-growing animals filter out plankton.*

An amphipod. This ancient lake holds 40 per cent of the world's amphipods – cleaners and scavengers.

The nerpa, or Lake Baikal seal – the world's only freshwater seal. It can dive down 300m (985 feet) after fish.

Underwater ice sculptures. Few see them as it is only possible to stay in the cold water for about 45 minutes.

The sun setting over the frozen lake. For five months, Baikal is sealed by an ice sheet more than a metre (3 feet) thick.

GIANT RIVERS

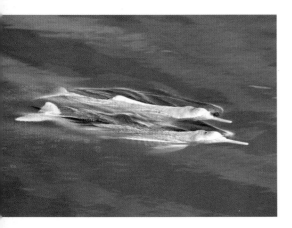

Most great rivers don't end their journeys in lakes but run great distances to the sea. From space, they appear as long ribbons of silver snaking across the continents. The top ten, ranked by how much water they carry, are headed by the Amazon – by far the largest, with more than four times the amount of water than the next biggest, the Congo. The third biggest is the Orinoco, followed by the Yangtze, Parana, Brahmaputra, Yellow, Yenisei, Ganges and Mississippi. The Nile in Africa is the world's longest river – one major tributary, the Blue Nile, rises in the Ethiopian Highlands and the other, the White Nile, in Lake Victoria – which empties 6695km (4150 miles) later into the Mediterranean.

Born in the Himalayas, the world's highest mountain range, are many other great rivers. The Ganges and Brahmaputra flow south through India, join forces to form the Padma – then effectively, the world's third largest river in volume of water and the first in terms of the amount of sediment it carries – and emerge in the Bay of Bengal to form the world's largest delta. Arising in Tibet and flowing across the north of China is the Yellow River, which is second only to the Padma in terms of sediment. Further south in China is the Yangtze, the longest river in Asia at 5150km (3190 miles) and probably the deepest in the world when it flows through the Three Gorges area.

THE AMAZON QUEEN

In the Americas, the Mississippi and its tributaries drain almost the whole of the US. But the queen of all rivers is the Amazon. Carrying almost a fifth of the world's flowing fresh water – the amount carried by the next ten biggest rivers combined – its river basin is larger than any other, draining a third of South America. It transports a billion tons of sediment a year, visible from space as a brown stain hundreds of miles out to sea.

Rising in the Peruvian Andes, its main trunk flows eastwards across Brazil. In places this monster of a river is 40km (25 miles) wide when in flood. Even 3700km (2295 miles) from the sea, it is navigable by ocean-going ships. Eventually, more than 6450km (4000 miles) from its source, the world's second-longest river drains into the Atlantic Ocean.

The Amazon's waters are wonderfully rich. To date, in excess of 3000 different species of fish have been identified – more than in the entire Atlantic Ocean – and scientists predict the count could eventually rise to more than 5000. In the depths lurk creatures that communicate through electricity. By altering the properties of the electric fields around their bodies, they can 'talk' to each other in the gloom, and the electric eel can deliver up to 600 volts – enough to render a human unconscious. Monster fish including pirarucu, or arapaima – the longest fish in South America at 2.5m (more than 8 feet) – also skulk in the gloom. Other oversized predators include the world's largest freshwater dolphin, otter and river turtle and the green anaconda, which can grow to more than 6m (20 feet) long.

The boto, or pink river dolphin, can weigh up to 100kg (220 pounds) and grow to more than 2.5m (8 feet) long. It is highly social and may live in groups of up to 20 individuals. In the breeding season, there is stiff competition for mates, and males will fight, inflicting serious bites. But they also display in front of watching females, rising up out of the water with rocks in their jaws, perhaps to prove how strong and dexterous they are.

ABOVE *Botos, or pink river dolphins. They are highly social, and in the murky Amazon, they communicate through an elaborate vocabulary of whistles and clicks. They also use echolocation (like bats) to find their way around and catch prey.*

TOP *A male boto shows off a lump of mud – a behaviour thought to be part of a courtship display.*

OPPOSITE *The planet's super-river, the Amazon. Its waters teem with fish and other animals and support a unique flooded-forest ecosystem. Only a third of the world's 177 large rivers remain free-flowing, unimpeded by dams or other barriers, and the Amazon is one of only 21 of those still running freely from source to sea.*

The Amazon provides food aplenty for botos. Migrating fish pass through their territories, including shoals of the dorado catfish. This species makes the longest migration of any freshwater fish – from the Amazon's delta to the Andean foothills, probably to spawn there – a journey of more than 4830km (3000 miles). During the *piracema*, the water literally boils with fish so densely packed that individuals may die through lack of oxygen. The botos follow the shoals and corral them in shallower water, where capture is easier.

The Amazon is also home to the tucuxi, a porpoise known locally as a 'river dolphin'. The tucuxi and boto are the only freshwater cetaceans not critically endangered. The four other species, all found in the largest rivers in the world, tend to live in muddy water, have reduced eyesight or are virtually blind and rely on highly developed sonar to catch fish. The two species on the Indian subcontinent are the Ganges dolphin, found from the foothills of the Himalayas to the Ganges-Brahmaputra delta, and the Indus river dolphin of Pakistan and India. The Yangtze river dolphin, or baiji, of China is the most threatened of them all. The development of the Three Gorges Dam, along with increased pollution, netting and river traffic, has pushed it to imminent extinction, with a handful of individuals left.

A river's final passage to the sea may still encounter obstacles. In the lower courses of the Iguaçu River on the border of Brazil and Argentina, where the waters have left hard rock and flowed over a softer layer, they have eroded a huge waterfall 2.5km (1.6 miles) across. You can hear the roar of the mighty Iguaçu Falls (Iguaçu means 'great water') 15km (more than 9 miles) away. The best way to view the head of the falls is by helicopter, where the river plunges over its semi-circular bowl down into the mist-filled chasm known as the Devil's Throat, but the spray and vicious updraft make it a hair-raising experience.

OPPOSITE *The Dardanelos Falls on the Aripuana River, Brazil. Great dusky swifts use the giant waterfalls in South America to their advantage. These acrobatic birds can dart behind the protective walls of water to nest on the rocks, safe from predators.*

THE BIGGEST OF ALL

Arguments have raged for centuries over which freshwater fish deserves to land this sought-after title. And one of the many problems is that sightings of giant creatures, like many a fisherman's tale, are usually not possible to verify.

North America's white sturgeon has a maximum recorded weight of 816kg (1803 pounds). But its European cousin, the beluga sturgeon, has been weighed in at 2070kg (4575 pounds). In Russia, a European catfish is rumoured to have reached 4.5m (nearly 15 feet) long. Asian contenders include the Chinese paddlefish from the Yangtze River. This filter-feeder has an elongated snout covered with electro-sensors and is said to have reached lengths of 7m (23 feet), though there are no authenticated records. Giant stingrays in the Mekong River are challengers, supposedly weighing more than 500kg (1105 pounds) and measuring up to 4.2m (14 feet). But the accolade of the longest freshwater fish *on record* goes to the critically endangered Mekong giant catfish, pictured here, which measured 2.7 metres long (nearly 9 feet) and tipped the scales at 293kg (646 pounds).

SWAMP AND MUD

In their final stages, rivers broaden and flow across their low-lying floodplains, and when they break their banks, they create wetlands. These cover 6 per cent of the Earth's surface and include bogs, marshes and swamps. Notable waterlogged areas are the Everglades in Florida, the Okavango in Botswana, Kakadu in northern Australia and the Amazon in Brazil. Important havens for wildlife, wetlands also act as the kidneys of the land, filtering out pollutants and rejuvenating the system. But agriculture and urban development continue to suck dry the remaining areas.

Each wet season in southwest Brazil, the Parana River undergoes a dramatic change. Fed by rainfall far away, the river swells and overflows its banks to flood an area the size of

England – approximately 130,000 sq km (50,000 square miles). This creates the largest wetland in the world, called the Pantanal from the Portuguese for swamp. For the next six months, the vast tracts of dry grassland and forest are transformed into a temporary waterworld of swamps, pools and water channels.

The Pantanal supports diverse forms of animals and plants. Its slow-flowing, nutrient-rich river water nurtures underwater forests of aquatic plants such as water hyacinth and Victoria giant water lily. This environment is the perfect nursery for fish. More than 300 species breed here, including freshwater stingrays and piranhas. Yellow anaconda and spectacled caiman up to 3m (10 feet) long also thrive here. Snorkelling in these clear, shallow waters is like being in a giant tropical aquarium. Carried along in the gentle current, you sweep past swathes of aquatic plants and schools of exotic-looking fish.

ABOVE *The world's largest wetland, the Pantanal, in southern Brazil. Its source is the Parana River, which overflows its banks to flood an area the size of England.*

OPPOSITE *Red-bellied piranhas patrolling the river channels. Schools of these notorious predators will attack large prey as a group.*

Fig trees overhanging the water's edge provide welcome food for shoals of hungry fish. The competition for falling fruits is intense, and schools of pacu and piraputanga spend hours moving up and down the river channels in search of them. So keen are they that they appear to have learned to shadow brown capuchin monkeys, waiting for them to dislodge fruit. Darting pacu and piraputanga cause a commotion, which in turn attracts dorado, the largest predatory fish in the Pantanal, known as river tigers because of their sharp teeth and powerful jaws. Ready to pick off their leftovers are the red-bellied piranhas, which pour out of the thick vegetation en masse and can strip a fish to the bone in minutes.

BELOW A yellow dorado – the area's largest predatory fish – and above it piraputangas. Home to more than 300 species of fish, the Pantanal is like a giant tropical aquarium.

ABOVE RIGHT A spectacled caiman in its element. In the dry season, caimans are forced to march long distances on land, reportedly in lines, in search of remnant pools of water.

OPPOSITE A yellow anaconda – one of the top predators in the Pantanal. It will even feed on caimans.

By April the rains cease, and the Pantanal begins to dry out, concentrating fish into a series of pools. These 'fish larders' supply the abundant waterbirds that breed at this time. There are more than 650 bird species in the Pantanal. The largest is the jabiru stork at 1.5m (5 feet) high, and herons, wood storks and roseate spoonbills form colonies 10,000 strong. The large numbers of growing chicks come under continuous attack from avian predators such as caracaras and turkey vultures, and any flightless chick that becomes dislodged from its nest is likely to fall into the waiting jaws of the spectacled caimans lingering below.

As the dry season heat intensifies, fish desperately attempt to escape from the drying pools into the deeper river channels, and caiman are forced to march away in search of fresh water, and do so in long lines. Then the rains finally break once more, the fish eggs lying dormant in the soil like seeds hatch out, and the richest wetland in the world rejuvenates.

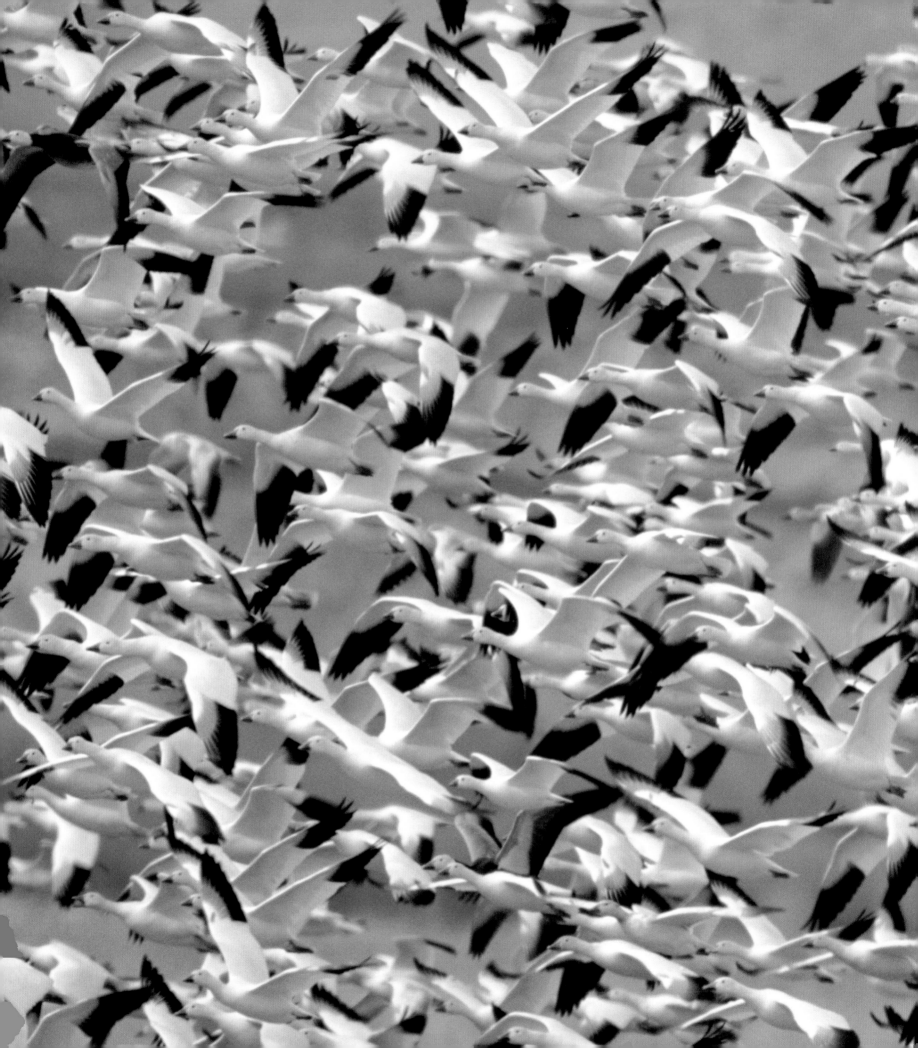

THE FINAL ACT

Down on the coastal plains, the gradient is now so shallow that the rivers begin to lay down their sediment. The growing banks of mud split the rivers into numerous channels, and where sediments build out into the sea, deltas are created. The largest deltas are, of course, created by the world's biggest rivers. They can take different forms – the bird's foot of the Mississippi delta or the fan of the Nile delta, for example. Though the Amazon appears more like an estuary in shape, its vast delta is under water, and it carries fresh water far out under the sea – fresh enough to drink more than 160km (100 miles) out.

The world's biggest delta is where the Brahmaputra and the Ganges pour into the Bay of Bengal. They deliver every year more than a billion tons of sediment eroded from the Himalayas – more sediment than in any other river system. The resulting delta stretches 75,000 sq km (29,000 square miles) across West Bengal and Bangladesh. Along its coastal fringes, the channels and mud banks have been colonized by mangroves to create the world's largest mangrove forest, the Sundarbans – visible from space.

The Indo-West Pacific region has the most extensive mangrove forests, but mangroves also take anchor across the tropical belt on protected coastlines, wherever river mud can accumulate. There are around 70 species, ranging from bush-sized plants to trees 25m (82 feet) tall. Though they can survive immersion by the tide, they also require fresh water, and for gas exchange, many have aerial roots that grow out of the waterlogged mud. At high tide, the underwater maze of mangrove roots provides shelter and creates important nursery grounds for fish. And when the tide retreats, another group of creatures emerges onto the exposed mud. These include mudskippers, armies of fiddler crabs and crab-eating macaques.

Not all rivers build deltas. In river mouths where a rising sea level has flooded the valley, the semi-enclosed area is called an estuary. The endless mudflats of estuaries may look like wastelands but are among the most productive environments on Earth. The mud dumped by the rivers is a nutrient-rich soup, in which an army of tiny creatures, from bacteria and protozoa to nematodes, breaks down the organic matter. Larger animals such as polychaetes, clams, and razorshells live in burrows or in permanent tubes. These in turn support great numbers of predators. Estuaries are vital breeding grounds for fish such as anchovies and mullet. And at low tide, huge flocks of wading birds, from oystercatchers, godwits and plovers to knots and sandpipers come to feed, each species with a beak fashioned to prise out or open the shellfish and other tasty creatures that inhabit the mud.

In temperate and subarctic estuaries, salt-marsh grasses replace mangroves in the mud. Along the North American Atlantic seaboard, salt marshes were once extensive. Now just pockets remain. Though hemmed in by an urban sprawl that stretches from Washington and New York, the tidal salt marshes around Chesapeake Bay and the Delaware estuary still provide rich feeding grounds – vital stopovers for the 400,000 greater snow geese that arrive each autumn to rest and refuel on their long migratory journeys south.

This is the end of the rivers' journeys. Collectively, they have worn down mountains and carried parts of them to the sea. And all along the way, their fresh water has brought life in abundance. All the great rivers also provide drinking water, food, irrigation, transport and now power to much of the world's population – though at a great cost to wildlife. Many predict that future world conflicts will be waged not over oil, but fresh water, arguably the world's most precious resource.

ABOVE *An Indonesian long-tailed macaque foraging in muddy mangrove water. Like the rest of its troop, it has learned to swim under water in search of submerged food.*

OPPOSITE *A 10,000-strong flock of greater snow geese. They stop over in the tidal salt marshes in the US to rest and refuel on their long migration down the Atlantic flyway to their wintering grounds.*

OVERLEAF *A satellite view of the world's largest delta, the Ganges-Brahmaputra, which stretches across East Bengal and Bangladesh. Every year, more than a billion tons of sediment, eroded from the Himalayas, is delivered to the ocean.*

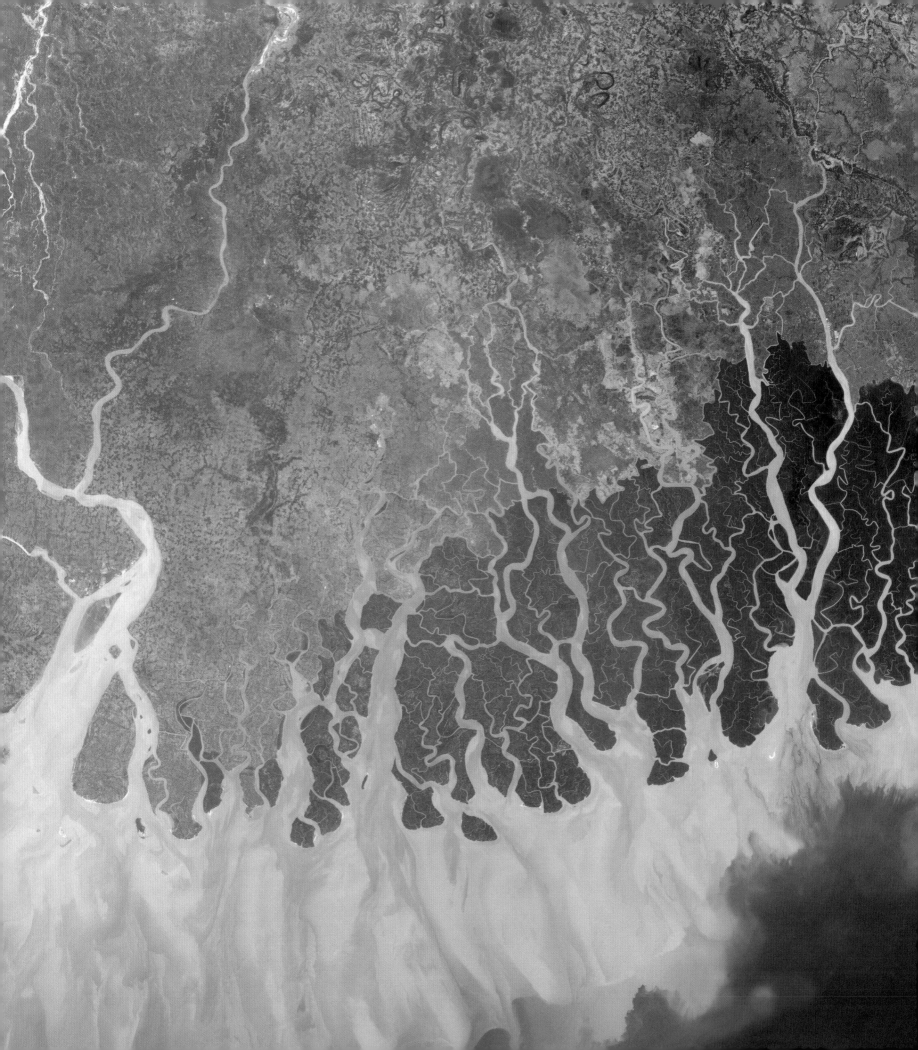

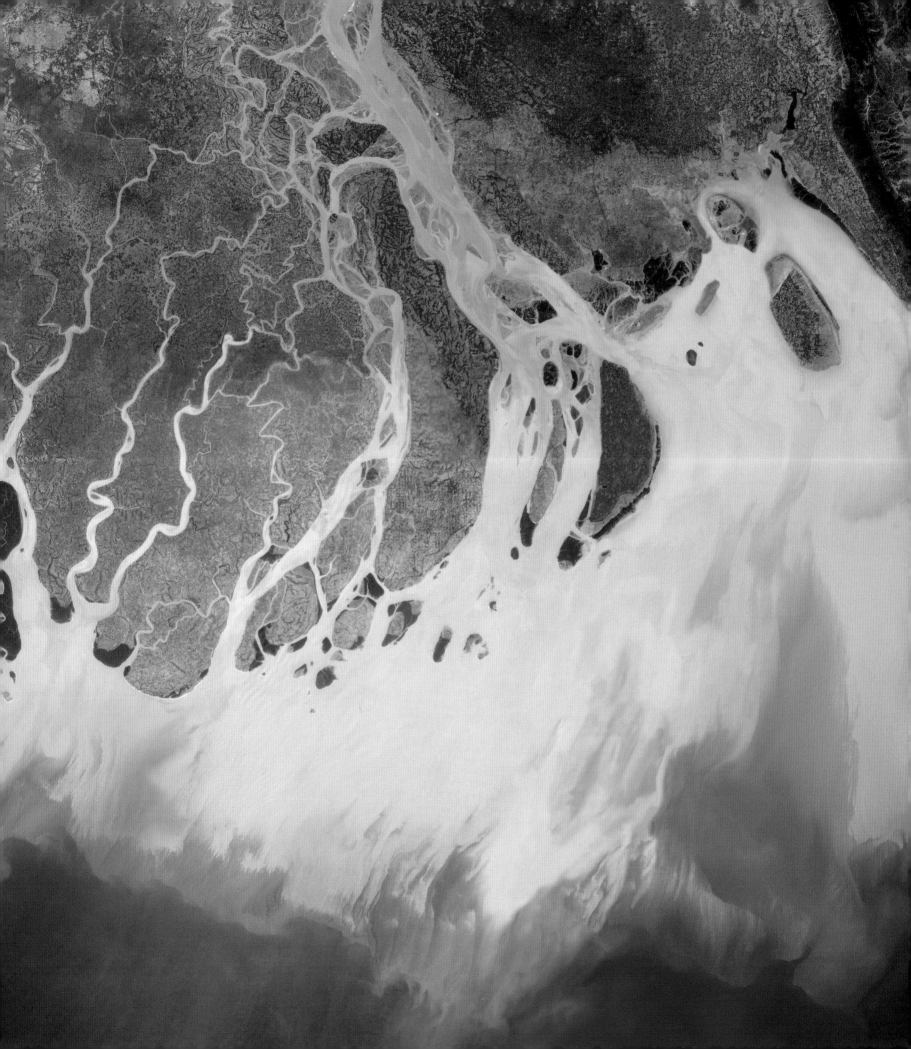

rainforests

Twelve hours of reliable sunshine all year round and regular downpours of rain provide the tropical regions of our planet with perfect growing conditions. The result is rich rainforest and a variety and complexity of life unmatched by any other habitat on Earth.

'Nothing but the reality can give any idea how wonderful, how magnificent the scene is.' This is what Charles Darwin wrote in his journal on visiting a tropical rainforest for the very first time. It was 1832, and he had just arrived in Brazil on the HMS *Beagle*. Twenty-five or so years later, Alfred Russel Wallace became the first European to explore a Southeast Asian rainforest. Like Darwin, he was overwhelmed by the complexity and variety of life he found. The struggles for survival both men observed all around them were to provide vital evidence for the theory of evolution, which they each developed independently.

For a first-time rainforest visitor lacking the experienced eye of a naturalist, the introduction can be less overwhelming. You are impressed by the profusion of plant life, but at first you see few animals. High up in the thick canopy, you might hear the crash of a nervous monkey or the loud, slow wing-beats of a passing hornbill. If you are very lucky, you may glimpse the jewel-like flash of a hummingbird. Surrounding you day and night are the incessant songs of cicadas, but you can't see them. The very fact, however, that rainforests share their secrets reluctantly makes them all the more intriguing. The longer you spend in them, the more fascinating they become.

Tropical rainforests hold the greatest diversity of life of any environment on Earth. The sheer numbers of species are extraordinary. One hectare (2.47 acres) of Malaysian rainforest was found to contain more than 180 different species of tree; in a similar area of deciduous temperate woodland, you would be lucky to find ten. So far, in the tiny Central American country of Panama, more than 1500 species of butterfly have been found; in the whole of the US, there is little more than half that number, while in the UK, there are only 56 native resident butterflies. In the Amazon River there are more than 3000 fish species – more species than in the whole of the North Atlantic Ocean. In fact, though the tropical rainforests cover just 3 per cent of the Earth's surface, they are thought to contain more than 50 per cent of all the animals and plants described or yet to be described.

THE PERFECT GREENHOUSE

Walking into a tropical rainforest for the first time can give you a physical shock. It is almost as if the humidity is punching you in the stomach. Sweat pours off your skin and you feel completely submerged in the weight of the air. Sometimes the ground cover can be so thick

ABOVE *A glasswing butterfly in Costa Rica using its transparent wings to camouflage itself while resting.*

OPPOSITE *Lowland dipterocarp forest in the Danum Valley, Sabah, Borneo, the mist rising off the trees in the early morning. The sounds that accompany it are the whooping calls of gibbons and the whoosh of the wings of hornbills setting off for the morning's treetop foraging.*

PREVIOUS PAGE, TOP *Lowland rainforest, Panama.*
BOTTOM *A Central American keel-billed toucan broadcasting its monotonous, metallic croaking call.*

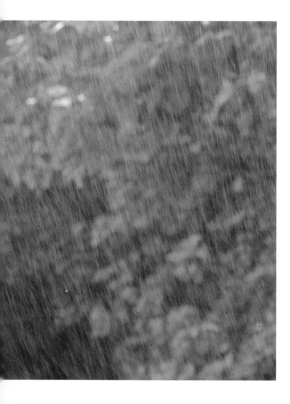

ABOVE *The daily afternoon downpour. A regular supply of water, warmth and sunlight powers the rainforest.*

OPPOSITE *Lowland rainforest on Barro Colorado Island, Panama, with the yellow and red flushes of trees in new leaf and jacaranda trees in flower.*

that, with every forward step, the vegetation seems to be making a grab at your ankles. If you dare to sit down on the forest floor, you wonder if the fungus will have eaten the sodden clothes off your body by the time you move on. It is hardly surprising then that rainforest can be one of the most demanding habitats to work in. But for the plants that dominate this sticky world, the conditions are perfect. The high input of energy from the sun and the continuous supply of rainfall are the key reasons for the enormous wealth of plant life found in the tropical rainforests of the equatorial regions. In these steamy hothouse conditions, vegetation grows faster than anywhere else on our planet.

The enormous quantity of rain that falls has also moulded the forests in another way. No one who has ever been drenched by a tropical storm in a jungle can fail to be impressed by its power. It starts quietly as the first heavy drops drum on the leaves far above. But soon the drum roll builds to a roar and water comes pouring down from the canopy. This regular torrent leaches nutrients and minerals out of the ground and leaves rainforest soils comparatively infertile. Yet it is this very shortage of soil nutrients and their patchy distribution that has encouraged competition and diversity among the plants.

The other key to diversity is the massive three-dimensional structure of the rainforest. Beneath the canopy of the enormous trees, their trunks and the trunks and branches of younger, shorter trees provide smaller plants such as climbing lianas and orchids with their own particular niches. The tangled framework that results provides nooks and crannies and feeding opportunities for animals.

Continuous sunshine is also crucial for diversity. Though the annual amount of sunlight at the equator is no more than that at the poles, it is delivered in 12-hour doses every day throughout the year. The sun always rises around six in the morning and always sets around six in the evening. One moment you can be walking among bright shafts of warming sunlight streaming down from the canopy, and the next it feels as if someone has switched off a light. The familiar sounds of daytime are instantly replaced with a new cacophony of night-time cicadas and courting frogs, and suddenly the forest becomes a far more frightening place to be in.

For wildlife, life in the tropics is comparatively easy. There are none of the seasonal extremes of climate experienced as you approach the poles, and with no changing seasons to disturb their life-cycles, insects in particular have proliferated. This has driven further diversity among the plants on which so many of them feed. As plants have evolved various defences, so the insects have changed their methods of attack, and the resulting arms races have further fuelled diversity. Similar arms races between predators and prey have encouraged enormous proliferation among the animals themselves. And with a relatively stable supply of suitable food, most species can develop and specialize further and further.

But cooperation, too, has driven the diversification of species. The forest canopy is so thick that little wind is available to pollinate flowers or spread seeds. So plants have developed intimate relationships with animals, bribing them with nectar to carry pollen from flower to flower and fruit to disperse the resulting seeds. Such mutually beneficial relationships are particularly common and complex in rainforests.

The final hothouse factor in this burgeoning of life is that the tropical climate has, for the most part, remained unchanged over thousands of years, giving many rainforest ecosystems time to develop a complexity unmatched anywhere else.

THE RAINFOREST BELT

Tropical rainforest is found, as its name suggests, between the tropics of Cancer and Capricorn, wherever the annual rainfall is more than 2500mm (98 inches) per year – an equatorial belt that extends from Queensland in Australia in the east to the vast rainforests of South America in the west. Up to 40 different types of rainforest have been described, but they all fall into five basic categories.

LOWLAND TROPICAL FOREST

The most extensive by far is the evergreen lowland tropical forest, which occurs up to around 1000m (3280 feet) and includes an unequalled abundance and variety of trees, including the giants so prized by loggers. The canopy often towers more than 45m (150 feet) above the forest floor, with occasional 'emergents' protruding to more than 60m (200 feet). This is the classic jungle of the Tarzan myth, where constantly moist air encourages the climbing creepers and lianas and a covering of epiphytes in the canopy. It makes up two thirds of the total area of tropical rainforest and includes the vast river basins of the Amazon and Zaire rivers. It is also found in Central America, West Africa and various parts of Southeast Asia, though here it has been broken up into fragments by extensive logging.

TROPICAL DECIDUOUS FOREST

Move a few degrees north or south of the equator, and the climate becomes more seasonal. Periods of heavy rain are interspersed with months of drier weather. Up to a third of the trees will shed their leaves each year, and in the 'monsoon forests' of Asia, the trees come into leaf with the onset of the monsoon season. There are few climbing plants and epiphytes, which need continuous moisture and cannot survive the drier spells. Though Indonesia still has reasonably large areas of tropical deciduous rainforest, elsewhere in Asia, Africa and South America, most of it has been logged or cleared for farming.

FLOODED FOREST

Many of the great tropical rivers rise and fall throughout the year, flooding vast tracts of lowland forest – known as swamp forest or flooded forest. The stresses of flooding cause the trees to be smaller than those of dry lowland forest, and the diversity of species is also lower. With the exception of stretches along the Fly and Sepik rivers in Papua New Guinea, most of the swamp forest of Southeast Asia has been cut down. But in South America, vast areas of flooded forest still remain. There are two distinct types. Várzea is found on the floodplains of white-water rivers such as the Amazon that are heavy with sediment washed down from the Andes. This sediment is trapped by the buttress roots of the trees and builds up as rich soil. Along the floodplains of the black-water rivers such as the Rio Negro is ipagó forest. These rivers carry no sediment, and so no soil builds up. But in the dry season, when the water-level falls, beautiful banks of sand are exposed, out of which the trees grow – mainly palms but also giants such as kapoks, with their spectacular buttressed roots.

ABOVE *Várzea flooded forest, Brazil, inundated with water from the Andes.*

TOP *In the Atlantic rainforest of Brazil, the orchid Cattleya intermedia presents its flowers to the insect community living high up in the canopy. The branch provides a perch, and the orchid gains moisture from any rain that falls.*

OPPOSITE *Dry, decidious forest, Central America. The quipo tree has shed its leaves in the dry season but is now flushed with baby leaves. These will stay orange-red until they are tough enough to deter herbivores and can be safely filled with green chloroplasts needed to make food for the tree.*

ABOVE *Dense cloudforest covering a 3000-m (9840-foot) peak of Volcano Baru in Panama.*

OPPOSITE, TOP *Mangrove forest. It fringes the coast and coastal rivers, the trees adapted to a life rooted in waterlogged and often salty mud. Special air-breathing roots are their survival secret. The habitat they create stabilizes and protects many low-lying coastal areas from the sea.*

PREVIOUS PAGE *The Amazon, as seen from space. It drains a third of South America and contains as much water as the next ten largest of the world's rivers combined.*

Climb up from the sticky humidity of the lowland forest floor and you enter a very different world. With every hundred metres, the temperature drops about half a degree centigrade. Soon you leave behind the towering trees of the lowland forest, and the canopy height drops to 15–30m (50–100 feet). Not only do the trees get shorter, but the leaves become smaller, too. Twisted, gnarled, multi-stemmed trunks replace the single, straight ones of the lowland forest, and when you get above 2000m (6560 feet), the trees are barely taller than a man.

The vegetation changes to that more reminiscent of temperate regions. In the Himalayas, for instance, you find the beautiful rhododendrons that we have transplanted to our colder northern climes. Cold temperatures bring mist that engulfs the forest in twisting cloud. Light levels are reduced, and condensation makes the leaves constantly run with moisture. Many of the branches are covered with dripping lichens, the forest floor is a carpet of wet, spongy moss, and the canopy is full of epiphytes – orchids and bromeliads – enjoying the permanently moist air. You are now in cool, damp cloudforest – a blessed relief from the oppressive sauna of the lowland rainforest below. In Southeast Asia, gibbons swing through the cloudforest branches and giant hornbills fly noisily across the steep valleys. In Central America, this is the world of hummingbirds and quetzals.

MANGROVE FOREST

Along sheltered tropical shores grows a highly specialized type of rainforest. Though mangroves are found as far north as 32 degrees, and even further in the southern hemisphere, the largest and most extensive mangrove forests are found alongside the equatorial rainforest belt. Mangroves are specially adapted for life in salty and tidal environments, with breathing roots that stick up out of the waterlogged mud into the air to absorb more oxygen. Of all the rainforest habitats, this has to be the least welcoming. At high water, the thick, scrubby vegetation is hard to penetrate even in a canoe. At low tide, you find yourself squelching through sticky mud. But it is this inaccessibility that makes mangroves so valuable for wildlife. The largest remaining mangrove forest in the east is found in the Sundarbans of the Ganges delta, where a healthy population of tigers still hides out. In the west, mangrove is still found along parts of West Africa, the coast of Central America and the Caribbean islands – in Trinidad, for example, mangroves provide a safe night-time roost site for hundreds of bright red scarlet ibis. In most of Southeast Asia, though, mangrove forest has been scrubbed out to provide ponds for prawn- and fish-farms.

THE GIANTS

The rainforest is essentially a gallery superstructure supported by trees. Each tree creates a framework for other plants and animals to live on and in. Giant emergents – trees that emerge from the top of the canopy – can reach 60m (200 feet) in height and 17m (56 feet) in girth. But most manage a more modest 30m (100 feet) in height.

Rainforest trees are usually evergreen with the same simple design: tall, slender trunks and simple, branching, umbrella-shaped canopies. Their root systems tend to be shallow, and so the trunks require extra support from buttresses (left). These are provided by roots that grow above ground and extend upwards and outwards from the trunk as thin flanges.

Unlike temperate trees, rainforest trees are able to grow all year round, and so they have no growth rings. Though they may live to be 1400 years old, they can take 60 years to reach maturity. Even then, a tree will not flower and produce fruit every year, rationing itself to every three to ten years, perhaps taking turns with other trees to use the services of animal pollinators and dispersers.

GOING UP, GOING DOWN

For scientists and film-makers alike, there has always been a problem getting to grips with the sheer scale and inaccessibility of the rainforest. On the forest floor, the animals you hope to work with disappear into the tangled darkness of the vegetation, while the forest canopy and its inhabitants always seem frustratingly beyond reach – providing nothing more than a cricked neck and the occasional frustrating glimpse of a monkey's tail. But modern technology has changed all that. Today a variety of specially designed hot-air balloons can carry you up and over the forest canopy. You can float just a few metres above the treetops with your feet literally dipping into the endless sea of green that forms the forest canopy. The trees arch into leaf at this level, and their foliage is crowded with life. They provide a platform for epiphytes (see page 240) and climbers that clamber through the countless umbrellas of leaves to bathe in the full glare of the sun. This is the powerhouse of the forest. Light and heat are at their greatest – temperatures may reach 32°C (90°F) – and so most of the photosynthesis takes place here. Flowers and fruit abound, the canopy buzzes with insect life, and the network of branches provides aerial walkways for monkeys and squirrels.

As plants scramble up towards the light, they tend to form layers of foliage. Each level filters out yet more light from the one below, forms a barrier to warmth from the sun and traps in moisture. The principle is the same in temperate forests, but what makes tropical forests so different is the spectacular range of strata, the enormous number of plants within each and the huge differences in light levels. It is a vast cathedral made up of many worlds, each with its own microclimate. To explore downwards, you need to take to ropes.

This can be a pretty terrifying business, but with modern climbing technology, it is easy to travel up and down. The worst moment is when you first step off the platform or branch high in the canopy and put your faith in a thin rope and a few pieces of metal. But as soon

BOTTOM LEFT *Male morpho butterfly. Males use the iridescent flashes of their upper wings to intimidate rivals and claim territory in the gloom of the forest, but they can also disappear with a flap of the wing, altering the angle of reflection to change the colour from blue to brown.*

BOTTOM RIGHT *A red-knobbed hornbill swallowing a fig in one. Hornbills in the rainforests of Southeast Asia eat large quantities of figs and are significant dispersers of their seeds.*

OPPOSITE *Reaching up from the forest floor, a tangle of shade-tolerant plants, lianas and young trees scramble for light. The trees provide climbing frameworks for lianas as well as surfaces for other communities of plants to grow on.*

OPPOSITE TOP LEFT *A young liana –*
a woody vine – starting the long
journey up its tree support, using
the twisting method of climbing.
Others use tendrils as supports or
even adhesion. Often, at least half
of rainforest trees are scaffolding
for lianas of one sort or another.
The trees get nothing in return except
slowed growth and sometimes
strangulation.

OPPOSITE TOP RIGHT *The flower of an*
Aristolochia woody vine, or pipe vine,
in Panama. It mimics the scent of
a carcass to summon dung beetles
and flies to pollinate it.

OPPOSITE BOTTOM *An ocelot,*
radio-collared so that its movements
can be tracked through the forest
strata, uses lianas as bridges and
ladders as it moves through its range.

as you know what you are doing, you start to enjoy the experience and begin to notice the different layers that slowly pass you by. Just below the canopy is an understorey of smaller or younger trees at different stages of growth, and passing through them, on their way up, are lianas and epiphytes. Some of these will complete their life-cycles halfway up, while others must climb to the very top. The smaller trees may spend many years here waiting in the wings for light and space. At this stage of their lives, they are shade tolerant and may grow very slowly. But when a fallen tree provides the opportunity to reach the sunlight, they will surge upwards to maturity.

When your feet are firmly down on the forest floor, life is very different. Only 2 per cent of sunlight penetrates down here, temperatures reach just 28°C (82°F) and the humidity soars to 90 per cent. In the murky light, only shade-tolerant plants can survive. In some forests, the floor may be so dark that little survives. In others, where there is more space and shafts of light filter down through the foliage, the ground is a tangle of young trees, shrubs and lianas. This is particularly characteristic of monsoon forests in Asia, which lose their leaves in the dry season, giving plants on the floor a short chance to establish themselves before the gloom sets in again.

THE RUSH FOR LIGHT

In a violent tropical storm, a tree crashes to the ground and perhaps more than a thousand years of interdependent plant and animal life comes to an end. And as the tree falls, it may bring other trees with it, creating a small clearing and bringing the sudden gift of light. Almost overnight, humidity plunges, temperatures rocket and even nutrients in the soil change. But though the stable environment of the forest floor has been shattered, the transformation is one that is vital for the regeneration and diversity of the forest.

All over the forest floor, seeds have been waiting for such a moment, some for many years. Large seeds, typical of primary forest trees of the Amazon, are designed to live off their reserves while establishing themselves slowly in the shade and then bursting into accelerated growth as soon as light appears. In this new, dynamic environment, competition is intense. Within days, animals moving into the clearing will have brought yet more seeds with them. A race is on to get a foothold before the dense ceiling of vegetation closes over again. Saplings already present respond to increased light by putting on a spurt of growth towards the canopy. The young jungle grows quickly. In less than ten years, it may not have the same height as the original forest, but it will already have the same leaf coverage.

THE CLIMBERS

In a world dominated by tall trees, it might seem impossible for any other plant life to penetrate this tight-knit community. Yet there are some that do so with such skill that they are able to make their way to the forest canopy. There are several ways to succeed at winding and grasping your way to the top. Some climbers such as rattans use thorns and brute force to get there, hooking onto the surrounding vegetation and reaching up to 200m (655 feet). Pitcher plants also climb like this, using special whip-like extensions of their leaves to lash

onto vegetation. These same leaves can turn into the pitchers – traps that catch and drown food such as insects and even reptiles and small mammals in a digestive broth.

Other plants such as lianas tether themselves by growing tendrils that sprout from their leaves or stems and act as guy ropes. These tendrils have evolved to reach away from light, waving around into the gloom in search of something to lash onto. When they brush against another plant, they are stimulated to curl and grasp with lightning speed. The tendrils of a tropical American gourd, for instance, will curl within 20 seconds of contact and can coil around its support within 4 minutes.

Some climbing plants use clasping roots to anchor themselves as they climb. These special sideways-growing roots develop adhesive hairs when they make contact with the surface. (Ivy works like this, and anyone who has had to pull it from a wall will know just how strong a grip these roots can exert.) Plants that use clasping roots may lose their ground-feeding roots and finish high up in the canopy, dependent on their side roots to keep them alive.

BELOW *An oak branch at 2000m (6560 feet) in La Amistad (a transboundary national park in Panama and Costa Rica). It is festooned with epiphytes, from orchids and bromeliads to mosses and lichens. Hummingbirds and a multitude of insects are feeding from the flowers, and another little community of animals is housed in the tangle of leaves and stems.*

GARDENS IN THE AIR

Gaining access to light without investing in long stems or roots is a popular strategy, and rainforest trees are often festooned with exotic gardens of orchids, cacti, aroids and bromeliads. These plants are epiphytes and they make a living by setting up camp high on the bark of tree branches.

Many lichens, mosses and ferns have evolved to do this. They are not parasitic, since their roots do not penetrate the bark for food, but their roots may absorb moisture from the air as well as their surroundings. Epiphytes do especially well in the moist conditions of the cloudforest, where they may form thick mats along the high branches of the canopy. Little pools of water form in the bromeliads, providing high-altitude homes for frogs. In fact, whole communities of small animals can live permanently in these gardens in the air. Many epiphytes form associations with ants – the Indonesian *Myrmecodia echinata* develops tuber-like lower parts that are inhabited by ants, whose activities release nutrients used by both plant and ants.

The epiphytic way of life is highly successful, and a quarter of all plant species in lowland forest are epiphytes. They are so numerous that, in places, their leaf output may be greater than that of the tree they are growing on. In one tree crown alone, their weight may reach several tons.

JUNGLE WARFARE

Plants not only create a dense, towering rainforest structure, they also produce vast quantities of edible food – leaves. A square metre (11 square feet) of lowland rainforest can produce a massive 11 square metres (more than 13 square yards) of leaves. Rainforest trees have evolved ingenious defences to avoid being stripped bare, but leaves are too valuable a source of food for animals not to fight for. In a battle that has raged for millions of years, both sides have gained and lost ground, producing extraordinary strategies along the way.

DIGESTIVE PROBLEMS

Plants have one great advantage: their leaves are made of cellulose, which is difficult to digest. Some animals such as caterpillars have got around this by breaking down the tough cell walls with relentless chewing. Large leaf-eaters, though, would find the amount of chewing necessary to get enough energy from the food impossible. Instead, they have added cellulose-digesting bacteria to their gut floras to do the job for them. But bacteria are not fast workers. Leaves digested in this fashion travel slowly through the gut, and as a consequence many large leaf-eaters, such as South American howler monkeys, are heavy and slow. Others, such as proboscis monkeys from the flooded forests and mangroves of Borneo, have large pot bellies in which they ferment their intake of tough leaves and seeds.

Hardly any birds are leaf-eaters, as the fermenting process would make them too heavy and slow to fly. A few, however, have persevered with this system of digesting cellulose, the most famous of which is the hoatzin of South America. This bird keeps a colony of cellulose-

ABOVE *South American hoatzins – among the few birds to feed on leaves. Using its crop as a fermentation chamber, the hoatzin employs bacteria to aid digestion. But a crop full of leaves makes flight difficult, and so the hoatzin spends much time digesting, resting its distended crop against a branch, cushioning it with a special callus at the end of its sternum.*

ABOVE LEFT *A howler monkey eating leaves. Nearly half its diet comprises leaves, particularly juicy young ones. It has a gut full of bacteria to help break down the cell walls, but even so, it will lose weight if there is a dry spell and it is forced to eat mature leaves, which are harder to digest.*

digesting bacteria in its enlarged oesophagus and crop, rather like the fermentation system in a cow's stomach. Perhaps not surprisingly, since the leaves it eats take almost two days to move through its body, the hoatzin produces a characteristic manure-like smell, giving it the nickname of stinkbird.

The leafcutter ants of Central and South America have become fungus farmers in their battle with plants. In their underground nests, they chew their leaf booty into a pulp and then add fungus spores, harvesting the fungus that subsequently grows.

PAINFUL AND STICKY ENDS

Being made of indigestible cellulose gives plants a ready-made deterrent, but they have also evolved other weapons. Many are armed with vicious prickles, spines and thorns to keep marauders at bay, while others use chemical warfare against the relentless army of chewers. The array of toxins and deterrents that rainforest plants have come up with is more proof of their extraordinary resourcefulness. Some use substances that trap or disable leaf-eaters. As soon as it is punctured, whether on its trunk or a leaf, the Brazilian rubber tree produces a sticky liquid, familiar to us as latex – the raw material for rubber. It is not only toxic but also oxidizes on exposure to air to form thick glue that gums up the mouthparts of insects. But some insects have managed to foil the defence, disarming the tree by punching small holes in the leaf around the bit they are eating or by severing the main latex duct.

CHEMICAL MANIPULATION

Many rainforest plants have resorted to even more ingenious ways of using chemicals. For instance, some mimic the juvenile hormones of their attackers to trick them into arrested development, forcing them to live out their lives as larvae, unable to reproduce. Others disrupt the various stages of development so that insects metamorphose into disfigured adults. Plants can even change the fertility of grazing mammals, producing oestrogen mimics that interfere with their fertility. In some cases, the chemicals used are powerful toxins that can kill humans: strychnine and cyanide are common in rainforest plants.

Yet the ingenuity of insects to outwit even these powerful deterrents is equally remarkable. In the chemical arms race, insects have evolved a battery of powerful enzymes to break down poisons, and for every plant poison, there is least one leaf-eater that can detoxify it. Some insects are even able to use plant poisons against their own enemies. Caterpillars of the huge birdwing butterflies of New Guinea feed on poisonous lianas and store the toxins, using them through to adulthood, displaying a vivid, colourful warning pattern, signalling to predators that they are toxic. More bizarrely, aphids that feed on plants from the Asclepiadaceae family use the plants' toxins to drug the spiders that eat them. The psychoactive properties of the toxins cause the spiders to spin crazy, disrupted webs. Other insects have a more personal use for their sequestered poisons – male danaid butterflies gather poisons from the plants they eat and modify them for use as aphrodisiacs.

As fast as plants can evolve new defences, the remarkable adaptive abilities of leaf-eaters will eventually allow them to overcome these, too. Successful damage limitation is the best that plants can hope for in the continually escalating arms race.

ABOVE *Seeds collected from just a small area of rainforest in Panama. Those landing near their mother trees will not have room to grow and are likely to be destroyed by their mothers' disease-causing microbes and pests. So most are packaged up for dispersal, mainly by animals, with just a few opting for spinning and wind (the rainforest being comparatively still).*

OPPOSITE *Atta leafcutter ants chopping up the leaves of a balsa sapling. Within a couple of hours of the scouts alerting the workers to the location of the sapling, it will have been stripped and the dismembered leaves carried back to the fungus farm at base camp. The fungus is fussy, and the ants know just what leaves it likes best to digest.*

ABOVE *A huge balsa-tree flower being visited by stingless bees. Monkeys and birds drink from it in the day, and bats and other mammals visit at night.*

TOP *A euglossine, or orchid, bee with pollen sacs (pollinia) on its back from the orchid it has previously visited. Orchids throughout the tropics use these bees for pollination.*

ABOVE RIGHT *A great rhinoceros hornbill grabbing a fig on a sweep-past at canopy height, startling a feeding red leaf monkey in the process. The fig seeds will be dispersed over the rainforest in the hornbill's dung as it flies from tree to tree in its huge feeding range in Kalimantan, Borneo.*

JUNGLE PARTNERSHIPS

There are times when plants go to great lengths to persuade animals to feed on them. To produce the fittest possible, genetically diverse offspring, they reproduce sexually – through cross-pollination – and so require a delivery system to ensure their pollen reaches another flower of the same species. In the still, windless environment of the rainforest, most plants rely on animals as couriers, often producing special flowers with food or other lures to attract specific helpers. Though many rainforest trees take 30 to 40 years to mature and rarely flower annually, when they do, they put enormous effort into the process. Their flowers and fruit are often spectacular and result in incredible quantities of seed – 1ha (2.5 acres) of lowland rainforest produces as much weight of fruit and seed as 12ha (30 acres) of temperate oak woodland. Plants can gain an edge over rivals by dispersing these seeds as widely as possible. Luscious fruits are therefore designed to attract highly mobile carriers, including monkeys, bats and birds, resulting in yet another complex web of relationships.

PERFUME MERCHANTS

Flowers in the rainforest tend to be large, colourful and highly scented. Those of the balsa tree, for instance, are 12cm (5 inches) long and 8cm (3 inches) across at the mouth. Many flowers use brilliant colours to attract their pollinators, especially if these are birds. The

Sarawak mistletoe, for instance, attracts flowerpeckers with bright red flowers which have petals that spring open when the birds brush by, revealing a nectar reward. In the still, moist forest air, scent carries over long distances, and rainforest flowers use it to draw in pollinators. The range and inventiveness of these scents is remarkable. Orchids in particular have complex flowers with a repertoire of sophisticated perfumes. The Madagascan comet orchid, for instance, attracts moths with a powerful scent resembling perfumed soap.

Others draw in pollinators such as flies or carrion beetles by mimicking the foul odours of putrescence. Quite a few flowers that trade at this end of the market add to the illusion with colours which mimic rotting flesh. The variety of fetid smells they produce is quite overwhelming. *Aristolochia* vines produce elaborate fly traps that smell like rotting fish. The flowers of the calabash tree open at night to release a smell of sweaty cheese, irresistible to bats. But the champion stinkers have to be the monster rafflesias, which grow in the forests of Southeast Asia. Not only does *Rafflesia arnoldii* produce the largest flower in the world at up to 0.9m (3 feet) across, but its flower also emits one of the most revolting smells in the plant kingdom. With just a few days to ensure pollen is collected and deposited, *Rafflesia* makes every effort to attract flies, growing a huge, red, carcass-like flower on the forest floor that reeks of rotting meat.

EVERYONE'S FAVOURITE FRUIT

Figs are among the most common rainforest plants, and lots of animals have developed a taste for their fruit. Across all three tropical continents, figs are the single most important source of food for rainforest fruit-eaters. In Central America, 26 species of bird have been found feeding from just one species, and in Malaya, in just three hours, 47 species of birds were seen feeding on one tree alone. The result is that fig seeds seem to get everywhere.

As many as 20 species of fig may be thriving in any one area of a forest, from small bushes to the stranglers with their extraordinary trunks and aerial roots. When a strangler-fig seed lodges in the branch of another tree, it grows by sending out long roots down to the ground and then producing aerial roots, eventually smothering the host. Each species of strangler has its own specific wasp pollinator, and all species produce masses of fruit – some upwards of 100,000 on a single tree. Since they produce fruit all year round, figs are a crucial source of food during times when other fruits are scarce.

ABOVE *Raggiana birds of paradise compete to outdo each other's displays in front of an audience of one – a female top centre-stage.*

OPPOSITE *Birds of paradise using colour and feather tricks to attract females to their display arenas. They can afford to invest energy in fabulous feathers as food is ever-present.*

CLOCKWISE, FROM TOP LEFT
A blue bird of paradise hanging upside down while displaying his elaborate tail and sending out an extraordinary, unbirdlike buzzing call.

A magnificent bird of paradise posing on his dance perch while resting between performances.

Lawes' parotia strutting his wire-like head plumes and iridescent cape.

A superb bird of paradise erecting his mesmerizing cape.

The best pollinators for long-distance dispersal are strong flyers such as birds, bats, hawk moths and insects that forage over long distances. The most common of these are bees, and in most rainforests, they perform the daytime pollination duties. Orchid bees, for instance, will use the same daily routes of more than 20km (12 miles) in search of food, collecting and refuelling at the same plants along the way. They may also have complex relationships with their providers. The Brazil-nut tree produces large, yellow flowers protected by a coiled hood. Female orchid bees are large enough to lift the hood and collect the nectar inside, inadvertently pollinating the flower as they do so. But the colourful males of these bees visit orchids, specific ones that usually grow on branches of the Brazil-nut tree. They collect perfume from the orchids, pollinating them as they move from flower to flower. When they have enough, they mass together in a swarm, buzzing and diving in a perfumed mass to attract the attention of the females feeding from the Brazil-nut tree flowers. It's an elegant system of mutual interdependence between the tree, specific orchids and specific bees.

Though insects are the most important daytime pollinators, birds are also busy in many rainforests. In South and Central America, hummingbirds have the monopoly, while in African and Asian forests, sunbirds do the same job. At night, the work falls to bats. Flowers specifically adapted to the needs of bats are easy to spot, being usually white or light-coloured (bats locate their flowers at a distance by sonar, not sight) and easily accessible, with large quantities of nectar. Those in the *Parkia* genus hang down from the canopy in pom-pom-like clusters on long stalks. Each cluster has a mass of pollen-bearing stamens, which shower a bat in pollen as it lands momentarily to sip the nectar.

HEAVY-DUTY DISPERSAL

With so little wind in the forest, most plants must also use animals to disperse their seeds and fruit, though this transaction is a little more complicated. While plants want animals to eat their fruit and consequently disperse their seeds, they want to protect the seeds themselves from being damaged or eaten or at least to ensure that some survive to germinate. The strategy of fig trees is to produce hundreds of tiny, gritty seeds in small, tasty, easily digested fruit, which many different animals enjoy. A fruiting fig tree is always a big event in the forest, drawing animals from all around. In Central Africa, for instance, it would be quite possible to see lowland gorillas, chimpanzees, three or four monkeys, squirrels and many different species of birds all feasting together in one tree. By flooding the market with millions of seeds inside tons of fruit, the fig tree has increased its chances of at least some progeny being dispersed. But this comes at a price – tiny seeds have very limited reserves and must germinate fast if they are to survive.

Most other plants in the forest choose to produce larger, more nutritious seeds, which are dispersed by specific couriers – specialist birds and bats that eat almost nothing but fruit. Toucans in South and Central America, large fruit-eating bats in Southeast Asia and the palm-nut vulture in West Africa are all specialist fruit-eaters that thrive on the rainforest's need to spread seeds. Fruits aimed at birds are often brightly coloured and conspicuous, while dull-coloured, pungent fruits such as wild bananas are meant for the more scent-conscious bats. The rainforest provides such an abundance of easy pickings that many fruit-eating animals are able to spend time and energy on other things. In the rich forests of New Guinea, for instance, birds of paradise are able to invest energy in spectacular and extravagant plumage and devote time to elaborate courtship displays.

In some cases, the relationship between a plant and its seed-disperser is so close that it becomes one-to-one. Though more than 20 species of bird feed on the fruits of the Costa Rican tree *Casearia corymbosa*, only one behaves in a way that makes it the perfect seed disperser. Tityras are small, silver birds with black face masks, easily spotted by hawks. To avoid being caught, tityras snatch fruit from the tree and dash off to eat it under cover, thus moving the seeds to places where they may have a better chance of finding room to grow. In their efforts to evade predators, tityras have become the only birds successfully to disperse *Casearia* seeds, and now the tree and birds are totally dependent on each other.

The Brazil-nut tree depends on the absent-mindedness of one particular animal, the agouti, to disperse its nuts. The agouti is the only animal that can break the hard outer shell of a Brazil-nut cluster. It will eat and destroy a good deal of the seeds inside, but it buries others and forgets where many of them are – absent-mindedness that gives the nuts a chance to germinate. Some of the largest trees produce huge seeds or nuts – far too big for any but the largest mammals to disperse. Their fruits drop to the ground, creating a feast just below the tree. In African rainforests, elephants will move in on such a bonanza, gorging themselves and later depositing the seeds in a rich manure of faeces some distance away.

ABOVE *Musky fruit bat feasting on figs in the Philippines. Rainforest fruit bats are provided with a year-long supply of food. The pay-off for the trees is the dispersal of their seeds.*

OPPOSITE *The largest predator in South America – the jaguar. It is bigger and stockier than a leopard and capable of killing large mammals, but its normal prey animals are small – anything from turtles to peccaries (small pigs).*

PREDATORY INTENT

Of all the rainforest animals, the most frustratingly elusive are the large meat-eating predators. You can spend years working in the jungles of South America without ever seeing a jaguar, and the leopards that prowl the forest of West Africa are far more difficult to spot than their shy relatives in the drier parts of Africa. Compared to the enormous diversity of rainforest plants and plant-eaters, there are relatively few predators, especially large ones. Yet their numbers are still greater than in other forests, largely because there are so many insects available to feed on. In fact, most rainforest predators are insectivores, and many of the predators are invertebrates themselves.

ABOVE *In a Brazilian coastal forest, the world's largest spider – a goliath bird-eating tarantula – pumps digestive juices into a snake it has pulled into its underground lair. The tarantula's potential legspan is up to 26cm (10 inches), and it will tackle anything that it can hold and impale with its venomous, downward-facing fangs.*

With so much insect food on offer, it is hardly surprising that there are insectivores in all the rainforest-animal groups. Many of the small mammal predators specialize in insects. Up in the canopy of the Amazon rainforest, tree anteaters attack the nests of ants and termites. These social insects have a daunting combined biting power, but thick furs protects the anteater, and the ant-eating pangolins of Africa and Asia add a defence of bony scales. Though many of the primates depend on leaves and fruit, some have become insect specialists as well. The shy lorises and pottos of Africa, for instance, use their dexterous fingers to deal with the tricky defence mechanisms many insects have developed. The chimpanzee – perhaps the ultimate jungle omnivore – has used its intelligence to exploit practically every source of food, including insects. Famously, chimps have learnt to shape special tools to dip into the termite mounds and extract the juicy inmates.

If you are a birdwatcher, the insect-eaters are probably among the easiest birds to spot. One of the most conspicuous sights in the forest of Central America is the brightly coloured jacamar, which sits bolt upright on a perch before dashing out to catch a passing butterfly. In the African rainforest, bee-eaters behave in much the same way and have developed a clever whipping technique to remove the stings from the bees they catch. Woodpeckers as a group are highly successful insectivores and occur in many rainforests. Some not only raid termite nests for food but also make their nests within these earthy structures. Even hummingbirds and sunbirds, which normally feed on nectar, recognize the high nutritional value of insects and catch them for their growing chicks. But the most impressive spectacle provided by the insect-eating birds must be the multi-species flocks that pass noisily through the forest, routing out their prey. You often hear them coming, because they call all the time to stay in contact. By creating a wave of movement, all the birds benefit from the resulting disturbance. Other birds specialize in following behind army and driver ants as they march through the forest. Any insects that fly from the jaws of the ants are snapped up by the antbirds.

ALL AS ONE, SMALL AS BIG

With so much invertebrate prey on offer, it is hardly surprising that there is an enormous variety of invertebrate predators in the rainforest. But without any doubt, the most impressive have to be the army ants of South America and driver ants of Africa. Both use the same rather terrifying blitzkrieg technique, in which the whole colony, many thousands strong, is constantly on the move across the forest floor in a black stream of hungry mandibles. Through strength in numbers, the ants can easily overcome large insects, lizards, small birds – almost anything that crosses their path. Stories of driver ants entering villages and eating babies in their cribs are probably exaggerated, but there is no doubt that, after army ants have passed through the forest, the floor can be denuded of all life for weeks.

BELOW *Army ants overwhelming a scorpion. The most numerous rainforest predators are ants. This species specializes in swarm raiding in their hundreds of thousands.*

The warmth of the tropics has produced other invertebrate horror stories. Many invertebrates are able to grow to such a size that they can be formidable predators even on vertebrates. The best example must be the tarantula spiders of South America, which can have a legspan width greater than 25cm (10 inches) and can easily take treefrogs or small birds. Mantids also grow to record sizes. In the rainforests of Malaysia you find large and beautiful flower mantids that are perfect mimics of the orchids in which they wait. Insects attracted to these 'flowers' discover themselves to be on the menu when the mantid strikes.

THE FLESH-EATERS

True flesh-eaters, like us, face a problem in the rainforest: they find it a tangled and impenetrable jungle. This is no place for running cheetahs or stooping falcons. Most have opted to be small and agile like the ocelots or margays of South America or slender like the civets and genets of Africa and Asia. There is only one exception in each of the continents – the jaguar in South America, the forest tiger in Asia and the leopard in Africa. All these large cats are limited in numbers by the comparative low density of large forest herbivores. Likewise, most of the birds of prey are limited in number and are usually small with rounded wings and the ability to jink quickly between the branches. Each major rainforest block, though, does have at least one large, spectacular eagle at the top of the predatory tree. The harpy eagle in South America, the monkey-eating eagle of the Philippines and crowned hawk eagle of Africa have all specialized in taking forest monkeys.

10

shallow seas

Though the shallow seas make up only 8 per cent

of the ocean's surface, they are by far the richest

parts of the ocean. It is here that you find the coral

reefs, the seagrass beds, the kelp forests and

90 per cent of the world's commercial fisheries.

ABOVE *A rich coral community, with oriental sweetlips and red bigeyes, off Ari in the Maldives – an Indian Ocean chain of volcanic atolls. The clear water that coral grows in enables fish to make full use of colour for communication.*

OPPOSITE *Humpback mother and baby in the tropical Pacific waters off Tonga. It is the perfect nursery – calm and warm, with a sandy bottom – but, like much of the ocean tropics, lifeless.*

PREVIOUS PAGE, TOP *A fast-moving school of southern rightwhale dolphins hunting off New Zealand.*
BOTTOM
A riot of Red Sea soft coral and a swirl of glassfish.

A newborn humpback whale calf suckles from its 40-ton mother in the clear tropical waters off the island of Tonga in the Pacific – a wonderfully peaceful scene. As the baby pulls away from the nipple, a puff of fat-rich milk clouds the water. The one-ton calf drinks around 450l (120 gallons) of milk each day, and for the next 12 months, it will be totally dependent on its mother. These shallow, calm, tropical waters provide the perfect nursery, but they are also relatively lifeless. There is no food for the mother, who must live for most of the year entirely off her own blubber. As soon as the calf is strong enough to follow her, they will leave the tropics on the longest migration of any marine mammal, in search of rich feeding grounds in the temperate and polar oceans. In this chapter, we will also journey through the length and breadth of the planet's shallow seas.

WHERE THE SHALLOW SEAS LIE

The world's shallow seas are, generally speaking, the ones that lie above the continental shelves – the submerged extensions of the continents. On average, a shelf extends out about 80km (50 miles), but off the Pacific coast of South America, it is less than 1km (half a mile) wide, and off the Arctic coast of Siberia, it can stretch for 750km (466 miles). Here the water is rarely more than 200m (650 feet) deep. The type of animals you find on the shallow seafloor – the richest regions of the ocean – depend principally on the type of substrate. For the most part, the continental shelf consists of large, flat areas of sand and muddy sediment. The animals that live here either burrow into the mud like clams or live close to the surface like brittlestars or flatfish. Sessile creatures (sedentary ones), such as sea anemones or plants such as seaweeds, with the exception of seagrass in the tropics, are rare as there is nothing for them to hold onto. Where the substrate is hard or rocky, allowing animals and plants a firm grip, very different communities develop. In colder temperate waters, you find the rich forests of seaweed and dense communities of colourful invertebrates plastering rocky walls. In the tropics, a rocky substrate provides a surface for coral larvae to settle on, without which most reefs cannot grow. The richness and variety of life you find in the waters above the continental shelves do, though, vary enormously, depending more than anything else on the quantity of sunlight and the available nutrients.

THE WARM SHALLOWS

The warm tropical waters that provide such a welcoming nursery for the newborn humpbacks are among the least productive of all the shallow seas. They are crystal clear because they contain low quantities of the phytoplankton that gives richer, more productive waters their tell-tale green, murky quality. Phytoplankton is responsible for 90 per cent of the primary production in the oceans, and it forms the basis of practically all marine food chains. The tropical seas – the equatorial band of warm water over 20°C (68°F) that lies between the tropics of Cancer and Capricorn – are for the most part marine deserts, because so little phytoplankton grows there.

Like all plants, phytoplankton needs two main ingredients to perform photosynthesis – sunlight and nutrients. In the tropics near the equator, there is no shortage of sunlight; year round there are 12 hours of reliable daylight every day. The limiting factor is lack of nutrients, especially nitrogen and phosphorus, which play a major role in controlling primary production. Without these nutrients, the phytoplankton cannot photosynthesize.

The problem is that, in the oceans, these nutrients are mostly found in deeper water, and in the tropics the water column is so still that there is very little mixing of surface and deeper layers. As all sailors know, the regions around the equator are known as the doldrums because of the lack of wind. This not only produces the calm conditions so enjoyed by the newborn humpback whale but also ensures that very few nutrients make it to the surface. The only tropical shallow seas that are not, for the most part, watery deserts are the coral reefs and the seagrass beds.

REMARKABLE REEFS

There can be few pleasures in nature that compare with snorkelling over a rich coral reef, and in terms of sheer variety and colour, few reefs can match the spectacle fringing the shores of the Red Sea. The surrounding land is a true desert. It is all the more surprising then to stick your head under water and discover a world so rich in wonderful designs and bright colours that you almost wonder if you have been affected by a hallucinogenic drug. The water is bath-warm and crystal-clear, and you can float along for hours entranced by an ever-changing kaleidoscope of fish, corals and other invertebrates.

The Red Sea reefs seem particularly colourful for two reasons. In the first place, they are extremely rich in soft corals, which come in an extraordinary range of bright colours, from soft, pastel pinks to rich, dark purples. Second, all along the reef there are endless shoals of goldfish-like anthias that surge back and forth from the reef's shelter in billowing bright clouds of orange. In fact these small fish are so numerous that some people believe the Red Sea may even have got its name from them.

The diversity and quantity of life that crams into every nook and cranny of coral reefs' three-dimensional structure make them by far the most productive habitat in the oceans. If you look at their productivity in terms of grams of carbon fixed every year per square metre of reef (11 square feet), the figure ranges from a minimum of 1500g (53 ounces) to a maximum of 3700g (130 ounces). Compare this with the tropical rainforests, which have a productivity range of 1000–3500g (35–125 ounces) of carbon per square metre per year,

ABOVE *A nudibranch (Chromodoris kuniei) – basically, a snail without a shell – on coral in Indonesian waters. Its defences are chemicals acquired from the sponges it feeds on, and its spectacular colour pattern lets predators know it is toxic.*

TOP *A male leafy seadragon (a relative of seahorses) carrying eggs. It is camouflaged for life among the seaweeds of the rocky reefs that fringe Australia's southern shoreline.*

OPPOSITE *A glassfish shoal swirling over a Red Sea coral-reef garden in crystal-clear, nutrient-poor water. In the darker, safer understorey of this forest of hard and soft corals grows a diversity of sponges as rich as that of the corals themselves. Nutrients from these plankton-eating colonial sponges in turn provide food for other animals.*

ABOVE *Lionfish among sea fans in a coral garden off the Solomon Islands. These nocturnal, predatory fish are in the top level of the coral food chain and have few predators of their own, mainly because of their armoury of venomous spines.*

OPPOSITE *Mass spawning of coral in the Maldives shortly after the March full moon, staining the sea red with millions of egg bundles – a bonanza for a multitude of coral fish.*

and it is clear that coral reefs are extraordinarily rich. This is even more remarkable when you consider that the majority of the world's reef-forming corals are found in the tropics, where the shallow seas as a whole are at their least productive. Coral reefs seem to have overcome the lack of nutrients in these waters by their close symbiotic relationship with zooanthellae – photosynthetic algae that live within the coral polyps.

All the world's coral reefs, however large, have been built by billions of polyps that look like tiny sea anemones no more than a few millimetres long. Each polyp lives in a small cup-like skeleton of calcium carbonate that it secretes itself, and over thousands of years, the layers of calcium carbonate build up to form coral reefs sometimes hundreds of miles long. Practically all reef-building corals get most of their energy from the photosynthetic zooanthellae living in their tissues. In return, the coral polyps provide their partners with a steady supply of the all-important nutrients such as phosphorus and nitrogen. Despite the relative lack of these nutrients in calm, tropical waters, coral reefs flourish because they have become very efficient at recycling. Rather than releasing their waste products in the sea, the polyps pass them on to the zooanthellae, which recycle the nutrients as part of their photosynthetic process. In fact, the whole community of animals that make up coral reefs has become very adept at nutrient recycling. It is also now known that, of all natural communities, coral reefs are among the most capable when it comes to fixing nitrogen. All the factors have combined to allow the world's most productive natural community to flourish in the desert-like conditions of the shallow tropical seas.

CORAL LIMITS

Coral reefs are restricted largely to the shallow, warm seas of the tropics. Reef-building corals are unable to reproduce and grow in waters that drop below 20°C (68°F), and most reefs occur in considerably warmer areas. On the eastern side of continents, surface currents tend to transport warm water away from the equator, extending the range of warm coral-growing conditions north and south. On the western sides, by contrast, the currents tend to transport cold water from the polar regions, and corals do less well. This explains why the Galapagos Islands have almost no coral reefs, despite their position so close to the equator. Up the west coast of South America, the Humboldt Current brings cold Antarctic water and bathes the islands in water too cold for coral growth.

The other key factor limiting coral growth is the clarity and depth of the water. Reefs can only grow to depths where sunlight can penetrate and their zooanthellae can photosynthesize. Different corals have different depth limits, but reefs rarely flourish in water deeper than 50m (164 feet). The clarity of water also depends on the quantity of sediment it carries. Sediment not only limits the penetration of light but can also smother the coral polyps. Off Brazil's coast, sediment from the Amazon and South America's other great rivers limits coral growth. Sediment also prevents coral reefs from developing along the coast of China and other nearby South Asian countries, where there are simply too many large rivers emptying into the sea. By contrast, the Red Sea reefs are the most extensive in the world because the land around is so dry that there are no rivers.

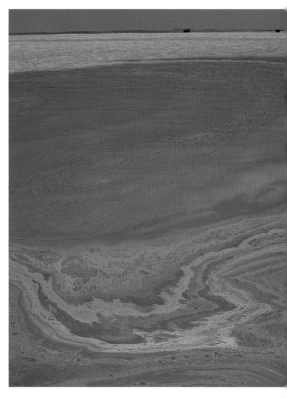

ABOVE *Staghorn coral releasing egg and sperm bundles during the March mass-spawning of coral on Ningaloo Reef off Western Australia.*

OPPOSITE *Land, sand, reef and sea off a Seychelles coral island in the Indian Ocean. Here volcanic intrusions have provided the hard base on which the coral has been able to grow.*

The coral reefs of the shallow tropical seas come in different shapes and sizes, depending on the geology of the seabed they have grown on, the temperature of the water and the impact of waves. It was Darwin who first came up with a way to classify them, which is still largely used today. He recognized three main types: fringing reefs, barrier reefs and atolls.

THE LONGEST REEF

Without doubt the most spectacular example of the first type is the 4000-km (2500-mile) reef that runs along the coast of the Red Sea – the longest single reef in the world. Fringing reefs, as their name suggests, run in a narrow band close to the coast. Typically, they start with an inner reef flat that runs out from the shore. This shallow area may be exposed at low tide and suffer from freshwater and sediment run-off, and so it tends to have little live coral. Its surface of sand or coral rubble is often covered in soft corals or seaweeds, which provide rich pickings for colourful herbivorous fish such as surgeonfish and parrotfish.

The real wealth is found at the reef crest, where the reef flat drops away into the blue and there are few problems with run-off. Wave action circulates the water and provides nutrients and zooplankton for the corals to feed on. To snorkel over these spectacular drop-offs can be a heart-stopping experience. One moment you are pottering slowly over the reef flat in shallow, warm, sunlit waters, and then suddenly you are suspended above an abyss, looking down over the coral cliff onto the silhouettes of distant sharks in the dark blue.

THE LARGEST REEF

Clearly visible from space is the world's largest (but not longest) reef, running 2000km (1250 miles) along the northeastern coast of Australia. The Great Barrier Reef is a system of more than 2000 separate reefs, sandy cays and islands covering more than 225,000 sq km (86,875 square miles). Its nearest rival in size is the barrier reef that runs along the coast of Belize in the Caribbean. Barrier reefs follow the coastline but tend to be further out to sea than fringing reefs – sometimes as far as 100km (62 miles) offshore. Protected by the reefs are lagoons, where you often find beds of seagrass and beautiful, isolated coral pinnacles.

The power of the waves that pound against its outer edge determines the structure of a reef system. The corals on the outer edge of a barrier reef occur in different layers, just like the vegetation in a rainforest. Those near the reef crest tend to be large, strong and compact, to withstand the force of the breaking waves. Just below that level, the coral growth is at its most luxuriant, with many different shapes, all of which tend to grow vertically upwards – probably in competition for space and sunlight – while in the gloom at the bottom of the slope, the corals tend to grow in flat sheets to collect as much light as possible.

ISOLATED ATOLLS

Darwin's third reef type – atolls – were to prove a real mystery. Unlike fringing or barrier reefs, these rings of coral around a central lagoon are not always close to a continental shelf. Many atolls are found far out to sea, where they rise straight up from the deep-sea floor. They range in size from a kilometre (more than half a mile) across to more than 30km

(19 miles), and the vast majority are in the Indian Ocean and the western Pacific. Their position out in the vast expanse of open ocean gives them crystal-clear waters for near-perfect diving conditions. In their isolation, they act as beacons for large pelagic (open-ocean) predators such as hammerhead and white-tipped sharks. The mystery was how these rings of coral formed in the first place. Coral can only establish itself in shallow, sunlit waters, and so there was no way the coral atoll could have grown up from the dark, deep-sea floor. Charles Darwin suggested that the atoll's ring of coral was originally a fringing reef around a deep-sea volcano that had grown up from the seafloor and emerged as an island. Gradually, over millions of years, the volcanic island slowly subsided. Throughout that time, the coral was laying down a reef of calcium carbonate that kept the ring of living coral at the surface. For a long time, scientists were not sure if Darwin was right, but eventually geologists, drilling into Enewetak Atoll in the Marshall Islands, found irrefutable evidence. Almost 1.5km (5000 feet) below a cap of calcium carbonate they discovered the volcanic rock on which the modern-day atoll had started to grow.

THE RICHEST PLACE ON EARTH

Coral reefs are easily the richest and most complex of all marine ecosystems. A reef's three-dimensional structure provides a wide range of different opportunities and niches for different species. Intense competition between these animals for space and resources further fuels the drive to increased diversity. Today the world's 'epicentre' of marine

BELOW *Part of the Great Barrier Reef off Queensland, Australia – the largest fringing barrier reef in the world, made up of 2500 individual reefs (here, Hardy Reef) and 400 species of coral.*

OPPOSITE *Golden damsels at the edge of a coral reef off Papua New Guinea with plant-like crinoids or sea fans – animals with calcium-carbonate skeletons.*

PREVIOUS PAGE *A pack of yellowsaddle goat fish hunting around a coral head off a small island in the Banda Sea, Indonesia. With them are opportunist blue-finned jacks grabbing escaping fish. And flushing out fish from inside the coral is a pack of sea kraits. Together, they are working as a hunting association.*

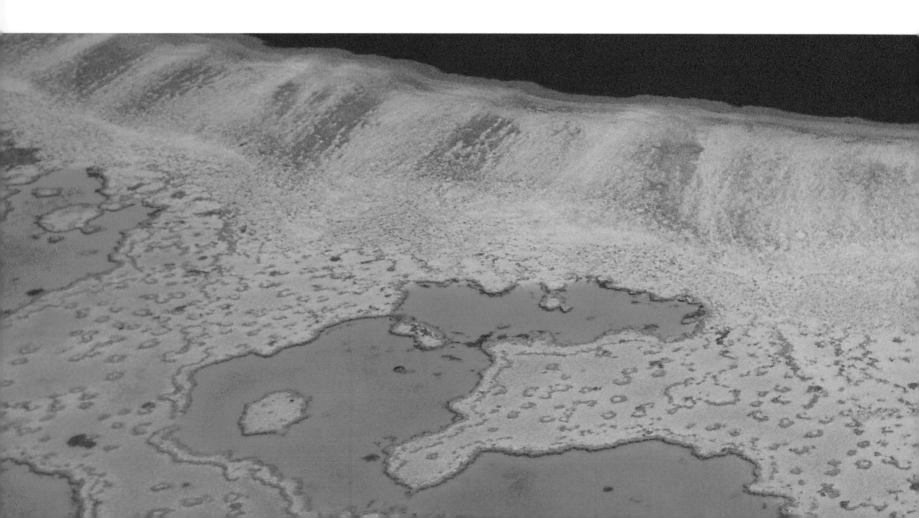

biodiversity is widely recognized as being the waters around the Indonesian archipelago.

In the triangle connecting Indonesia, the Philippines and New Guinea, more species of fish have been identified than anywhere else on the planet – so far, more than 2800, and the waters remain relatively unexplored. As you go further away from this epicentre, the diversity gradually decreases. Hawaii, for instance, has only 500 identified fish species. And as far east as Easter Island, the numbers are down to just 100.

So why have these Indo-Pacific waters developed into this centre for marine biodiversity? Several reasons have been suggested. In the first place, this region has enjoyed a long period of evolutionary stability. During the last ice ages, when drops in surface temperatures killed corals in many places around the world, Indonesian waters were far less affected, and once the last age was over, coral species spread out again from the Indonesian epicentre. By that time, an isthmus had formed between North and South America, blocking the spread of speciation (evolution of new species) from Indonesian waters. So today there are just 65 species of coral in the Caribbean, compared with more than 450 in the Indo-Pacific.

Another reason why the Indonesian waters are so diverse is the enormous variety of habitats that this vast archipelago provides. Recent expeditions have explored Raja Ampat, a group of islands off Papua New Guinea, and marine biologists believe that this may be the absolute centre of biodiversity in this very rich region. On one single dive, marine biologists counted 400 species of coral and 248 species of fish. They estimate that in this small group of islands there may be as many as 3000 fish species and 465 types of coral.

SEA SNAKES

Among the most interesting predators found on coral reefs are the sea snakes. They are all carnivorous and have some of the most powerful venom found in any snakes. About 60 species are found only in the tropical Indian and Pacific oceans. They are highly adapted to underwater life, with nostril valves that keep out the seawater and flattened bodies and paddle-shaped tails for efficient swimming. Their lungs, which run almost the whole length of their long bodies, are far larger than in their land-based relatives and allow the sea snakes to stay under water for up to two hours.

Though some sea snakes – the kraits (here, a banded krait) – lay eggs on land, most live a totally marine existence and give birth to live young at sea. These cunning predators search for their prey of small fish, fish eggs and eels among the crevices in the reef, and their small heads allow them to work their way into the narrowest corners. Sometimes sea snakes hunt in bands 20 or 30 strong, scouring the reef together. Recently, they have even been observed to do this in close association with other predatory fish (see page 262); perhaps both the fish and the snakes benefit from the disturbance caused by so many hungry mouths working the reef together.

THE SEASONAL SEAS

OPPOSITE TOP *Dusky dolphins working cooperatively to herd and feed on anchovies.*

OPPOSITE BOTTOM *An anchovy shoal. In temperate regions, winter storms whip up the water, bringing nutrients to the surface. When spring comes, plankton multiply in the nutrient-rich waters, which in turn draws in huge numbers of migratory fish, from sardines and herrings to anchovies.*

After four months nursing their calves in warm tropical waters, humpback whale mothers have to start their long migrations towards higher latitudes to find food. Some of the southern hemisphere populations, such as those that visit Tonga, journey south for more than 6000km (3720 miles) to reach Antarctica. The northern hemisphere populations, such as the ones that breed off Hawaii, head north towards the Arctic. Throughout the nursing period and on their long journeys, the whales do not feed at all. They time their migrations to reach the high latitudes at the height of summer and arrive just as feeding conditions are at their best. The summer sun has injected new energy into the marine ecosystem, and the long days allow the whales to feed round the clock. The whales are attracted here because these temperate seas, which form a band between the tropical and polar extremes, are the most productive of all shallow seas. Each year plankton blooms in massive annual explosions that support vast numbers of fish, seabirds and whales.

But these are also highly seasonal seas. When the sun leaves in the autumn and the plankton bloom is finished, the feast is over for the whales. Most will leave and journey once more towards the equator and their tropical nursing grounds.

RICH FISHING

The temperate seas that attract the humpbacks are familiar to those of us in temperate climes. After years of bucket-and-spade beach holidays, we know these waters are cold and rough in the winter and, even in summer, are barely warm enough for swimming. Those brave enough to stick their heads under water know the visibility is minimal. Yet it is just these conditions that make the temperate seas so rich. They are murky because they contain far greater quantities of phytoplankton than the crystal-clear waters of the tropics.

Though the amount of sunlight falling on temperate seas varies between the dark of winter and long summer days, year-round the total quantity is about the same as in the tropics. The big difference is the quantity of nutrients in the surface layers of the ocean where photosynthesis takes place. While tropical seas remain calm for most of the year, in higher latitudes, powerful winter storms whip up the waters, bringing nutrients from deeper layers. This process is particularly effective in the shallow seas because the proximity of the seabed has stopped the nutrients sinking too far down in the first place. Waters near the land also benefit from the fact that they are constantly being replenished with nutrients brought down by rivers. Strong currents created by the tides can also help recycle nutrients. It is hardly surprising then that the shallow temperate seas are the world's fishing grounds.

The temperate seas are highly seasonal. During the winter months, when the sun's influence is off in the opposite hemisphere, there are only a few hours of light each day. In the summer, when the sun returns, the opposite is true, and the seasonal seas enjoy up to 20 hours of daily sunlight. Not only does this produce enormous fluctuations in the amount of energy available for photosynthesis, but it also changes the temperature of the water. In the summer the sun warms the ocean, but because water conducts heat inefficiently, this

only affects the upper layers. A boundary – or thermocline – is formed between the warm surface layers and the colder water beneath. This has a powerful influence on life in the temperate seas because its formation restricts the movement of vital nutrients from the deeper water and makes it harder for small animals to journey down in search of food.

SPRING BLOOMS

In spring, the surface waters of the seasonal seas are rich in nutrients, whipped up by the winter storms, and the increase in daylight injects new energy. The result is a phytoplankton bloom, which in its turn feeds vast blooms of zooplankton. Copepods – small crustaceans that make up 70 per cent of the zooplankton – start to appear in enormous numbers. They are food for a wide range of other animals, including large zooplankton such as jellyfish. Off the coast of Scotland, there can be swarms of moon jellyfish so dense that you can swim for minutes through a wall of pulsating jelly. These jellyfish plagues are closely linked to the amount of their copepod prey, and when the plankton blooms start to die off at the end of spring, the jellyfish invasion soon disappears as well.

In the southern hemisphere, spring brings a similar spectacle to the Poor Knight Islands off New Zealand, but here it is not jellyfish but ctenophores – comb jellies – that clog the water with life. These voracious predators propel themselves through the water with lines of beating combs along the sides of their bodies. Many have deadly, sticky tentacles that they suspend in the water column to ensnare their prey. Among the spring invasion of ctenophores are also beautiful paper nautiluses and giant salps up to 10m (33 feet) long that resemble enormous pink condoms. The salps capture plankton by pumping water through a sieve-like sac or a fine mucous net that filters out their prey.

The spring plankton bloom also attracts enormous shoals of plankton-eating fish such as herring, sardines and anchovies, which form the basis of most commercial fisheries in temperate waters. These fish are mostly migratory and spend the winter months in deeper, more sheltered waters, returning to the shallows each spring in massive numbers.

A good example is the annual gathering of southern anchovies on the Patagonian shelf off Argentina. Rough winter seas whip up nutrients, and these are supplemented by the Falklands current, which runs up the Atlantic coast of South America, bringing cold, nutrient-rich waters from Antarctica. The sun's return to the southern hemisphere in September fuels a phytoplankton bloom, which in its turn attracts the southern anchovies. A whole range of predators including dusky dolphins, fur seals, sealions, sharks and the world's largest colony of Magellanic penguins rely on this spring bonanza and often work together to attack the anchovies. The dolphins search out the fish in 20-strong groups, zig-zagging backwards and forwards and leaping out of the water to try to spot birds diving. Once they find a sizeable shoal, some of the dolphins will start to concentrate the fish near the surface, while others leap high out of the water – possibly the way dolphins call in others to help deal with the swirling fish. The anchovies gather in enormous shoals hundreds of metres across which twist around together in dense and highly synchronous swarms that blacken out the sky from below. After a while, hundreds of dolphins have congregated, and together they drive the enormous shoal towards the surface. Eventually, with the swirling shoal concentrated and contained, the dolphins can feed with ease.

OPPOSITE *Blue sharks taking large mouthfuls of anchovies from a baitball (a school of fish rounded up by predators). Off the California coast, huge schools of anchovies can be found where upwellings of cold water bring nutrients.*

BELOW *Moon jellyfish attracted into temperate waters by the spring plankton bloom.*

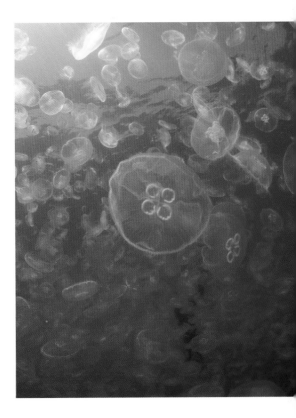

ABOVE *Courting tufted puffins. In spring, coastal waters provide food for millions of cliff-nesting seabirds.*

OPPOSITE *A spy-hopping humpback, revealing acorn barnacles encrusting its throat. Having spent the summer feeding in plankton-rich Alaskan waters, the humpback has returned to the warm but plankton-poor courtship and nursery grounds off Hawaii.*

SUMMER FEASTS

Summer brings maximum day length and calmness to the shallow seas. You might expect this to be a period of great productiveness, but after the frantic phytoplankton bloom of spring, things gradually start to slow down. The sun on the surface layers of the ocean creates a thermocline between warmer surface layers and the colder water below. This barrier starts to slow the upward flow of nutrients from the depths, and once the winter nutrients have been used up, the phytoplankton starts to die. Despite the slowdown, the fish remain in the shallows in enormous numbers, migrating to follow the patterns of blooming plankton. Off Scotland the swarms of moon jellyfish have disappeared, but other solitary jellyfish remain. The giant lion's-mane jellyfish can grow to more than a ton, catching fish and other jellyfish with its 50-m (165-foot) tentacles.

Summer is also a very busy time for seabirds with hungry chicks to feed. They spend the winter far out to sea but each spring return to traditional nesting sites in coastal waters. The distribution of the breeding colonies is largely related to the availability of food nearby. Each year the Aleutian Islands, which run off the southwestern corner of Alaska, host the world's largest concentration of breeding seabirds – more than ten million. One island, Kiska, has an estimated population of 2.5 million least and crested auklets. When these birds return each evening from feeding at sea, the flocks are so dense they look like swirling clouds of smoke.

The sheer scale of these colonies is impressive evidence of the richness of the surrounding seas. About 2 billion kilograms (4.5 billion pounds) of pollock are taken from the waters around the Aleutians each year, and the rich phytoplankton bloom also attracts vast quantities of salmon, atka mackerel and herring. These fish in their turn are food for humpback whales from Hawaii that return to Alaska each year for their annual feast.

One of the most impressive spectacles off the Aleutians is the whales surging up through the dense shoals with their enormous baleens spread wide to gulp mouthfuls of fish. Accompanying the whales are hundreds of thousands of sooty shearwaters, which turn the surface of the ocean black almost as far as you can see. The shearwaters can only duck-dive a few metres below the surface and are obviously benefiting from the fish the whales drive upwards. Extraordinarily, once the summer is over in Alaska, these shearwaters will follow the sun all the way to the southern hemisphere to benefit from the plankton bloom down there.

WINTER DEPTHS

Autumn brings ever-shortening days to the temperate oceans, but there may be just one more short phytoplankton bloom. The first of the autumn storms can break down the summer thermocline, and a fresh injection of nutrients from the depths may give the marine ecosystem one final kick. Eventually, though, the days become so short there is no longer enough energy in the system, and primary production grinds to a halt. Having completed their breeding, the seabirds and seals head for the open ocean, where they will spend the winter foraging for what they can. By dispersing in this way, they increase their chances of finding food.

As autumn turns to winter, storms become more violent, and life in the shallow seas is increasingly difficult. Many fish and even some invertebrates are forced to make annual migrations into deeper water, where they find shelter from the turbulent churnings above.

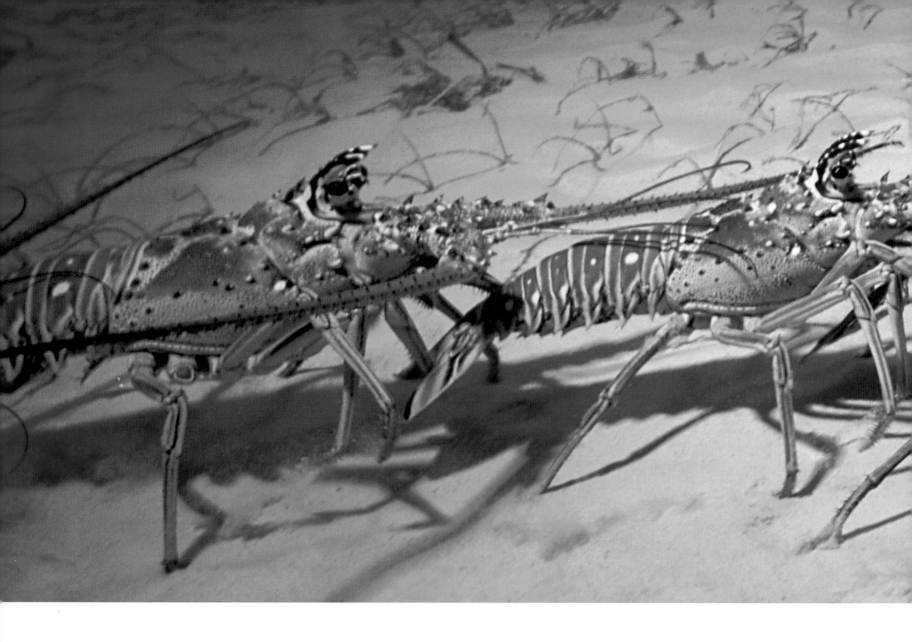

ABOVE *Migrating spiny lobsters.*
In late autumn, storms in Bimini,
in the Bahamas, cool the water and
whip up sediment from the shallow
bottom – a mosaic of coral heads,
seagrass patches and hard substrate –
triggering a migration of tens of
thousands of spiny lobsters. Using the
Earth's magnetic field as a compass,
the lobsters travel for several days to
deeper shallows, marching in line,
each follower keeping touch-contact
with the one in front.

Atlantic lobsters, for instance, come to shallows in the summer so that their developing eggs can benefit from the warmth. But in the winter they have to trek slowly back over 150km (93 miles) to a more sheltered haven in the depths. Basking sharks that spent the summer slowly cruising coastal waters, with their massive mouths wide open to trawl for copepods, also escape to deeper water. During the winter they have to stop feeding altogether as they grow a new set of gill rakers in preparation for the summer's plankton trawling. Those not heading to deeper water will seek shelter on a leeward shore away from the full force of the storms. Every winter 8 billion Atlantic herring cram into Norway's deep fjords, where the steep, towering walls provide calm, protected waters. There they patiently sit out the winter, disturbed only by pods of killer whales that follow them into the fjords to feed.

The herring shoals are so dense that the orcas have had to develop a special hunting technique. Rather than just going straight into the swirling masses they slap the edge of the shoal with their powerful tails. This seems to stun the herring, which then float helpless in the water column – easy pickings for the hungry whales. For all the animals that remain in temperate waters, winter is a time to batten down the hatches and wait for the fresh opportunities that spring will bring. The ocean itself is recharging its batteries as the winter storms whip up the nutrients for the following year.

UPWELLINGS

Upwellings that bring nutrients to the surface from the depths are a key to stimulating productivity in the shallow seas. The most important upwellings are found along the western coasts of the continents that fringe the Indian, Pacific and Atlantic oceans. Here the prevailing winds tend to blow offshore and so push the surface waters out to sea. Replacing the surface waters are upwellings of cold, deeper waters so rich in vital nutrients that almost half of the world's fisheries are found where these west-coast continental upwellings occur.

Probably the most famous of these is along the west coast of South America, where there is a massive anchovy fishery. These fish also sustain enormous numbers of seals and seabirds. There are islands off Peru completely covered with so many breeding boobies and cormorants that their droppings support an industry which mines this guano for fertilizer. In El Niño years (every three to seven years), when the offshore winds fail and the upwellings stop bringing cold, rich water to the surface, the fishery completely collapses, and thousands of birds just starve to death.

Other important upwellings occur along the California coast, off Namibia and Senegal on Africa's west coast and along Australia's northwestern seaboard.

LIFE ON THE CONTINENTAL SHELF

Compared with the vast, relatively lifeless expanses of the deep-ocean floor, the narrow strip of shallow seabed on the continental shelves is very rich indeed. The main reason for this is that these shallow seas have a much more reliable supply of nutrients. The seas above a continental shelf are rarely deeper than a few hundred metres, and wave action can bring up waters from as deep as 200m (650 feet). Near the coast, tidal currents further help the mixing process, and there are constantly fresh supplies of nutrients coming down from the rivers.

In the deeper ocean, temperatures tend to remain relatively stable. But as you travel from the equator towards the poles, water temperatures in the shallow seas tend to drop, and this has a strong effect on the quantity and variety of life. Interestingly, this means that the seabed in the tropics tends to have a larger number and variety of residents than in colder waters at higher latitudes. The other key factor that influences life on the shallow seabed is the substrate, which can be either rocky or more uniform sand and mud.

RIGHT *A dense aggregation of common brittlestars off the Scottish coast feeding on the huge amounts of organic matter suspended in the water. They have tube feet on their arms, used more for feeding than walking.*

OPPOSITE TOP *A field of sea pens – corals specialized for living on soft bottoms, with bulbous bases as anchors – filtering plankton out of the water. The seastar is feeding on them.*

OPPOSITE BOTTOM *Sand dollars (related to brittlestars and sea urchins) littering a sandy seafloor off the east coast of the US. Their tube feet are used for feeding on organic matter and burrowing into the sand. Feeding on them and other sea-bottom creatures are flatfish and horseshoe crabs.*

SOFT BOTTOMS

The vast majority of the continental-shelf seabed is covered with sand and muddy sediment. The animals here are similar to the ones on a sand beach or tidal mudflat, but being beyond the reach of the tides, they do not face the daily risk of desiccation or the cycle of changing salinity with the tides. So life is easier and more abundant. But with the exception of the tropical seagrass beds, sessile animals and plants are rare out on the uniform plain of sand or mud because there is simply nowhere for them to get a purchase. Without plants, there is little primary production. So animals here tend to live off detritus deposited on the seafloor, and many burrow into the sand. Polychaete worms such as lugworms and trumpet worms

SEAGRASS BEDS

The most productive of all the soft-bottom communities are the seagrass beds. In fact, they rank among the most productive habitats in the ocean. There are only about 50 different species of seagrasses, and most of these are found in the tropics and subtropics. They are particularly important in Caribbean and Indo-Pacific waters, where they can cover vast areas in thick, verdant mats of green.

Seagrasses are the only plants in the ocean that flower and the only marine plants with roots, which they use to secure their position in the soft, sandy, sheltered bays and lagoons where they flourish. The roots not only help to stabilize the sand but also allow the seagrass to extract nutrients from the substrate (seaweeds do not have roots and so cannot benefit in this way). A whole community of detritus feeders and herbivores depend on the seagrass for their food – sea urchins, turtles and even some parrotfish graze the beds, and many tiny creatures live on and around their leaves. But surely the most impressive residents are the manatees of the Caribbean and West Africa and the dugongs (above) of the Indo-Pacific. These gentle giants are the only truly herbivorous marine mammals, able to eat 40kg (85 pounds) of seagrass in a day.

reach out from their burrows to collect detritus with their tentacles. Others, such as razor-shells or cockles, are suspension feeders, using their siphons to draw water through their burrows and filter out what they need. Others scavenge on the surface. Shrimps do this in enormous numbers, and sea urchins such as the sand dollar have become flattened with short spines – adaptations for seabed life. In richer waters, the ground can be completely covered by brittlestars, which in their turn attract larger predatory echinoderms such as starfish.

Seabed life at normal speed seems quiet and peaceful, but time-lapse photography can show these invertebrate predators for what they are. Particularly impressive are the 50-cm (20-inch) diameter sunstars found in temperate waters. They move across the seabed on their tube feet, causing waves of brittlestars to scatter in every direction. Other predators include important commercial fish. Flatfish such as plaice, flounders and sole have adapted their whole body structures to a life on the seabed. They are totally flattened, and one eye has migrated to join the other on the upper side so they can hide just beneath the surface with both eyes peeping out and grab at any passing prey. Cod also hunt down here, using two sensory barbules on their chins to feel out food on the seafloor. The richness of the continental seabed is reflected by the fact that cod can grow up to 80kg (175 pounds) and used to occur in vast numbers, before they were devastated by commercial fisheries.

OPPOSITE *California sealions playing in the nutrient-rich shallow water in a forest of kelp off the Channel Islands, California. They hunt for fish and other sea creatures among the huge seaweeds, which are anchored to the rocky bottom.*

ABOVE *A Canadian coastal tidepool rich with rocky-surface creatures, from giant green anemones and purple sea urchins to ochre seastars.*

OPPOSITE *A species-rich bull kelp forest off the Cape of Good Hope, South Africa, with a diversity of rock-hugging creatures, sheltering shoals of fish and larger predators. Encrusting the kelp fronds is a miniature community of creatures.*

ROCK BOTTOM

Rocky substrate tends to occur only as an extension of a rocky coastline. But where it does occur, rocky-bottom communities are rich and productive, as this is a place where plants and sessile animals can get a firm foothold. Indeed, there is enormous competition for space here: the seaweeds need to be in a sunny position so they can photosynthesize, and the filter-feeding animals benefit from being out in the current where they can extract plankton.

Swimming along a rich rocky wall is one of the great pleasures of cold-water diving, with a density of life and variety of colours that match anything you see on a coral reef. Seaweeds waft in the water in a riot of reds and browns, bright yellow sponges and pink soft corals cling to the rocks, and jewelled sea anemones are dotted everywhere. Look more closely and you see the delicate glassy structures of sea squirts and, the really special prize, the brightly coloured warnings of predatory sea slugs (nudibranchs). But of all the rocky communities, the most productive – indeed one of the ocean's most productive areas – are the kelp forests.

UNDERWATER JUNGLES

Imagine what it would be like to float through a tropical rainforest just below the canopy, passing effortlessly by feeding monkeys or looking into the nest of a forest eagle. A very similar experience is possible in the kelp forests of the temperate shallow seas. Off the west coast of North America, kelp grows in such abundance that in some places you find whole forests of these beautiful golden-brown seaweeds 60m (200 feet) or so tall. On a good day, when the water is clear, shafts of bright California sunshine illuminate the underwater forest like the light in a cathedral. Just as in a tropical forest, life is hiding everywhere. Every corner seems home to one sort of invertebrate or another, shoals of fish shelter in the golden fronds, and harbour seals appear from nowhere to gambol around you as you float along.

Worldwide, there are hundreds of species of kelps, all of which are restricted to cool temperate waters. The largest of them all and the world's largest seaweed is the giant kelp, which can grow 50cm (20 inches) in one day and has single fronds up to 100m (330 feet) long. While coral reefs have a greater range on the eastern side of the world's continents, kelp forests tend to do better and have a far greater range on the western sides. This is because prevailing ocean currents on the western seaboards carry cold water down from the polar regions, and kelp enjoy these cooler conditions. In terms of primary productivity, a kelp forest is roughly equivalent to a tropical rainforest, and like a rainforest, it is a three-dimensional world, with each species having its own particular place in the structure.

Kelp plants are attached to the rocky substrate with holdfasts that are like the roots of a rainforest tree, and in the mess of twisted holdfasts, lots of different polychaete worms, small crustaceans and brittlestars make a living. The kelp fronds themselves are completely plastered with tube-dwelling polychaetes (worms) and bryozoans (colonial, coral-like animals). One clever amphipod is called the kelp-curler because it makes itself a shelter by curling the kelp over and weaving it together with silk. Shoals of plankton-eating fish such as blacksmiths hide from sharks in the forest, only venturing into open water to feed when the time is right. Other fish, such as the brightly coloured orange garibaldi fish, feed off the invertebrate life. Sealions, harbour seals and sea otters also hunt among the kelp. Even grey whales stop off to feed there as they migrate up and down the coast of California.

open ocean depths

Beyond the beaches, coral reefs and fertile shallow

waters of the narrow continental shelves lies the deep

and open ocean, covering more than 60 per cent of

the planet's surface. It regulates our climate,

conditions our atmosphere and contains some of the

least known and most extraordinary animals on Earth.

BELOW *Plankton – the ocean-riders –*
here including copepods and larvae of
crustaceans (shrimps and the like).

OPPOSITE *A baby green turtle*
sheltering in sargassum weed.
In the open ocean, free-floating
sargassum and flotsam provide
the only hiding places.

PREVIOUS PAGE *Huge manta rays*
filter-feeding on plankton.

When the heavy hatch door is screwed firmly shut, a strange silence descends. The familiar sounds of breaking waves, clanking machinery and calling gulls are gone. It is very cramped inside the submersible, with just room for three passengers side by side, sardine-like – but nobody talks. All of them are engrossed in their own thoughts. You know you are about to undertake a journey far more dangerous in some ways than even space travel. The deep ocean is a cold, dark place, and the extreme pressure of working at depth, often more than 300 times that at the surface, makes far greater physical demands on the submersible than ever experienced by a spacecraft. Waiting nervously for the dive to start, you think about what it will be like exploring the least known habitat on Earth and the chance you have of seeing an animal new to science. Suddenly the silence is broken as a massive crane takes hold of the tiny submersible, less than 8m (26 feet) long, and manhandles it off the ship's deck and down onto the surface of the open ocean. As you roll around at the surface waiting for permission to dive, it is impossible not to feel extremely small and vulnerable. The nearest land is more than 322km (200 miles) away, and beneath you the ocean drops away to a depth of more than 3km (2 miles). It will take more than two hours to reach the ocean floor, and on the way down, you will pass through different worlds.

LIFE AT THE SURFACE

As the submersible bobs around in warm, blue, sunlit seas, lots of life is visible through the tiny viewing ports. Shrimps bang up against the thick glass, chains of glassy salps float by and, in the distance, you spot the occasional silvery flashes of little fish. It takes the submersible just a matter of minutes to descend the first 200m (655 feet), but in that short time, the light begins to fade as you leave behind the productive ocean layer. Even in clear tropical seas, there is no longer enough light below the top 200m for most plants to photosynthesize, and so practically all the primary production takes place in the thin surface layer.

In the open ocean, there is no firm ground for plants such as seaweeds or sea grasses to attach to, and so virtually the only plants (with the exception of the mats of floating seaweeds you find in some tropical water such as the Sargasso Sea) are planktonic and tiny. But what these plants lack in size, they make up in numbers. Phytoplankton – the term for

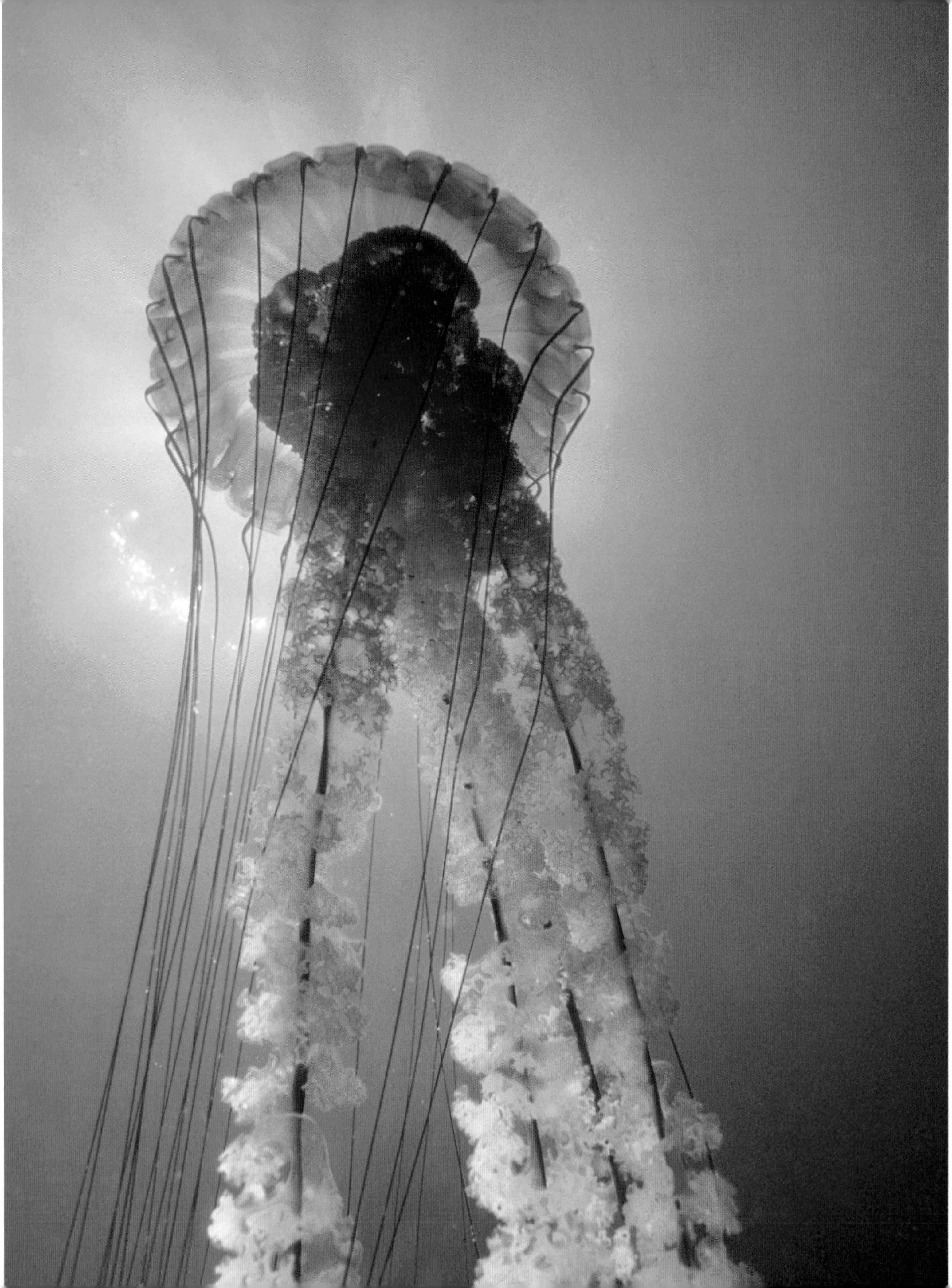

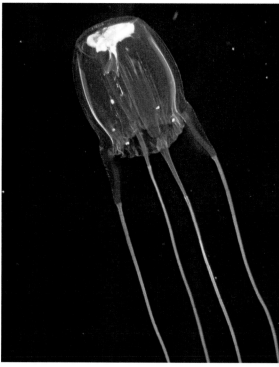

these free-floating, photosynthesizing plants, mainly algae – occurs in vast quantities and probably produces half the mass of all the world's living matter, releasing half the atmosphere's oxygen in the process. In shallow coastal waters, energy can come from elsewhere – rivers bring organic material down into estuaries and valuable food floats in from the shore. But out here in the open ocean, almost the only source of energy for animals comes from the photosynthesizing phytoplankton at the surface. It is hardly surprising then that almost all ocean life is found in the shallow surface layers.

A WORLD WITHOUT WALLS

For the animals living in the open ocean, the world has no walls. The deep-ocean floor is so far below that few ever reach it. Most live their entire lives without ever encountering a firm surface. There is nowhere to burrow, no sharp coral to avoid and no place to hide. Instead they live a wandering life suspended in liquid. Though some parts of the open ocean tend to be more productive than others, it is difficult to predict the best places to find food. There are few reliable upwellings. Conditions change on an almost hourly basis, shifting with the currents that distribute the all-important nutrients. So the animals are forced to be permanently pelagic – wandering the vast expanse of the open ocean in search of food.

There are two basic approaches to such a lifestyle: going with the flow or swimming. The multitudinous planktonic animals have little or no ability to propel themselves and just float along where wind and currents take them. Shrimps, jellyfish and even the sluggish but enormous ocean sunfish also lead a planktonic lifestyle. But the free-swimming, or nekton, animals are capable of directed wanderings, and they include most of the fish, squid, marine

ABOVE *A box jellyfish slowly digesting a meal in its bell as it floats along. It is capable of jet-propelling itself through the water and uses some of the most powerful toxins in the ocean to paralyse prey, injecting them from stinging cells on its long tentacles.*

ABOVE LEFT *Lobate comb jellies propelling themsleves using rows of fused cilia (hairs) along their bodies. These beating 'paddles' create rainbow colours when caught in the white light of a diver's torch.*

OPPOSITE *A sea-nettle jellyfish drifting along. Its trailing tentacles are effectively a deadly net, with stinging cells that can paralyse small fish and even other jellies.*

ABOVE *A chain of salps. Such chains are colonies, which can be more than 10m (33 feet) long. Individuals in a colony may be identical or, in some cases, have different roles and designs.*

OPPOSITE *A sea angel, or pteropod – a mollusc (related to slugs and snails) adapted for life in the open ocean. It is camouflaged by being nearly transparent, and it has delicate 'wings' to help it stay where it needs to be in the water column.*

mammals (dolphins, whales, seals and so on), turtles, sea snakes and even penguins.

At the bottom of the planktonic food chain, responsible for eating most of the phytoplankton, are enormous quantities of single-celled creatures – zooplankton – that are far too small even to catch in a net. The larger net zooplankton, so called because you can catch them in a net, are dominated by small crustaceans, particularly copepods, which make up 70 per cent of net zooplankton and are probably the most abundant animal group on Earth. The other important crustaceans in the open ocean are krill. These shrimp-like animals, which can grow up to 6cm (2.4 inches) long, occur in vast aggregations. Krill are particularly important in Antarctic waters as food for penguins, seals and great whales.

Though crustaceans dominate the open-ocean plankton, the most beautiful planktonic animals have to be the transparent wanderers – the salps, larvaceans, pteropods, ctenophores, siphonophores and jellies. One of the most dangerous ways to go diving in the open ocean, but also the most enjoyable, is to drift at about 20m (66 feet) down. As the current carries you gently along, a whole array of different transparent creatures pass by – each more extraordinary and exquisitely beautiful than the other. A salp looks like a transparent jet engine, extracting phytoplankton by pumping water though a fine mucous net in the hollow centre of its body. Salps can be solitary but may also join together in long, pulsing chains several metres long. Pteropods are beautiful snails that have adapted to life in the liquid blue. The snail foot has been reshaped into two transparent 'wings' that keep it afloat and make it look like a tiny ocean angel. A larvacean floats inside a 'house' made of mucous. It uses its tail to draw water through the open-ended house and over mucous filters that capture minute phytoplankton. Some larvaceans even secrete a mucous net outside their bodies that can stretch out as far as 2m (6.5 feet). When the filters of a mucous house become clogged, a larvacean simply throws away the house and builds a new one in a matter of minutes.

There are some powerful planktonic predators drifting in the open ocean as well. By far the largest are the siphonophores, colonies of polyps that can be many feet long. What makes them so fascinating is that the members of the colony have different roles. Some may form gas-filled floats that keep a colony near the surface. Others form long tentacles with rows of deadly stinging cells that hang down in the water. The most famous siphonophore is the Portuguese man-of-war, *Physalia*, which has one massive polyp adapted into a gas-filled float above the surface. This float, which may be up to 30cm (12 inches) long, catches the wind and carries *Physalia* along, dragging its trail of stinging cells behind.

A jellyfish's rounded body, or bell, gives it only limited swimming ability, and so for the most part, it is carried along either by the wind or by the currents like all the other plankton. Some of the jellies with the largest bells are among the most dangerous marine animals, such as the lion's-mane jelly, with bell diameters up to 2.4m (8 feet). The box jellyfish, which is as large as a human head, has 2m (6.5 feet) tentacles with stinging cells containing a powerful toxin. In humans, this causes immediate, extreme pain, and death due to heart failure may occur within minutes.

Of all the transparent killers drifting on the open-ocean currents, the most beautiful have to be the comb jellies, or ctenophores. They get their name from eight rows of fused cilia that run along their bodies and provide limited manoeuvrability. Caught in the white lights of the submersible, their rows of beating paddles flicker like dynamic rainbows before they disappear away into transparent obscurity.

ABOVE *A sperm whale – one of the biggest predators in the ocean and probably the deepest-diving mammal, pursuing squid and other prey to at least 2000m (6560 feet).*

OPPOSITE *A streamlined mako shark – the fastest of all the sharks, able to catch even billfishes such as marlin.*

The open-ocean animals that control their movements, the nekton, are far less abundant than the plankton. But they do include the largest, most spectacular animals in the sea. Practically all nekton are carnivorous, and among those that eat plankton are small fish such as herrings, sardines and anchovies, which can occur in enormous numbers. One school of herring, for instance, covered just over 4.5 million cubic metres (159 million cubic feet). More solitary plankton predators include the world's largest fish, the whale shark, which reaches up to 14m (46 feet) in length, and the largest ray, the manta, with its beautiful wings that stretch 5m (more than 16 feet) across. Both these giants are designed for slow, energy-saving wanderings in search of plankton and prove that such a feeding technique can be effective if you are suitably streamlined. At the top of the plankton food chain are the baleen whales (with baleen plates for filter-feeding), which travel enormous distances over the open ocean, mostly searching for krill. These mammals have lost all their hair and have almost perfectly streamlined shapes to minimize drag in the water.

Most of the nekton, though, do not consume plankton. Instead they feed on each other in a classic predatory food chain, where small fish are eaten by bigger fish, only to be eaten by even bigger fish. They include the fastest-swimming predators – the billfish and the tuna.

These 'racing cars' of the ocean are highly streamlined and packed with muscle to carry them over enormous distances at great speed. At the very top of the food chain are the whales and sharks. The sperm whale is the largest nekton-eating whale and dives deep in search of giant squid that can be more than 10m (33 feet) long. Killer whales are highly intelligent dolphins that catch fish, penguins or seals and sometimes work together to run down baleen whales over twice their size. And the mako shark, the ocean's fastest shark, even takes large billfish such as marlin and sailfish.

All the animals that live in the surface layer of the open ocean, from the tiniest plankton to the mighty blue whale, have to deal with two key problems unique to this habitat. In the first place, they all have to make sure that they can stay near the surface. Not only is the vast majority of food to be found in this warm, sunlit layer, but as you get deeper, the water can also get too cold and the oxygen level too low for many of these animals to survive. And as all animal cells and tissues are denser than water, open-ocean animals face a constant struggle to stay afloat. This pressure has shaped their lifestyles and even their body designs. The second big challenge is finding food in their unpredictable, ever-changing world. Inhabitants of the open ocean have no option but to wander continuously in search of a meal.

AVOIDING THAT SINKING FEELING

Oceanic animals have adopted two basic strategies to stop them sinking into the depths. They either increase their drag on the water to slow down their sinking rate or they increase their buoyancy. Tiny planktonic animals are already at an advantage when it comes to drag as their small size gives them a proportionally higher surface area. They increase this surface

area further by spines and projections. This explains why many of the tiny larvae of bottom-living animals such as lobsters and seastars resemble spiky satellites – they are designed to float near the surface so they can be dispersed by wind and currents. The open ocean's only resident insect has adapted a similar technique. The marine water strider has elongated legs and uses the water's surface tension to skate on the surface. The wide bells of jellyfish act as umbrellas to increase their drag through the water. And the long chains of some salps and siphonophores also slow down sinking. Sometimes salps will go one step further by wrapping up their long chains into flat circles that produce yet more drag.

Oils and fats – lipids – are lighter than water, and many oceanic animals store lipids for that extra lift, and most fish eggs contain drops of lipids to keep them floating near the surface for efficient dispersal. The livers of many sharks and tuna are enlarged and rich in oils. In the case of warm-blooded marine mammals such whales and seals, a thick layer of buoyant fat (blubber) beneath the skin not only helps keep them afloat but also provides insulation. Another way to stay buoyant is to trap pockets of air. Even the tiny bacteria in the plankton have air pockets within their single cells. The advanced version of this is the gas-filled swim bladder, which many fish use to control buoyancy. Like the buoyancy aids worn by divers, swim bladders constantly need adjusting as the fish vary their depths. Fish do this in different ways, but few can make fast adjustments to the quantity of air. Dynamic predators such as sharks and billfish that must dive quickly after prey tend to have poorly developed swim bladders but make use of enlarged livers to help keep them afloat.

HIDE-AND-SEEK

Throughout the vast space of the open ocean there is no place to hide and no predictable place to hunt. There is no sandy bottom to bury into, no kelp frond to hide behind, no coral reef from which to ambush fish and no shallow bay for good hunting. Predators and prey must take part in the most demanding game of hide-and-seek there is – and every day the rules change. Prey animals need to find a way to hide themselves in a world without walls. The predators need highly tuned senses and endurance to search over vast areas.

The surface layers are well lit, and so many oceanic animals – even zooplankton – have large, efficient eyes. The turbidity of water, though, means that, even in the clearest tropical seas, visibility is limited. Oceanic dolphins that tend to hunt in large groups have, however, learnt to leap out of the water to get a better view, perhaps spotting for seabirds diving into fish schools or even signalling to each other where a good feeding site is.

Water carries vibrations well, which means it is also important to be sensitive to water movement. Most fish have lateral lines along the lengths of their bodies that are highly sensitive to vibrations. These allow billfish to locate injured fish thrashing near the surface and also enable prey fish to react at the last minute to lunging predators. Lateral lines may also play a vital role in coordinating the movements of shoals of schooling fish. Just as roosting starlings gather in enormous flocks to provide safety in numbers from birds of prey, so many small fish form giant circling schools – 'bait balls' that may contain hundreds of thousands of densely packed fish swimming in synchrony. For any individual fish within the shoal, there is at last something to hide behind.

Other ways of concealment in the open include transparency, adopted by many plankton animals, such as the jellies and even snails. For a nekton, which needs muscles to move around, it is impossible to be transparent. Instead, many open-ocean fish have opted for counter-shading. The tops of their bodies tend to be dark blue while the bottoms are light and silvery. Looking down from above, the tops merge with the darkness of the deep water, while looking from below, their silvery bottoms are hard to see against the flickering light from the surface. Silvery sides act as mirrors, reflecting back the light and helping the fish merge into the blue. Mackerel also have stripy sides to further break up their silhouettes. But the ultimate disappearing trick is that of the flying fish. When chased by speed merchants such as tuna or sailfish, they accelerate through the surface and open their massively elongated pectoral fins. Once airborne on these 'wings', flying fish rapidly beat their tails for extra power and, with a good following wind, they can easy 'fly' at least 100m (328 feet) and, with luck, land well beyond their predators' reach.

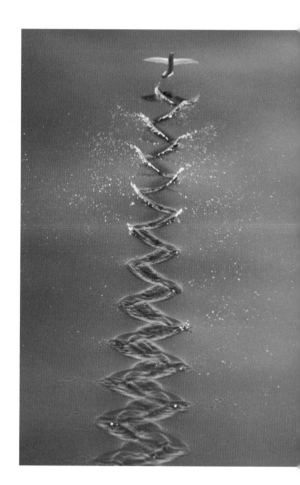

ABOVE *The pattern on the water surface is created by the flying fish's specially extended tail, which it beats to get extra power. This enables it to 'fly' for distances up to 100m (328 feet) to avoid predators below the water.*

OPPOSITE *Rarely seen whale shark behaviour. Hanging almost vertically near the surface, the shark is surrounded by a swarm of tiny fish, which seem to be sheltering behind it to avoid the hungry tuna that are attacking them.*

The fastest fish in the sea

The fastest and most spectacular fish in the sea are tuna and billfish. The upper jaw of each of the 11 species of billfish is elongated into a bony spear that can be well over 1m (3 feet) long. The biggest is the blue marlin, which can weigh more than 900kg (1990 pounds), and the fastest is the sailfish, with bursts of speed up to 110kph (68mph).

Tuna and billfish are not just sprinters but can also travel vast distances fast in search of prey. One bluefin tuna tagged off the coast of Japan was re-captured almost 11,000km (6820 miles) away off Baja California, Mexico. Another tagged bluefin crossed the Atlantic in just 119 days – an average straight-line distance of 65km (40 miles) a day, though the tuna would have covered a far greater distance in its search for food.

To achieve impressive speed and endurance, tuna and billfish are almost perfectly streamlined. Their bodies are sleek and compact, and most species have no scales, keeping them very smooth. Their eyes do not protrude and are covered with transparent lids to reduce drag. Their fins are stiff and narrow and can be quickly tucked away in grooves along the body so as not to break up the streamlining. The exact purpose of the bill remains something of a mystery, but it probably helps them slip through water, just as the needle on the nose of a supersonic aircraft slips through air. Many tuna and billfish also have keels, and finlets near the tail direct the flow of water across their bodies in such a way as to reduce drag – another trick used by supersonic-jet engineers.

Streamlining is important for speed, but you also need a powerful engine. Billfish and tuna both have large, high tails with swept-back tips that give them the maximum propulsion for minimum effort. They are also both packed with muscle and, in particular, red muscle rich in myoglobin, which stores a lot of oxygen and provides enormous endurance. Muscle works best when warm, but in the cold ocean, most fish lose the heat generated by their muscles through their skin. Tuna and billfish, however, have their blood vessels arranged in a counter-current system.

Cold veins run parallel with warm arteries so that the venous blood is warmed as it returns to the heart. Swordfish that specialize in hunting in deep, cold waters even have specially warmed muscle behind their eyes and brain to keep these vital organs as active as possible. Bluefin tuna have become warm blooded to such an extent that, in water as cold as 7°C (45°F), they can maintain a core temperature of more than 25°C (77°F). This allows them to venture deep into cold, temperate waters that are rich in life – unlike other tunas, which are generally restricted to warm but less productive tropical waters.

ABOVE *A southern blue tuna, built for speed and endurance swimming. For perfect streamlining, the stiff, narrow fins can be tucked away quickly in special grooves along their bodies.*

LEFT *A blue marlin – the largest of all the 11 species of predatory billfish, weighing up to 900kg (1985 pounds).*

OPPOSITE *A sailfish with its fin raised. While hunting and possibly during courtship, sailfish constantly raise and lower their impressive dorsal fins. As part of this display, they may also change colour rapidly, from blue to dark black and many shades in between.*

JOURNEY INTO THE DEEP

The submersible spends just a few minutes at the warm, sunlit surface, which is lucky because, even on a calm day, the tiny submarine rolls violently back and forth, leaving you feeling like a load of washing in a tumble dryer. As permission to dive comes crackling over the radio, the pilot allows water to flood into the buoyancy chambers, and the submersible slips smoothly away from the surface. The two-hour journey down to the seabed 3km (2 miles) below has begun. Even when diving in clear tropical waters, it is surprising how quickly it seems to get dark. Within just a few minutes, you are deeper than 150m (492 feet), and to the human eye at least, most of the light seems to have gone. You have left the photic zone, the surface layer where almost all life is found, and are journeying into the deep.

The scale of the deep ocean far exceeds that of the open ocean. It is by far the largest habitat on Earth and, by volume, makes up almost 80 per cent of the space on our planet available for life; the land, by comparison, represents just 0.5 per cent. So far we have explored just 1 per cent of this vast space, making the deep ocean the last true frontier.

The main reason the deep has proved so difficult to explore is the pressure of water. At the surface, we are subjected to one atmosphere of pressure, the equivalent of 1kg per sq cm (2.2 pounds to less than half a square inch). But with every 10m (33 feet) we descend into the deep, the pressure increases by another atmosphere. It is this change in pressure that restricts most scuba divers to the top 30m (98 feet) of the ocean. Even highly experienced technical divers rarely go much below 50m (165 feet) and then only for a matter of minutes.

The only way to go any deeper is to travel in submarines built to withstand these pressures. But most submarines are not able to dive much deeper than 500m (1640 feet). The pressure there is already 50 times that at the surface, and large submarines, designed to carry lots of people and weapons, would simply break up. Luckily, our submersible is far smaller than most naval ones. Three passengers squeeze into a sphere just 3m (10 feet) in diameter – an ideal design for resisting pressure. The walls are made of an extremely strong mix of steel and titanium 5cm (2 inches) thick, and the tiny portholes use strengthened glass 18cm (7 inches) thick. It is capable of descending to an extraordinary depth of 6km (nearly 4 miles) from the surface. Though 60 per cent of the ocean is more than 1.6km (a mile) deep, there are barely 10 submersibles worldwide that can dive to that depth – hardly surprising then that so much remains to be explored.

THE TWILIGHT ZONE

Though you are looking through the tiny portholes of the submersible, the light seems to have mostly gone by the time you reach 150m (492 feet), but in the clearest tropical waters, small quantities of light do penetrate far deeper. This gloomy layer of the deep ocean, down to the 1000-m (3280-foot) limit, is known appropriately as the twilight zone. Practically no plants are found here, and as you quickly start to notice inside the submersible, water temperatures drop rapidly to around 5°C (41°F).

At about 500m (1640 feet), you also pass through the oxygen-minimum layer. In this

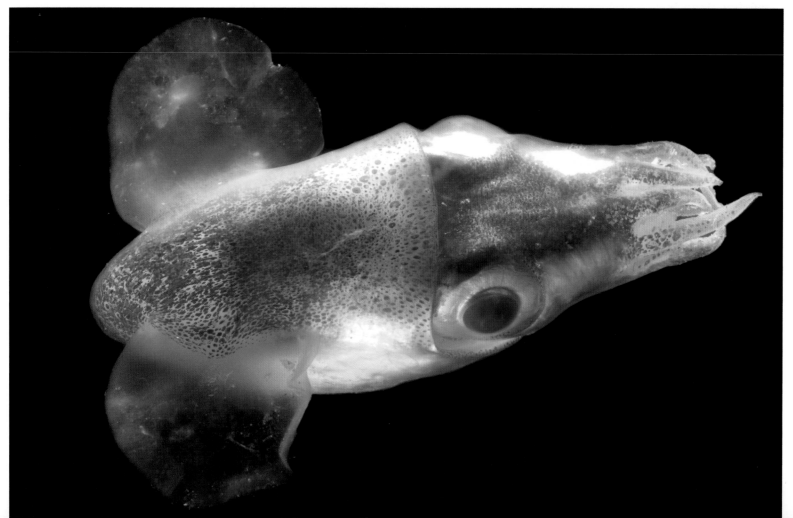

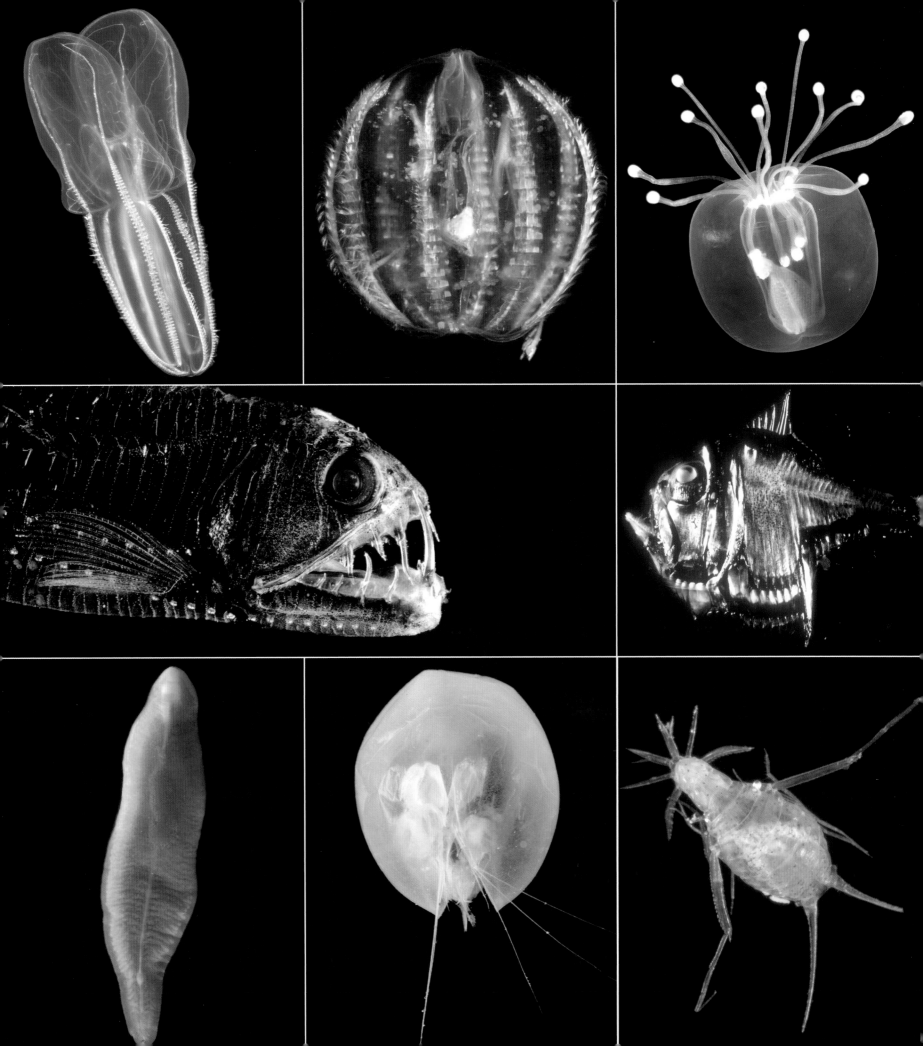

zone, the little oxygen that makes its way down from the surface is almost entirely used up by the few animals that live here. Without photosynthetic plants to replenish the supplies, oxygen levels drop close to zero.

Inside the submersible, we put on thick fleeces to stay warm and make use of our tanks of oxygen. But the combination of the cold, lack of light and oxygen and the change in pressure make it very difficult for other visitors from surface waters. Those that do manage to dive into these murky depths are specially adapted to do so. For instance, the only deep-diving turtle is the leatherback. Most marine turtles have rigid shells, but the leatherback has a flexible shell that allows it to survive the changing pressure. Even so, leatherbacks only make quick foraging trips down to 500m (1640 feet) and back in just 10 minutes.

Swordfish, impressive fish that grow up to 500kg (1105 pounds) and have broad, sword-like bills, have immense eyes to see in the gloom. They also have lots of fat and use the counter-current system to keep them warm. But even they cannot dive beneath the minimum-oxygen layer.

Among the deep-diving champions are the elephant seals, which can stay down as deep as 1500m (4920 feet) for up to two hours. A thick layer of blubber keeps an elephant seal warm, and huge quantities of blood provide the oxygen. Even so, it slows down its metabolism to a minimum and beats its heart only six times a minute while diving.

For the permanent residents of the twilight zone, the biggest problem is lack of food. Only 20 per cent of the energy fixed in the photic layer above makes it down to these depths. So there are far fewer animals here than there are in the surface layers, and most are much smaller. What they lack in size, however, they make up for in ferocious looks. The aptly named viperfish, for instance, has a huge set of needle-like teeth that are too long to fit inside its mouth and extend up to its eyes. Like many twilight-zone residents, the viperfish's strategy is to save energy by sitting and waiting for a meal to come along. As it cannot afford to be choosy, its highly extendible jaw and sharp teeth are adapted to deal with even very large prey.

The battle of hide-and-seek we saw in the surface water is even more keenly fought down here. Predators need even better vision to spot their prey. *Dolichopteryx*, for instance, looks rather like a deep-sea bushbaby, each of its eyes being almost half the width of its head, while *Benthalbella* has tubular eyes with a binocular overlap. These remarkable eyes are not only very sensitive but also allow the fish to determine the range of their prey.

The little light that does reach the twilight zone always comes from the surface, and so many animals here have eyes designed to look up. The squid *Histioteuthis* has one large eye and one small one, and it is thought that it positions itself in the water so that the large eye can watch for the silhouettes of prey illuminated by the faint glow from the surface.

If the predators go to extreme lengths to spot their prey, so the prey do what they can to avoid being spotted. Hatchetfish are small, highly flattened fish that look like silvery postage stamps. Their whole bodies are reflective and act as mirrors when seen from the side, bouncing back any light from the surface and making the fish invisible against the dark blue. When seen from below, they are thin enough to be virtually non-existent. But to make absolutely sure they are invisible, they use light-producing cells called photophores. These can change colour to match the intensity of daylight seeping down from above, however high the sun is in the sky. Other twilight-zone residents – fish, squid and shrimps – use photophores as a form of counter-illumination to break up their silhouettes.

OPPOSITE TOP, LEFT TO RIGHT
Bolinopsis – a lobate ctenophore, or comb jelly. It is an active hunter that swims using its comb plates but which can also expand its lobes and swim by jet propulsion. It can be up to 15cm (about 6 inches) long and eats mainly copepods, which it funnels into its mouth with its expandable lobes.

The rainbow colours of a sea gooseberry – interference patterns caused by the beating rows of cilia along its body. Despite its beauty, a sea gooseberry is an effective predator, which uses two long sticky tentacles to ensnare its copepod prey.

A midwater jelly, one of a wide range of jellies, salps and ctenophores that interact in a complex food chain, or jellynet – predators and prey in a world without walls.

MIDDLE, LEFT TO RIGHT
A viperfish. Twilight predators often have large teeth – their meals come along so rarely that they need to be able to deal with prey of all sizes.

A hatchetfish. Its flattened, silvered body acts like a mirror – perfect camouflage for the twilight zone.

BOTTOM, LEFT TO RIGHT
A nemertine worm. Most worms are found in the sediment on the seafloor, but this species hangs in midwater.

Gigantocypris – the largest known ostracod, or mussel shrimp, about the size of a pea. The two golden discs are its sensitive eyes, and its antennae are used as oars. It can retract its body parts inside its hinged outer 'pod'.

Lanceola – a bioluminescent amphipod (relative of shrimps), often found with jellies. In the darkness of the twilight zone, its red colour would appear black, helping camouflage it.

ABOVE *A bristlemouth displaying a mouthful of brush-like teeth. Bristlemouths are among the most numerous fish in the twilight zone. Every night they swim a huge distance towards the surface in search of food.*

Many animals in the twilight zone are happy to sit and wait for their food to come to them. Those that are not predators feed on scraps falling from the rich pickings up above in the surface layers. These detritus feeders include most of the plankton, chiefly copepods and krill, which live off the faecal pellets and dead bodies of surface dwellers.

Other twilight-zone residents, however, have a different strategy altogether. Every night, they migrate hundreds of metres up into the rich, shallow waters of the photic zone in search of food. The problem is that the surface waters are also rich in predators, which is why the mammoth journeys only take place under cover of darkness. The sheer scale of this daily migration is breathtaking. It involves millions and millions of tons of animals and far outstrips the annual migrations of birds or wildebeest. A wide range of animals is involved, from the tiniest zooplankton that may journey tens of metres to fish that manage as much as 1000m (3280 feet) up and down each night. Two of the most common fish taking part are bristlemouths (one species, *Cyclothone signata*, is possibly the most abundant fish in the oceans) and lanternfish. These little fish, 5–15cm (2–6 inches) long, have large eyes and strong muscles to help them on their nightly journeys. They are so numerous that, when sonar was first being developed during the Second World War, echo-soundings from the swim bladders of millions of these little fish were mistakenly read as sound bouncing back from the sea bottom.

THE DARK ZONE

After about half an hour of gradual descent, the submersible slips below 1000m (3280 feet). The thermometer shows that water temperature has now dropped to just above 2°C (36°F), and the water looks black as ink. We have entered the dark zone. The pressure here is more than a hundred times that at the surface, and absolutely no light penetrates this deep. The pilot keeps the external lights off to save batteries, but even if they were on, you would be lucky to have even the occasional glimpse of life.

This vast space, which contains three quarters of the water on our planet, is home to some of its strangest animals, none stranger than anglerfish. These really are monsters of the deep and have names such as black devilfish and triple-wart sea devil to prove it. They

BIOLUMINESCENCE

It is now thought that up to 90 per cent of the animals in the deep sea create their own light. This bioluminescence is produced by a chemical reaction in which the substance luciferin is oxidized, or burnt, using the catalyst luciferase. Most animals produce blue light, which penetrates well through the water, but yellow, green and even red bioluminescence occurs. It has a number of purposes.

Deep-ocean animals such as anglerfish may use bioluminescence to attract prey. And the prey may use it to confuse their predators. An *Atolla* jellyfish lights up its body like a firework when attacked. Others such as some of the deep-sea copepods spew small quantities of bioluminescence out of their bodies to confuse their predators, who chase after these mysterious lights, leaving the copepods to slip away unseen into the black. In the twilight zone, a vast array of different animals (lanternfish, in the picture above) produce bioluminescence in organs called photophores. These are carefully arranged on their bodies to produce camouflage and counter-illumination. Special patterns of photophores may also help with the difficult job of finding a mate in the darkness, as different species and even the opposite sexes put on different light shows to attract the right partners.

are perfectly adapted for life in total darkness. For a start, they are black, as are most dark-zone fish, though dark red is an equally effective camouflage, and many shrimps here are blood red. Anglers are also small, usually only a few centimetres long, which is hardly surprising considering that only 5 per cent of the energy from the photic layer makes it down this deep. Like most other fish here, anglers are designed to save energy by just sitting and waiting for their food to come to them and so have little muscle and non-functional swim bladders (no animals in the dark zone migrate vertically because the distances up to the photic zone and the changes in pressure are just too great). Because their meals are so irregular and unpredictable, all anglers have huge mouths and highly extendible stomachs that allow them to handle prey of almost any size.

Vision is less useful in the dark, and so anglers have tiny eyes, but they are often very sensitive to vibrations in the water – one group, the hairy anglers, are covered in antennae that pick up even the slightest movements of their prey. Anglerfish are, of course, most famous for fishing for their prey. The females have lures suspended in front of their giant mouths. What makes a lure so attractive is that its tip glows in the dark, and in a world of total darkness, any light is fascinating. The bioluminescence is created by symbiotic bacteria that live in the tip of the lure. Anglers and other dark-zone predators have come up with a wide variety of different and often bizarre designs for their lures. Those of whip-nosed anglers are on the ends of fishing poles four or five times longer than the fish themselves, while other anglers suspend their lures from the roofs of their mouths right in between their long and terrifying teeth.

THE DEEP-SEA FLOOR

After two rather peaceful hours, the submersible starts to approach the bottom. The pilot still has not turned on the external lights, but an alarm starts to ring as the sonar picks up the vague contours of the seabed. Inside our tiny sphere, it has really become very cold, and the Russian pilot resorts to his secret weapon – sheepskin boots from Siberia. The submersible's gauges tell us the outside temperature is just below 2°C (36°F) and the depth is almost 3000m (9840 feet). Down here, two miles from the surface, the pressure has increased 300 times, and if even a tiny hole appeared in the submersible, we would be dead in seconds.

Just metres from the bottom, the pilot finally turns on the powerful external lights. Outside, the water is crystal clear and you can see a good 50–60m (165–200 feet) into the distance, and yet what you see will be very limited. The deep ocean is so vast and our tiny submersible so small that our exploration is little more effective than an astronaut searching the surface of the dark side of the moon with nothing but a hand torch.

First impressions of the deep-sea floor are hardly overwhelming. For the most part, it appears muddy, flat and lifeless. But as you look more closely, you start to see signs of animal life – tracks and trails have been left all over the sediment. Most of these have been made by sea cucumbers – largely white echinoderms, whose name well describes their shape. Sea cucumbers are the vacuum cleaners of the deep-sea floor, sucking in sand at one end and extracting what algal life and bacteria they can, before excreting the processed sand as droppings. They are so numerous that they are thought to make up 95 per cent of the biomass on the deep-sea floor. Other common echinoderms are the brittlestars and

ABOVE *A deep-sea anglerfish, or monkfish, Lophius piscatorius, more than 100cm (39 inches) long, in the act of swallowing a fish. It is resting on the sea bottom, close to the remotely operated vehicle that is illuminating it. In the dark of the deep sea, its eyes are used for spotting bioluminescence and detecting movement using a highly developed sensory system.*

sea urchins, which come in a variety of shapes and sizes. Usually these animals are solitary, but occasionally you will spot what appears to be a small herd of sea urchins travelling together. Such aggregations are probably to do with reproduction – once you have found a mate in this vast space, it is important to stick together.

Food is the other factor that draws large numbers of animals together down here. Only 2 per cent of the energy created in the photic layer makes it down to the deep-sea floor. Most tasty morsels have been snapped up by animals living in the water above, and benthic animals living on the bottom have to make do with marine snow – particles of bodies and droppings drifting down from above. Occasionally, larger food such as the carcass of a dead fish or marine mammal makes it unscathed right down to the depths, and many of the benthic animals are specially adapted to scavenge on these rare deliveries. Gone are the delicate, vertical migrants of the twilight zone or the strange monsters of the dark zone. Here the fish are large and muscular with long tails and big heads. The rat-tails, or grenadier fish, are typical. With strangely shaped triangular heads that contain a battery of sensory cells, they look like large, ugly tadpoles and are designed to wander slowly over large distances, literally sniffing out their potential prey.

VOLCANOES IN THE DEEP

As the submersible creeps along at just a few knots, the shape of the deep-sea floor begins to change. We are gradually forced to climb up an increasing incline. The featureless flat bed of sediment is replaced with rolling clumps of dark rock resembling the outside surface of an enormous cauliflower. This is unmistakably a volcanic landscape, and passing below us is mile after mile of lava that looks remarkably fresh. The relaxed atmosphere in the submersible changes as the eerie silence of the abyss is broken and we start to hear a distant industrial roar. The once-clear water becomes black with billows of passing smoke. And then, suddenly, right in front of us, emerging through the smoke is a massive chimney far taller than the submersible itself.

Black smoke thunders out of the top, and it is clear from the heat haze that the water is very hot. The pilot manoeuvres very carefully now and, using one of the submersible's manipulating arms, he places a specially designed thermometer inside the water gushing from the chimney. It gives a reading of 375°C (707°F) – hotter than molten lead and easily hot enough to do serious damage to our submersible. We have reached the legendary black smokers – the volcanic hot vents found all along the mid-oceanic ridges of the deep-sea floor.

The mid-oceanic ridges are the largest geological structures on our planet and run almost 45,000km (28,000 miles) round it like the seams on a cricket ball. Here, new seabed is being formed as molten lava seeps up through the Earth's crust and flows out to form mountains. These mountains can stand up to 3.2km (2 miles) above the seafloor, and the mid-oceanic ridges they form can be 80km (50 miles) wide. Black smokers have now been found on almost all the world's mid-ocean ridges, but they were not discovered until 1977. In that year, geologists diving with a submersible on the East Pacific Rise just off the Galapagos Islands saw active chimneys for the very first time. They were thrilled by the

BELOW *A unique view of the deep-sea anglerfish* Lophius piscatorius *swimming, its fishing lure folded down on its head. It spends most of its time lurking buried in the sediment, the bioluminescent end of its lure wriggling enticingly above its huge mouth.*

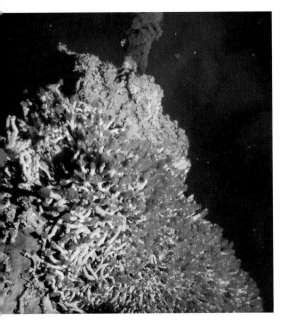

ABOVE *Rifta tubeworms covering a 'smoker'. Their red gills carry carbon dioxide, oxygen and sulphides down to bacteria in their tubes, which convert them into organic matter and then exchange them for chemicals.*

ABOVE RIGHT *A Pompeii worm, one of a cluster living on the very edge of a hydrothermal vent where the hottest water is emerging. It gets its name from its ability to survive extraordinary temperatures up to 80°C (176°F).*

OPPOSITE TOP *A deep-water coral community at about 1600m (5250 feet) on Davidson Seamount, an inactive volcano off California. Species spotlit by the submersible include yellow sponges, basket stars and bubblegum coral.*

OPPOSITE BOTTOM *Giant Neolithodes spider crabs, up to 1m (more than 3 feet) across, living 1800m (5900 feet) down in the Gulf of Mexico. Their spines may provide protection from predators, and their colour is typical of many deep-sea animals – as no light penetrates to these great depths, a red animal appears black and so is perfectly camouflaged.*

geology, but even they knew that it was the biology that was going to prove really amazing.

When the submersible leaves the gushing summit of the chimney and slowly drops down its side – which at times can be as high as a 16-storey building – you suddenly start to notice an extraordinary profusion of life. In the eastern Pacific, this profusion is dominated by thick clusters of white tubeworms that grow 2m (6.5 feet) tall and can be as thick as your arm. Flowering out of the top of each tube are beautiful, bright-red plumes that waft delicately in the hot currents from the vent. Look carefully among the tubeworms and you start to notice a variety of shrimps, limpets, amphipods and the occasional extraordinary pink fish. At the base of the chimney are thick beds of mussels, which are themselves covered in white polychaete worms delicately sifting food particles from the water. Even when the submersible moves away from the chimney, there is still a lot of life to be seen, including white clams as big as dinner plates.

When biologists finally visited the hot vents off the Galapagos, they could hardly believe that such density of life – which rivals anything found on even the richest coral reefs – could exist in the total darkness of the deep-sea floor. Photosynthesis was obviously impossible, and the gentle drift of marine snow could never provide enough energy to fuel the system. Eventually, it was discovered that the entire complex ecosystem is ultimately dependent on specialized bacteria that fix the energy in the sulphides pouring out of the vents in the smoke and hot water as hydrogen sulphide.

Geologists have now discovered hot vents on almost all of the mid-oceanic ridges they have explored. The different vents are thousands of miles apart, but amazingly all have developed their own ecosystems based around fixing energy from sulphides. What has fascinated biologists is that, though these ecosystems are similar, they each contain unique animals. So far, we have visited about 1 per cent of the deep-ocean floor, and there are still 300 million sq km (116 million square miles) to go. There can be little doubt that there are other completely new ecosystems down there waiting to be discovered.

INDEX

Page numbers in *italic* indicate pictures

aardvarks 114, *114*
acacia trees 129
Africa: deserts 119, 120
 Great Rift Valley *144*, 146, 208, *208*
 mangrove forests 235
 mountains 145, 146–8
 rainforests 231, 246, 248, 249, 251
 savannahs 21–2, 92, 98–9, 107–14
agave *133*
agouti 248
airplant 132
Alaska 66, 96, 270
alerce (Patagonian cypress) 84
Aleutian Islands 270
algae 258, 285
Algeria 123
Alps 76, 77, 159
Amazon Basin 128, 216, 238
Amazon River 199, 212, *213*, 221, 227, 231, 232–3, 259
amphibians, in deserts 136
amphipods 210, *210*, 278, *296*
Amundsen-Scott research station, South Pole 34
Amur region 77, 86
 tiger 69–70, *71*
 leopard 86, *87*
anacondas: green 212
 yellow 217, *219*
anchovies 267, 268, 269, 273, 288
Andes 84, *142–3*, 148, 149–54, *150–1*, 215
 canyons 204
 effect on climate 120
 pumas 153
 rivers 212
 torrent ducks 200, *200*
 tree line 149
 volcanoes 149
Angel, Jimmie 199, 200
Angel Falls *198*, 200
anglerfish 299–300, *302*, 303
Antarctica *32–5*
 altitude 36
 birds 45–7, 50, 55–6
 ice 37, 43, 199
 isolation 37–9
 krill 286
 mountains 37
 penguins 50
 seasons 28, 31, 34
 temperatures 34–6, 45
 whales 48, 49
 winter conditions 58–9
anteaters, tree 250
antelopes 135
 chiru 100
 kob 100, *100*
 pronghorn 115, *115*
 saiga 100–1, *101*
ants 240, 250
 army 251, *251*
 driver 251
 leafcutter *242*, 243
aphids 243
Aphyonus gelatinosa 301
Arabian desert 118, 121, 126

arachnids 135–6
aragonite *186*, 192
araucaria (monkey-puzzle) trees 84, 85
Arctic: birds 50–4, 56, 57
 caribou migration 57, 96, *97*
 food chain 47–9
 seasons 28, 34, 47
 temperatures 36, 39
 tundra 28, 92–6, 99
 winter conditions 57–8
 see also polar bears
Arctic Ocean 39
Argentina 85, 215, 269
Aripuana River *214*
Aristolochia vines *239*, 245
Arizona 133, 139, 204
art, prehistoric 195
Asia: continental drift 159, 162
 influence of Tibetan plateau 105
 rainforests 231, 246, 248
aspens 70, 75
Assam 106
astronauts 13, 118, 187
Atacama Desert 118, 120, *120*, 121, 132
Atlantic Ocean 28, 128, 212, 273
atmosphere: and deserts 119
 formation of 13–14
atolls 260–4
auklets 270
auks 50
 little 50–4, *50*
auroras 17, *29*
Australia: bats 178
 coral reefs 260, *264*
 deserts 118, 119, *119*, *124–5*, 126, 136
 rainforests 231
 wetlands 216
avalanches 154, *156*, 157
El Azizia 122

baboons *110*
bacteria: bioluminescence 300
 in caves 181, *181*, 192
 cellulose-digesting 241–3
 in hot ocean vents 18, 211
 hydrothermal vents 304
Baikal, Lake 207, *207*, 210–11, *210–11*
balsa trees *242*, 244, *244*
Baltoro Glacier 157, *157*
bamboo 166, *167*
Banda Sea *262–3*
Banks Island *94*, 95
Barrenlands 96
barrier reefs 260
Barro Colorado Island 229
Bat Cleft Cave, Australia 178, *178*
bats 175–9, 245, 246
 free-tailed 176
 little bent-winged 178, *178*
 long-nosed 131
 wrinkle-lipped *170–1*, 175, *177*
bears 69, 70, 96, 166
 cave 195, *195*
 grizzly 154, *154*, *202*, 203
 Tibetan brown *104*, 105
 see also polar bears

Bedouin 121
bee-eaters 250–1
beech trees *74*, 75, 76, 79
bees 246, 251
 euglossine *244*
 orchid 246
beetles 245
 dung 110, 115
Belarus 79
Bellamar caves, Cuba *186*
belugas 49, *49*
Bengal, Bay of 157, 212, 221
Benthalbella 297
Bielowieza 76–7, 77–9
Big Bang 13
billfish 288–9, 291, 292, *292*
bioluminescence 299, *299*, 300
birch trees 65, 70, 75
birds: boreal forests 68–9, 70
 caves 181–3
 deserts 136–9
 estuaries 221
 migration 79, 95
 mountains 165, 169
 polar regions 39, 45–7, 50–6, 57
 rainforests 246, 248, 250–1
 seabirds 270, 273
 seed dispersal 248
 temperate forests 79
 tundra 92
 wetlands 218
 see also individual names
birds of paradise 248
 blue *247*
 Lawes' parotia *247*
 magnificent *247*
 Raggiana *246*
 superb *247*
bird's-nest soup 181–3
bison 79, 100, *100*, 115
black-fly larvae 200
black smokers 303–4, *304*
blind animals, in caves 179–80
blubber 291
bluebells *74*, 79
 desert *133*
bluefish, false *301*
boarfish 288–9, 291, 292, *292*
bogs 200, 216
Bolinopsis 296
boreal forests 26, 66–70, 85
Borneo *21*, 172, 175–9, 181–3, 226
botos (pink river dolphins) 212–15, *212*
Botswana *23*, *93*, *111*, 113–14, 216
Bracken Cave, Texas 176
Brahmaputra River 105, 106, 204, 212, 215, 221, *222–3*
Brazil 212, *214*, 215, 216–17, *216–17*, 231
Brazil-nut trees 246, 248
bristlemouths 298, 298
Britain *74*, 77, 187
brittlestars 274, 277, 300–2
broadleaf trees 75, 77, 86, 89
bromeliads 240
Brood X, cicadas 75–6, *76*
Bryce Canyon 127
bubble nets, humpback whales 48
Buddhism 169
budgerigars 136

buffalos 106, 113
Buffon, Comte de 145
Bunaken Island, Sulawesi *20*
buntings: Lapland 57
 snow *50*, 57
buoyancy, oceanic animals 290–1
burrowing mammals 114–15
butterflies: birdwing 243
 danaid 243
 glasswing 227
 morpho 236
 in rainforests 227
 red admiral 31, *31*

cacti *120*, 129–31, *130*
caddisfly larvae 200, 203
caimans, spectacled 217, 218, *218*
calabash trees 245
calcite 184, *185*, *186*, 192, *192*
calcium carbonate 172–5, *190–1*, 258, 264
California 80, 82, 120, 121, 273, 278
camels 127, 135, 139
 Bactrian *135*, 139–40
Canada 39, 65, 66, 69, 80, 95, 96, 203, 278
canyons 204, *204*
Cape Adare 50
capercaillie 66, *66*
carbon dioxide: cave formation 175, 184
 coral reefs 21, 257
 deserts 22
 rainforests 21, 257–8
 removal by forests 65, 66
 storage in cacti 131
carbonic acid 172–5, 192
Caribbean 208, 235, 260, 265, 277
caribou 31, 57, 69, 92, 96, *96*, 99
Carlsbad Caverns *172*
Casearia corymbosa 248
Caspian Sea 207
catfish: dorado 215
 Mekong giant 215, *215*
Cauvery River 205
cave angels 180, *180*
Cave of Swallows, Mexico *174*, 175
cave swiflets, white-nest 181–3, *182*, *183*
caves 172–95
 animals 179–80
 bats 175–9
 birds 181–3
 cavemen 195
 exploring 187–92, *188*
 food chains 175–6
 formation of 172–5, *172*, 192
 prehistoric art *194*, 195, *195*
 snottites 181, *181*
 stalactites and stalagmites 184, *184–6*
cellulose 241–3
Central America: figs 245
 mangrove forests 235
 rainforests 230, 231, 234, 246, 250–1
Central Asia: deserts 118, 120
 steppes 92, 100–1
Chauvet Cave *194*, 195, *195*
cheetahs 98–9, 110, 115

chemical defences, rainforest plants 243
Chesapeake Bay 221
Chile 85, 118, *142–3*, *148*, 149–53
chimpanzees 250
China: dolphins 215
 forests 77, 86
 gorges 204
 limestone 172
 mountains 200
 pandas 166, *167*
 rivers 212
chiru (Tibetan antelopes) 100
Chitral Gol 164, *164*
chlorophyll 74
Chobe National Park *112–13*, 113–14
cicadas 75–6, *76*, 227, 228
cichlids 208–9, *209*
climate: deserts 23, 118, 119–21
 effect of mountains 162
 equatorial 21
 on plains 92
 polar regions 28, 36–9
 rainforests 228
 seasonal changes 31
 Tibetan plateau 105
 tree line 65
 tropical 21–2
climbing plants, rainforests 231, 238–40, *239*
cloudforest 162, 234, *234*, 240
clouds 18, *18*
cockroaches 176
cod 277
Colca Canyon, Peru 204
colonies: penguins 55, 60
 seabirds 50–1
 siphonophores 286
Colorado River 204, *204*
comb jellies 269, 285, 286, *296*
Congo River 212
conifers: forests 22–6, *64*, 65–8, 67, 75
 Mediterranean region 89
 temperate rainforests 80
continental drift 17, 159, 162
continental shelves 254, 274
copepods 47, 49, 269, 272, 282, 286, 298, 299
Copper Canyon, Mexico 204
coral reefs *20*, 252–66, 254, 257–66
 carbon fixing 21, 257
 deep water 305
 ecosystems 264–5
 fish 257, 265
 polyps 258
 spawning *259*, 260
 staghorn coral 260
 types of 260–4
cormorants 50
crabs: giant spider *302*
 Neolithodes 304
cranes, demoiselle 168, 169
creosote bush 129
crinoids 265
Cro-Magnons 195
crocodiles 205–6
 mugger 205, *205*
 Nile 206, *206*

crossbills 68, 69
crustaceans 282, 286
ctenophores (comb jellies) 269, 285, 286, 296
Cuba, caves 184, 186
Cueva San Martin Infierno, Cuba 184
currents, ocean 259, 278
cypress trees, Patagonian 84, 89

Dallol Springs, Ethiopia 14–15, 145, 146
Danakil Depression 14–15, 145–6, 145
Danum Valley, Sabah 226
Darwin, Charles 84, 227, 260, 264
Dasht-e Lut Desert 127
Davidson Seamount 305
Death Valley 120, 121
deciduous trees 22, 75–7, 79–80, 231
deer 86
    pudu 85
Deer Cave, Sarawak 175–9, 176
defences, oceanic animals 291
deforestation 77
deltas 221, 222–3
deserts 23, 118–41
    animals 131–40
    climate 23, 118, 119–21
    dust storms 127–8, 128–9
    erosion 122–3, 127
    plants 128–33, 132–3
    sand dunes 122, 123–6
Devil's Mountain 198, 200
doldrums 257
Dolichopteryx 297
dolphins 291
    botos 212–15, 212
    dusky 267, 269
    Ganges 215
    Indus River 215
    killer whales 289
    southern rightwhale 252–3
    Yangtze river 215
Domesday Book 77
dorados 196–7, 218
    yellow 218
Doyle, Arthur Conan 199
drought 21, 110
ducks:
    eider 57
    harlequin 200
    mandarin 86
    torrent 200, 200
dugongs 277, 277
dung: in caves 175–6, 176
    recycling 110
dung beetles 110, 115
dust storms, deserts 127–8, 128–9

eagles 92, 251
    golden 169
Earth: energy from Sun 17–18
    formation of 13
    formation of Moon 15–17
    regions 21–8
    seasons 28–31
    structure 13
earthquakes 159, 162–4
Easter Island 265
Eavis, Andy 187
echinoderms 300–2
echolocation 183
Egg River 94, 95
Egypt, Western Desert 126, 127

eider duck 57
electric eels 212
elephants: African 23, 93, 110, 112–13, 113–14, 248
    in deserts 140, 141
    Indian 106
elk 69
Ellison's Cave, Georgia 175
Empty Quarter 126
energy, from Sun 17–18
Enewetak Atoll 264
epiphytes 81, 231, 234, 236, 238, 240, 240
equatorial regions 21, 119
erosion: caves 175
    deserts 122–3, 127
    glaciers 157
    mountains 157
    rivers 204, 215
    sediment 221
estuaries 221
Ethiopian Highlands 142–3, 145, 146, 212
Eulychnia cactus 120
Europe: ice ages 76–7
    steppes 27
    woodlands 22, 26, 76–9, 76–7, 79
Everest, Mount 102, 158, 159, 162, 169
Everglades 216
evergreens, rainforests 231
evolution 145, 227, 228, 265
extremophiles 181, 192
eyes, marine animals 291, 292, 297, 300

Falklands current 269
Fantastic Pit, Georgia 175
ferns 240
figs 218, 236, 244, 245, 245, 248, 248
finches 70
fish: biggest 215, 215
    cichlids 208–9, 209
    in caves 180, 180
    coral reefs 254, 257, 265
    counter-shading 291
    in estuaries 221
    flatfish 277
    lakes 208–9, 211
    lateral lines 291
    mangrove forests 221
    migration 298
    mountain streams 200
    open oceans 288–9, 291–2
    in rainforests 227
    rivers 205, 212–15
    in shallow seas 278
    shoals 269, 272, 291
    swim bladders 291, 300
    temperate seas 269, 270
    in wetlands 217–18
    see also individual names
flatworms 211
flies 96, 245
fllooded forests 231, 231
floodplains 216
flowerpeckers 245
flowers: rainforest plants 244–5
    see also plants
flying fish 291, 291
fog 80, 121, 121, 132
Fogg, Tim and Pam 187
food chains: in caves 175–6
    marine 31, 257, 288

polar regions 47, 49
forests 65–89
    boreal forests 66–70, 85
    cloudforest 162, 234, 234, 240
    jungles 89
    mangrove forests 221, 235, 235
    monsoon forest 21
    seasonal forests 65–6
    temperate woodlands 22–6, 62–3, 75–80, 76–7, 86
    see also rainforests
foxes: Arctic 50, 50, 56, 58, 95, 95, 96
    fennec 134
    Tibetan 104
France 77, 145, 186, 195
Franz Josef Land 51
fringing reefs 260
frogs: burrowing 136
    sandhill 136
    treefrogs 178, 178
fruit bats 248
    musky 248
fruits, rainforest plants 248
fungi: recycling ability 66
    in temperate woodlands 79, 79
fur, desert animals 134–5

Galapagos 259, 303–4
Ganges River 105, 157, 212, 215, 221, 222–3, 235
Gangetic Plains 102, 105, 106
gaur 89, 89
gazelles 92, 135
    Mongolian 99, 115
    Thomson's 107
geese 70
    snow 94, 95, 95, 220, 221
geladas 146–8, 147
'General Sherman' (redwood) 82
geophytes 132
Gigantocypris 296
giraffes 111
glaciers 157–8, 157
glassfish 252–3, 256
glow-worms, cave 179, 179
goat fish, yellowsaddle 262–3
goats 153
    markhor 164, 164
    walia ibex 146, 148
Gobi Desert 23, 118, 118, 122, 139–40
golden damsels 265
golomyanka (oil fish) 211
Gomantong Cave, Sabah 181–3, 182
gorges 204
goshawks 70
gourds 240
Grand Canyon, Arizona 204
Grand Cenote, Mexico 185
grasses 90, 99, 132
grasslands *see* plains
gravity, Moon's 17
Great Barrier Reef 260, 264
Great Lakes 77, 207
Great Rift Valley 17, 144, 146, 208, 208
Great Sandy Desert, Australia 118
Greenland 50
ground squirrels 99, 114, 134
groundhogs 70
grouse, blue 66
Grumeti River 206, 207
guanaco 152, 153, 153
guano 175–6, 176, 273
guigna (kodkod) 84, 85

guillemots 50, 56
    Brunnich's 46–7, 51
Gulf of Mexico 304
    gulls 95
    glaucous 50
    ivory 33
    kelp (Dominican) 50
gunnera 85
gypsum 184, 189, 192

Ha Long Bay 172, 173
hatchetfish 296, 297
Hawaii 265, 266
hawks, bat 176
hellgrammite nymphs 200
herds, plains animals 115
herrings 269, 270, 272, 288
hibernation 66, 154
Hillary, Sir Edmund 169
Himalayas 118, 145, 158–62
    birds 165, 169
    canyons 204
    erosion 221
    forests 234
    formation of 17, 102, 159
    mammals 166–7
    and the monsoon 105, 120, 159
    Mount Everest 102, 158, 159, 162, 169
    plants 165
    rivers 157, 212
Hindu Kush 159, 162
hoatzins 241–3, 241
hogs, pygmy 106, 106
hornbills 234, 236
    great rhinoceros 244
Humboldt Current 259
hummingbirds 131, 227, 234, 240, 246, 251
hydrogen sulphide 181, 192, 304
hydrothermal vents 17–18, 211, 303–4
hyenas 92, 110
    spotted 98, 99

ibex, walia 146, 148
ice: in Andes 149–53
    glaciers 157–8, 157
    icebergs 40–1
    Lake Baikal 210–11, 211
    polar regions 34, 36–7, 39, 43, 199
ice ages 76–7, 195
Iguaçu Falls 215
India: continental drift 159, 162
    dolphins 215
    forests 21, 89
    monsoon 105, 106
    plains 102, 106
    rivers 205
Indian Ocean 105, 162, 261, 264, 265, 273, 277
Indiana 75–6
Indonesia 231, 265
Indus River 105, 157, 162
insectivores: plants 200
    in rainforests 249–51
insects: boreal forests 70
    deciduous trees 75–6
    deserts 134, 135–6
    rainforests 228, 243
invertebrates: rainforests 251
    shallow seas 270–2, 277
Iran 127
iron, Earth's core 15–17
islands, atolls 264

jacamar 250
jackals 98–9, 110
jackrabbits 134
jacks, blue-finned 262–3
jaguars 249, 249, 251
Japan 77, 200
jellyfish 285, 290, 291
    Atolla 299
    box 285, 286
    lion's-mane 270, 286
    midwater 296
    moon 269, 269, 270
    Octophialucium funerarium 295
    Portuguese man-of-war 286
    sea-nettle 284
jungles *see* rainforests
Jupiter 13, 17

K2 162, 163
Kakadu 216
Kalahari Desert 118, 119, 132
Kali Gandaki Canyon, Nepal 169, 204
kangaroos 134
Karakoram Mountains 156, 159, 162–4, 163
Kashmir 164
Kazakhstan 100–1
Kaziranga National Park 106
kelp 17, 276, 278, 279
kiang 26–7, 102–3
Kilauea Volcano 13
killer whales 45, 272, 289
Kipling, Rudyard 89
Kiska 270
kob (antelopes) 100, 100
kodkod 84, 85
Kong Karls Land 42, 45
kraits, sea 262–3, 266, 266
krill 43, 48, 49, 50, 286, 288, 298
Krubera Cave, Abkhazia 188, 188
Kukenon tepuis 199, 200
Kunlun Mountains 104
Kutiah Glacier 157

lagoons 260
lake flies 208, 209
lakes 199, 207–11
    fish 208–9, 211
    giant lakes 207–8
Lanceola 296
lanternfish 298–9, 299
Lapland 68
larches 66
larvaceans 286
lateral lines, fish 291
latex 243
leaves: decomposition 75, 80
    digestion 241–3
Lechuguilla Cave, New Mexico 181, 186, 188–92, 189–93
lemmings 57, 68, 114
leopards 98–9, 110, 249, 251
    Amur 86, 87
    snow 164, 165
lianas 228, 231, 238, 239, 240, 243
Libya 122
lichens 39, 58, 240
life: energy from Sun 17–18
    evolution of 14–15
light: bioluminescence 299, 299, 300
    photophores 297
    see also sunlight
limestone 172–5, 172, 184, 192
lionfish 258

lions 92, 98–9, 110, *112–13*, 113–14
　Namib 140, *140*
living stones 128–9
lizards, shovel-snouted *134*, 136
loach, Tibetan stone 200
lobsters 290
　Atlantic 272
　spiny *272–3*
locusts 133
lorises 250
lynxes 69

macaques, long-tailed *221*
mackerel 270, 291
Madagascar 172, *172*
magnetic field, Earth's 17
mahseer fish 205
mahua trees 89
Malawi, Lake 208–9, *208, 209*
Malaysia 227, 245, 251
Maldives 259
Mali 122, *122*, 140
mammals: Arctic 57
　boreal forests 69–70
　burrowing 114–15
　deserts 131–5, 139–40
　giant 69–70
　mountains 146–8, 153–4, 164,
　　166–7
　plains 92, 115
　rivers 205
　temperate forests 79
　tundra 92
Mammoth Cave, Kentucky 175
Manas National Park 106, *106*
Mangawhatikau Cave, New Zealand
　179
mangrove forests 221, 235, *235*
mantids 251
maples 75, 76
markhor 164, *164*
marlin, blue 292, *293*
Mars 13, 14
Marshall Islands 264
marshes 216, *220*, 221
marsupials, temperature control 134,
　135
mayflies 179
Mediterranean 89, 212
Mekong River 215
Mercury 13, 14
metabolic water, desert animals 139
Methuselah tree (bristlecone pine) 82
Mexico: canyons 204
　caves *174*, 175, 181, *184, 185*
　deserts 139
mice, pocket 134
mid-ocean ridges 303, 304
migration 31
　birds 50, 79, 95
　in boreal forests 70
　caribou 57
　fish 215
　invertebrates 270–2
　on plains 92–100, 107, 110, 206
　polar regions 39
　salmon 203
　on tundra 28
　vertical migration in oceans 298
　whales 31, 49, 266
Mississippi River 212, 221
mistletoe, Sarawak 245
Mojave Desert 120, 188
Mongolia 23, 99, 100–1, 107–14, 139
monito del monte *84*, 85

monkey-puzzle trees 84, 85
monkeys 251
　baboons *110*
　brown capuchin 218
　geladas 146–8, *147*
　golden snub-nosed *62–3*, 86
　howler 241, *241*
　macaques *221*
　proboscis 241
　Yunnan snub-nosed *166*
monsoon 102, 105, *160–1*, 162, 231
monsoon forest 21
Moon 16
　astronauts on 13, 15
　formation of 15–17
　importance of to life on Earth
　　15–17
moose 69, 70, *71*
moraine 157, *157*
mormyrids 209
mosquitoes 96
mosses 240
moths: army cutworm 154
　woolly bear 66
mountain goats, American 154, *155*
mountains 145–69
　animals 146–8, 153–4, 164, 166–7
　Antarctica 37, 46
　birds 165, 169
　earthquakes 159, 162–4
　effect on climate 18, 120, 162
　erosion 157
　formation of 17, 145–6, 149, 159
　glaciers 157–8, *157*
　streams 199
　underwater 303
mouth-brooding 208–9, *209*
mudflats 221
murrelets, marbled 80, *80*
musk ox 56, 57
mussels 304, *304*
Myrmecodia echinata 240

Naica mine, Mexico *184*
Namib Desert *22*, 118, 119, 120,
　121, 126, 129, 132, 136, 140
narwhals 49
nekton 288–9, 291
Nepal 159, 165, 169
Neptune 13
Ness, Loch 207
New Guinea 231, 243, 246–7, 248,
　265, *265*
New Zealand 179, 269
Ngorongoro Crater 107
Nicaragua, Lake 207–8
Nile, River 212, 221
Ningaloo Reef *260*
El Niño 273
nitrogen 18, 28, 257, 258
North America: deserts 118, 120,
　123, 127, *127*, 129, 131
　kelp forests 278
　mountains 154, *155*
　plains 27, 92, 100, 114–15
　temperate rainforests 80–5, *81*
　woodlands 22–6, 77
North Pole 28, 34, 36
Norway 272
nudibranchs 257, 278, 287
nunataks 38, 46
nutcrackers, Clark's 69, *69*

oak trees 75, 76, 89, *240*
oceans 282–304

buoyancy 290–1
currents 259, 278
deep ocean 294–304
　as deserts 22
　energy from Sun 18
　fish 288–9, 291–2
　formation of 14
　hot vents 17–18, 303–4
　plankton 282–8
　polar regions 37–9
　sea-floor 300–3
　seasonal changes 31
　shallow seas 254–78
　submersibles 282, 294–7, 299, 300,
　　303–4
　temperate seas 28
　vertical migration in 298
　water cycle 18
　water pressure 294, 300
ocelots 239, 251
octopuses *301*
Ogof Ffynnon Ddu, Wales *185*
oils, in oceanic animals 290
Okavango *19*, *110*, 113, 216
Olympic Peninsula 80
orcas (killer whales) 45, 272, 289
orchids 228, *240*, *244*, 245, 246
　Cattleya intermedia 231
　comet 245
Orinoco River 200, 212
oryx 135, *137*, 140
ostracods 296
ostriches 115
otters, smooth-coated 205, *205*
owls 70, 79
　burrowing 115
　great horned *130*
　snowy 57, 68
oxygen: in oceans 294–7
　production by forests 65, 66

Pacific Ocean: black smokers
　304, *304*
　coral reefs 264, 265
　salmon migration 203
　seagrass beds 277
　upwellings 273
paddlefish, Chinese 215
Pakistan 157, *157*, 159, 162–4, 215
pampas 27, 92
Panama 227, 229, *234*
pandas: giant 166–7, *167*
　red 166, *167*
pangolins 250
Pantanal, Brazil *216–17*, 217
Papua New Guinea 231, 265, *265*
　see also New Guinea
parakeets, slender-billed 84
Parana River 212, *216–17*, *216–17*
Parkia 246
Patagonia 119, 120, *148*, 149, 269
peacocks 88, 89
Pench Reserve 89
penguins 50, 286
　Adélie *43*, 47, 50, 52–3, 56
　chicks 55, 56, 61
　chinstrap 50
　colonies 55, 60
　emperor *29*, 33, 39, *40–1*, 45,
　　59–61, *59–61*
　gentoo 50, 56
　Magellanic 269
　migration 39
peregrine falcons 50
permafrost 26

Peru 121, 204, 273
petrels: giant 55
　snow 46–7, *46*
　southern giant 57
pheasants: blood pheasant 165
　Himalayan monal 165
　satyr tragopans 165
phosphorus 18, 28, 98, 257, 258
photophores 297, 299
photosynthesis: rainforests 236
　in seas 257, 267, 282
　zooanthellae 258, 259
phytoplankton 22, 28, 31, 47, 49,
　257, 267, 269, 270, 282–6
pikas, black-lipped 105, *105*, 114
pines: bristlecone 82, *82*
　whitebark 69, *69*
piranhas 217
　red-bellied *216*, 218
pirarucu 212
pitcher plants 238–40
plains 27, 92–115
　African savannahs 21–2, 107–10
　burrowing mammals 114–15
　Gangetic Plain 106
　herds 115
　migration on 92–100, 107, 110, 206
　speed of animals 115
　Tibetan plateau 26–7, 102–5, 120,
　　162
　waterholes *112–13*, 113–14
planets, formation of 13
plankton *280–1*, 282–8, *282*
　blooms 128, 266, 269, 270
　buoyancy 290, 291
　detritus feeders 298
　food chain 286, 288
　migration 298
　in temperate seas 266, 267, *267*
　in tropical seas 257
plants: cellulose content 241–3
　defences 243
　in deserts 128–33, *132–3*
　geophytes 132
　grasses 99, 132
　insectivorous 200
　in open oceans 282
　phytoplankton 282–6
　polar regions 39
　rainforests 227–34, 236–48
　in shallow seas 277, 278
　in temperate woodlands 79
　in tropical rainforests 21
　see also individual plant names
poaching 101
poisons: jellyfish *285*, 286
　nudibranch 257
　rainforest plants 243
　see also sea snakes
Poland 79
polar bears 36–7, 39–43, 45, *45*, 50,
　58
　breeding 42, *44*
　hunting ability 42–3, 54, *54–5*, 55
　social life 58
　in winter 58
polar regions 29, 34–61, 118
　climate 28, 36–9
　migration 39
　seasons 31, 39
　see also Antarctica; Arctic
pollination, rainforest plants 228,
　244–6
pollock 270
Pompeii worm *304*

Poor Knights Islands 269
porcupines 66
porpoises 215
Portuguese man-of-war 286
pottos 250
prairie dogs 114–15
prairies 22, 27, 92
primates 146–8, 250
　see also monkeys
ptarmigan 57
pteropods 286
pudu 85
puffins, tufted *270*
pumas, Patagonian 153, *153*
pycnogonids *301*

quipo trees *230*

racoons 176
Rafflesia arnoldii 245
rainfall: deserts 23, 118, 120–1, 127
　forests 65
　monsoon 21, 102, 105, 106, 162
　on plains 92, 110
　rainforests 228, *228*
　seasonal changes 31
　taiga 26
　Venezuelan tepuis 200
　water cycle 18
rainforests 21, *21*, 227–51
　birds 246, 248, 250–1
　carbon fixing 257–8
　layers 236–8
　numbers of species in 227
　plants 227–34, 236–48
　predators 249–51
　temperate rainforests 80–4, *81*
　trees 228, 235, 237, 238, *244*
　types of 231–5
　see also individual names
Raja Ampat 265
rat tails *301*, *302*
rats, kangaroo 139
rattans 238
ravens, common 57
rays, manta *280–1*, 288
razorbills 50
recycling, coral reefs 258
Red Sea 146, *252–3*, 256, 257, 259,
　260
redpolls: Arctic 57
　common 57
redwoods, coastal 26, 80, *81*, 82
reefs *see* coral reefs
reindeer 69
　see also caribou
reptiles, in deserts 134, 136
rhinos 101
　greater one-horned 106, *106*
rhododendrons 165, 234
rivers 199–206
　animals in 205
　deltas 221, 222–3
　erosion 157, 204, 215
　estuaries 221
　fish 205, 212–15
　flooded forests 231, *231*
　giant rivers 212–15
　gorges and canyons 204, *204*
　influence of Tibetan plateau 105,
　　160–1
　mangrove forests 221, 235, *235*
　mountain streams 199–200
　salmon migration 203
　sediment 212, 221

wetlands 216–18
see also individual rivers
roadrunners 139, *139*
Rockies 120, 154, *155*
rocks: caves 172–5, 184
  erosion 123
  mountains 145
rodents, in deserts 134
roots: climbing plants 240
  desert plants 129
  mangroves 221, 235, *235*
Rose Dunes, Mali *122*
Rub' al-Khali 126
rubber trees 243
Russia 66, 69, 72–3, 77, 86, 100–1

Sabah 181–3, 226
saguaro cactus *130*, 131, *131*
Sahara Desert 121, 122–3
  dust storms *24-25*, 26, 127–8
  mammals 134, 139, 140
  reptiles 136
  sand dunes 118, 123
  trees 129
sailfish 291, 292, *293*
salamanders: giant 200, *201*
  Texas blind cave 180, *180*
Salar de Uyuni *118*
salmon 203, 270
  sockeye 203, *203*
salps 269, 282, 286, *286*, 290
salt deserts *118*
salt marshes *220*, 221
sand: dunes *122*, 123–6
  dust storms 127–8, *128–9*
sand dollars 275, *277*
sandgrouse, Namaqua 139
Sarawak 175–9
Sarawak Chamber, Borneo 175
Sardanelos Falls *214*
sardines 269, 288
sargassum weed *283*
Saturn 13
savannahs 21–2, 92, 98–9, 107–14
Scandinavia 66
scent, rainforest plants 245
scorpions 134
Scotland 207, 269, 270
sea angels *see* sea slugs
sea cucumbers 300
sea gooseberries *296*
seagrass 254, 257, 274, 277, 282
sea pens *275*
sea slugs (nudibranchs) 257, 278, *287*
sea snakes *see* kraits
sea spider *300*
sea urchins 302
seabirds 50–4, 270, 273
seadragons, leafy *257*
sealions 269
  California *17*, *276*
seals 42–3, 270, 286, 290–1
  crabeater 43–5, 59
  elephant *297*
  harp 39, 42
  hooded 42, *42*
  hunted by polar bears 54
  leopard *43*, 45, 56
  migration 39
  nerpa 210–11, *210*
  ringed 42
  Weddell 39, *39*, 59
seas 254–78
  continental shelf 274
  coral reefs 254–66, *257–66*

phytoplankton blooms 269
substrate 274–8
temperate 266–72
upwellings 273
see also oceans
seasonal forests 65–6
seasons 17, 28–31
  African savannah 110
  boreal forests 70
  polar regions 39
  temperate woodlands 79–80
seaweeds 254, 260, 277, 278, 282
sediment: and coral reefs 259
  in rivers 157, 212, 221
  on seabed 274
sedimentary rocks 172
  see also limestone
seeds: in deserts 132–3
  dispersal *243*, 244, 248
  rainforest plants 238, 244, 248
selenite 184, *189*
sequoia 82
  see also redwoods
Serengeti 92, 99, 107, *108–9*, 110, 206
Seychelles *261*
shags, Antarctic (blue-eyed) 50
sharks 269, 290, 291
  basking 28, 272
  blue *268*
  bull 207–8
  hammerhead 264
  mako 289, *289*
  whale 288, *290*
  white-tipped 264
shearwaters, sooty 270
sheathbills 55
shrimps 277, 282, 285, 297, 300
Siberia 207, *207*, 210–11, 254
Sichuan province 86
Sierra Nevada 82, *82*, 120
Simien Mountains 146–8
Simpson Desert *119*, 126
siphonophores 286, 290
skuas: Arctic 33
  polar 46–7
skunks 176
Smarthvaren 46
snails 75, 210
snakes: hunting bats 176, 178
  Peringuey's sidewinding adder 138
  sea snakes 262–3, *266*
snottites 181, *181*
snow: avalanches 154, *156*, 157
  boreal forests 68
  eating 139–40
  melt-water streams 200
  polar regions 34
soil, rainforests 228
solar system 13
solar wind 17
solifugids *134*
Sonora Desert 120, *130*, 131, *131*, *186*
South Africa 27, 100, 279
South America: anchovy fisheries 273
  continental shelf 254
  deserts 120
  grasslands 27
  mountains 149–54
  pampas 92
  rainforests 231, 246, 249, 251
South Pole 28, *29*, 34–7, 118
Southeast Asia: mangrove forests 235
  rainforests 21, 231, 234, 248

Southern Ocean 37, 49
speed, plains animals 115
spiders 136, 243, *250*, 251
sponges 210, *210*
springboks 100, *101*
squid: giant 289
  Heteroteuthis 295
  Histioteuthis 297
stalactites and stalagmites 184, *184–6*
steppes 27, 92, 99, 100–1, 107–14
stingrays 215, 217
storks, jabiru 218
storms: dust 127–8, *128–9*
  temperate seas 28, 267, 270, 272
  tropical 228
Stratosphere Giant (redwood tree) 82
streams 199, 200
sturgeon 215
submersibles 282, 294–7, 299, 300, 303–4
Sudan 100
sulphides 304
sulphur *14–15*, 146
sulphur tuft 79
sulphuric acid 181, 192
Sun: energy from 17–18
  formation of 13
  polar regions 34
  seasons 17, 28–31
sunbirds 246, 251
Sundarbans 221, 235
sunfish 285
sunlight 18
  and coral reefs 259
  rainforests 228, 236, 238
  temperate seas 267
  tropical seas 257
  under water 282, 291, 294
sunstars 277
Superior, Lake 207
Svalbard archipelago 42, *45*
swamp forests 231, *231*
swamps 216
swift, European 31
swim bladders, fish 291, 300
Switzerland 157–8
swordfish 292, 297

taiga 26, 66, 72–3
Tanganyika, Lake 208, *208*, 209, 210
tarantula spiders 251
  goliath bird-eating *250*
teak forests 89
tectonic plates 145–6, 159, 162, 210
temperate regions 22–7, 31
  forests and woodlands 22–6, *62–3*, 75–80, *76–7*, 86
  rainforests 80–4, *81*
  seas 266–72
temperatures: black smokers 303–4
  in deep ocean 299, 300
  deserts 121–2, 131–6, 146
  planets 14–15
  polar regions 28, 36, 39, 42, 45
  rainforests 236, 238
  shallow seas 267–9, 270, 274
  tropics 21, 22
Tenzing Norgay 169
tepuis, Venezuela *198*, 199–200, *199*
termites 110, *250*, 251
terns: Antarctic 50
  Arctic 50
Thailand *177*
thermocline 209, 269, 270
Three Gorges Dam, China 212, 215

thrushes 70, 79
Tibet 169, 204, 212
Tibetan plateau 26–7, 92, *92*, 100, 102–5, 120, 162
tidepools 278
Tiger Leaping Gorge, China 204
tigers 106, 235
  Amur 71
  forest 251
  Siberian 69–70, 86
Tillandsia latifolia 132
tityras 248
toads, spadefoot 133, *136*
toadstools 79
Torres del Paine *142–3*, *148*, *152*, 153
toucans 248
  keel-billed *224–5*
transparency, as defence 291
tree line 65, *65*, 84, 149
trees: autumn colours *74*, 78
  in deserts 129
  oldest 82
  tallest 82
  see also forests, rainforests *and individual names*
Trinidad 235
troglobites 179–80
Tropic of Cancer 22, 29, 31, 118, 120, 231, 257
Tropic of Capricorn 22, 31, 118, 120, 231, 257
tropics 21–2
  caves 175
  climate 31
  coral reefs 258, 259
  deserts 118–20
  rainforests 89, 227–51
  shallow seas 257
Tsingy de Bemaraha Strict Nature Reserve 172
Tuareg people 121
tubeworms 304, *Rifta 304*
tucuxi (porpoise) 215
tuna 288–9, 290, *290*, 291, 292
  bluefin 292
  southern blue 293
tundra 28, 92–6, 99
turtles: green 283
  leatherback 297

ultraviolet radiation 17
United States of America 75–6, 80
upwellings 273, 285
Uranus 13
urine, desert animals 139

Valdivian coastal rainforest 84–5
veldt 100
Venezuela 198, 199–200, *199*
Venus 13, 14, 17
verbena, sand *133*
Victoria, Lake 207, 208, *208*, 212
Vietnam 172, *173*
Villa Luz Cave, Mexico 181, *181*
viperfish *296*, 297
vlei lily *132*
Volcano Baru 234
volcanoes 13, *13*, 14, 17–18, 149, 264, 303–4
voles 57
Voltaire, François Marie Arouet de 145

Wallace, Alfred Russel 227
walruses 54–5, *54–5*

Watchung Mountains 145
water: cave formation 175, 184
  in deserts 128–33, *132–3*, 139
  erosion 123, 127
  fresh water 199–221
  temperate rainforests 80
  water cycle 18, 31, 199
  see also lakes; oceans; rainfall; rivers; seas
water strider, marine 290
waterfalls 198, 200, *214*, 215
waterholes *112–13*, 113–14
weather *see* climate
Welwitschia mirabilis 132, *132*
wetlands 216–18
whales: baleen whales 49, 288
  belugas 49, *49*
  blubber 290–1
  blue 49, 289
  bowhead 49
  fin 49
  humpback *30*, 48, *48*, 49, 254, *255*, 266, 270, *271*
  migration 31, 49
  minke 49
  narwhals 49
  in polar regions 48, 49, 54, 286
  sei 49
  southern right 49
  sperm 288–9, *289*
wildebeest 22, 92, 98–9, 113, 114, 206, *206*
willowherb 50, 79
willows 70
wind: erosion 123, 127
  monsoon *160–1*, 162
winter, in polar regions 57–9
wolverines 68, 69, 70, *70*
wolves 79, 92
  Arctic 96, *96*, 99
  Ethiopian *146*, 148
  grey 57
woodlands *see* forests
woodpeckers 251
worms: nemertine *296*
  polychaete 274–7, 278, 304
  Pompeii *304*

yaks 92, *104*, 105
Yangtze River 105, 212, 215
Yarlung Tsangpo Gorge 204
Yellow River 105, 212
Yeti 105

zebras 107, *107*, 113, 114
zooanthellae 258, 259
zooplankton 269, 286, 291, 298

University of California Press, one of the most distinguished university presses in the United States, enriches lives around the world by advancing scholarship in the humanities, social sciences, and natural sciences. Its activities are supported by the UC Press Foundation and by philanthropic contributions from individuals and institutions. For more information, visit www.ucpress.edu.

University of California Press
Berkeley and Los Angeles, California

First published in the UK by BBC Books, BBC Worldwide Ltd., Woodlands, 80 Wood Lane, London W12 0TT to accompany the BBC television series *Planet Earth*, first broadcast in 2006.

Cataloging-in-Publication Data for this title is on file with the Library of Congress.

ISBN-13: 978-0-520-25054-3 (cloth) — ISBN-10: 0-520-25054-0 (cloth)

Commissioning editor: Shirley Patton
Project editor: Rosamund Kidman Cox
Designer: Bobby Birchall, DW Design
Picture researcher: Laura Barwick
Production controller: David Brimble

Printing and colour origination by Butler and Tanner Ltd, Frome, England

15 14 13 12 11 10 09 08 07
10 9 8 7 6 5 4

PRODUCTION TEAM
Susan Aartse-Tuyn
Penny Allen
Justin Anderson
Vanessa Berlowitz
Lesley Bishop
Mark Brownlow
Andy Byatt
Huw Cordey
Dave Cox
Samantha Davis
Alastair Fothergill
Tom Hugh-Jones
Amanda Hutchinson
Kathryn Jeffs
Jonny Keeling
Mandy Knight
Mark Linfield
Conrad Maufe
Emma Peace
Joanna Verity
Sarah Wade
Martin Whatley
Jeff Wilson
Lisa Wilson

CAMERA TEAM
Doug Allan
Doug Anderson
David Baillie
Barrie Britton
Keith Brust
Gordon Buchanan
Richard Burton
Simon Carroll
Rod Clarke
Martyn Colbeck
Steve Downer
Goran Ehlme
Justine Evans
Wade Fairley
Tom Fitz
Rob Franklin
Ted Giffords
Jeff Hogan
Mike Holding
Michael Kelem
Simon King
Richard Kirby
Peter Kragh
Ian McCarthy
Alastair MacEwen
David McKay
Mike Madden
Justin Maguire
Michael Male
Henry Mix
Shane Moore
Toshihiro Muta
Gavin Newman
Didier Noirot
Matt Norman
Ben Osborne
Haroldo Palo Jr
Mark Payne-Gill
Andrew Penniket
Mike Potts
Adam Ravetch
David Reichert
Mike Richards
Rick Rosenthal
Peter Scoones
Tim Shepherd
Andrew Shillabeer
Warwick Sloss
Mark Smith
Colin Stafford Johnson
Paul Stewart
Gavin Thurston
Jeff Turner
Nick Turner
John Waters
Mark Wolf

FIELD ASSISTANTS
Karel Allard
Glen Allen
Stan Allison
Reza Azmi
Claire Baker
Paul Beilstein
Ralph Bower
Paul Brehem
Milo Burcham
Tom Chapman
Tom Clarke
Dan Eatherley
Andy Eavis
Tim Fogg
Joel Heath
Chris Hendrickson
Daniel Huertas
Chadden Hunter
Richard Jones
Noah Kadlak Kartike
Jean Krecja
Huw Lewis
Paul Lickte
John Lucas
Trevor Lucas
Rob McCall
Gil Malamud
Nisar Malik
Frederique Olivier
Anatoly Petrov
Jason Roberts
Juan Romero
Graham Springer
Raj Suwal`
Joanna van Gruisen
Josh Westerhold
Emilio White
Greg Winston
Paul Zakora

PRODUCTION
Alison Brown-Humes
Tom Clarke
George Chan
Sharmila Choudhury
Sue Flood
Anne McCarthy
Anna Mike
Hugh Miller
Jo Morton
Sue Storey
Nick Smith-Baker
Amy Young

POST-PRODUCTION
Ruth Berrington
Miles Hall
Jennifer Silverman

MUSIC
George Fenton
BBC Concert Orchestra
Sam Watts

FILM EDITORS
Andrew Chastney
Tim Coope
Martin Elsbury
Jill Garrett
Stuart Napier
Andy Netley
Jo Payne
Dave Pearce

SOUND EDITORS
Kate Hopkins
Tim Owens

DUBBING MIXERS
Graham Wild
Andrew Wilson

COLOURIST
Luke Rainey

GRAPHICS
Burrell Durrant Hifle
Tim Brade
Nick Brooks
Steve Burrell
Carys Hull

PICTURE ONLINE
Chas Francis
Steve Olive

ACKNOWLEDGEMENTS

The television series that this book accompanies was a massive team effort. The authors of the book (producers of the series) are extremely grateful to the production, post-production and camera teams for their talent, dedication and determination. The result of their hard work on this challenging series is not only obvious in the television programmes but also in these pages. The stories they unearthed and the trips they organized were the inspiration for much of the text, and many of their unique images illustrate the book.

The names listed are, though, only the very tip of the iceberg. *Planet Earth* took four years to make, and during that time, we filmed in more than 200 locations worldwide. Everywhere we went we received enormous amounts of help. The Japanese Deep Sea Research organisation, JAMSTEC, allowed us to use their remote-operated vehicle to film hot vents 2000m (6560 feet) down at the bottom of the ocean. The Australian Antarctic Division hosted our camera team for a year, enabling them to overwinter with emperor penguins. The captain and crew of HMS *Endurance* carried our cameras on their Lynx helicopters over spectacular iceberg scenery. The Nepalese air force flew us right beside the summit of Everest. And the helicopter pilots of the Pakistan air force took us into the heart of the Karakorum Mountains.

We never would have found the elusive snow leopard without the help of local trackers in Pakistan. We only managed to get close to Bactrian camels in the Gobi Desert with the help of a brilliant local expert. The forest people of Papua New Guinea allowed us to film birds of paradise on their land. The list goes on and on. All round the world, many people – from scientists to trackers, pilots to field assistants – have given freely and generously of their time and expertise. The authors of this book thank them all for everything they did.

Finally, we would like to thank Shirley Patton at BBC Books for commissioning this book, Roz Kidman Cox, our editor, Laura Barwick, our picture researcher, and Bobby Birchall, the designer, for all the long hours and devotion they put into this project.

PICTURE CREDITS

1 NASA-BDH / BBC-Planet Earth; **2–3** NASA-BDH / BBC-Planet Earth; **4–5 top, left to right**: Jorma Luhta / naturepl.com; NASA-BDH / BBC-Planet Earth; David Tipling / naturepl.com; AFLO / naturepl.com; **4–5 middle, left to right**: Anup Shah / naturepl.com; Richard du Toit; David Noton; Tim Laman / National Geographic Image Collection; **4–5 bottom, left to right**: Peter Scoones; Christian Ziegler; Chris Newbert / Minden Pictures; Howard Hall; **7** Adam Gibbs; **8–9** National Geographic Collection; **10–11** NASA-BDH / BBC-Planet Earth; **12** AFLO / naturepl.com; **13** Doug Perrine / naturepl.com; **14–15** Martyn Colbeck; **16** Tom Murphy / National Geographic Image Collection; **17** Randy Morse / SeaPics.com; **18** StockTrek / Getty Images; **19** Ben Osborne / BBC-Planet Earth; **20** Fred Bavandam / Minden Pictures; **21** Frans Lanting; **22** NASA-BDH / BBC-Planet Earth; **23** Ben Osborne / BBC-Planet Earth; **24–5** NASA-BDH / BBC-Planet Earth; **26–7** Milo Burcham; **28** Alan James / naturepl.com; **29** Fred Olivier; **30** Doug Allan & Sue Flood; **31** Stephen Dalton / NHPA; **32–3 top** Pal Hermansen; **32–3 bottom** David Tipling / naturepl.com; **34** Pete Oxford / naturepl.com; **35** Kevin Schafer / SeaPics.com; **36–7** Pal Hermansen; **38** Simon King / naturepl.com; **39** Norbert Wu / Minden Pictures / FLPA; **40–1** Fred Olivier; **42** Gerald Lacz / FLPA; **43 top** Kevin Schafer; **43 bottom** Tui de Roy / Minden Pictures/FLPA; **44–45** Jason C Roberts; **46–7** Jan Vermeer; **48** Tim Voorheis / SplashdownDirect.com; **49** John KB Ford / Ursus / SeaPics.com; **50 top to bottom**: Winifred Wisniewski / FLPA; Kevin Schafer; M Watson / Ardea.co.uk; Pal Hermansen; **51** Pal Hermansen; **52–3** Kevin Schafer; **54–5** BBC-NHU; **56** Michio Hoshino / Minden Pictures / FLPA; **57 top** Sue Flood & Doug Allan; **57 bottom** Frans Lanting / Minden Pictures / FLPA; **58** Sue Flood / naturepl.com; **59** Fred Olivier; **60–1** Doug Allan / naturepl.com; **62–3 top** AFLO / naturepl.com; **62–3 bottom** Xi Zhi Nong / naturepl.com; **64** Adam Gibbs; **65** Thorsten Milse; **66** Jorma Luhta / naturepl.com; **67** Carr Clifon / Minden Pictures; **68** Tom Clarke; **69 left** Michael S Quinton / National Geographic Image Collection;

69 right Dietmar Nill / naturepl.com; **70** Paul Nicklen / National Geographic Image Collection; **71 top** Michio Hoshino / Minden Pictures; **71 bottom** John Goodrich / WCS; **72–3** NASA-BDH / BBC-Planet Earth; **74 top to bottom**: David Noton; AFLO / naturepl.com; David Noton; **76 top** Mark Linfield; **67–7** Tom Clarke; **78** Tim Fitzharris; **79** Angela Bird / naturepl.com; **80** Mark Moffet / Minden Pictures; **81** Gerry Ellis / Minden Pictures; **82 left** Art Wolfe; **82 right** Paul Schermeister / National Geographic Image Collection; **83 left** DCI / Martin Klimek; **83 right** Penny Allen; **84 top and bottom** BBC-NHU; **85** Tui de Roy / Minden Pictures; **86 top, left to right** BBC-NHU; **87 bottom** Toshiji Fukuda; **88** Art Wolfe; **89** Toby Sinclair / naturepl.com; **90–1 top** Jim Brandenburg / Minden Pictures / FLPA; **90–1 bottom** Anup Shah / naturepl.com; **92** Milo Burcham; **93** Ben Osborne / BBC-Planet Earth; **94** Chris Hendrickson; **95** Chris Hendrickson; **96 top** BBC-NHU; **96 bottom** Art Wolfe; **97** Michio Hoshino / Minden Pictures; **98** Richard du Toit; **99** Shin Yoshino / Minden Pictures; **100 left** Jim Brandenburg / Minden Pictures; **100 right** Bruce Davidson / naturepl.com; **101 left** Richard du Toit / naturepl.com; **101 right** Igor Shiplenok / naturepl.com; **102–3** Joanna van Gruisen; **104–5** Milo Burcham; **106 top** Ian McCarthy; **106 bottom** Art Wolfe; **107** Gerry Ellis / Minden Pictures; **108–9** Mitsuaki Iwago / Minden Pictures; **110** BBC-NHU; **111** Ben Osborne / BBC-Planet Earth; **112 top left to right** BBC-NHU; **112 bottom** Ben Osborne / BBC-Planet Earth; **113 bottom** Ben Osborne / BBC-Planet Earth; **114** Anthony Bannister / NHPA; **115 top** Art Wolfe; **115 bottom** Tim Fitzharris; **116–17 top** M&P Fogden; **116–17 bottom** Tony Heald / naturepl.com; **118 top** Rhonda Klevansky / naturepl.com; **118 bottom** Huw Cordey; **119** NASA-BDH / BBC-Planet Earth; **120 top and bottom** BBC-NHU; **121** Altitude / Yann Arthus-Bertrand; **122** Altitude / Yann Arthus-Bertrand; **123** Tom Hugh-Jones; **124–5** NASA-BDH / BBC-Planet Earth; **126** Dan Rees / naturepl.com; **127** M&P Fogden; **128–9** BBC-NHU; **130 left and**

right John Cancalosi / naturepl.com; **131** Jeff Foott / naturepl.com; **132 left** M&P Fogden; **132 right** Nigel J Dennis / NHPA; **133 left** Tim Fitzharris; **133 right** Tim Fitzharris; **134 left and right** M&P Fogden; **135** Henry M Mix; **137** Richard du Toit; **138** M&P Fogden; **139** Rolf Nussbaumer / naturepl.com; **140** BBC-NHU; **141** Paul Brehem; **142–3 top** David Noton; **142–3 bottom** Chadden Hunter; **144** Altitude / Yann Arthus-Bertrand; **145** Martyn Colbeck; **146** Elio Della Ferrera / naturepl.com; **147** Ingo Arndt / naturepl.com; **148–9** Colin Monteath / Hedgehog House / Minden Pictures; **150–1** NASA-BDH / BBC-Planet Earth; **152** Konrad Wothe; **153** Jeff Turner; **154** BBC-NHU; **155 left** Sumio Harada / Minden Pictures; **155 right** Art Wolfe; **156** Colin Monteath / Minden Pictures / FLPA; **157** Jeff Wilson; **158–9** Martyn Colbeck; **159** NASA-BDH / BBC-Planet Earth; **160–1** NASA-BDH / BBC-Planet Earth; **163** Jeff Wilson; **164** Jeff Wilson; **165** BBC-NHU; **166** Xi Zhi Nong / naturepl.com; **167 top** Mitsuaki Iwago; **167 bottom** BBC-NHU; **168** N.Shigeta / The Yomiuri Shimbun; **170–1 top** D Brown / PanStock / Panoramic Images / NGSImages.com; **170–1 bottom** Tim Laman / National Geographic Image Collection; **172** Frans Lanting / Minden Pictures / FLPA; **173** Huw Cordey; **174** DCI / Ed Carreon; **175** Kevin Downey / **176** BBC-NHU; **177** Alastair Shay / osf.co.uk; **178** Bruce Means; **179 top** M&P Fogden; **179 bottom** Francis Furlong / SAL / osf.co.uk; **180 left** Dennis Belliveau; **180 right** BBC-NHU; **181** Kenneth Ingham; **182** Jean-Paul Ferrero / Ardea.co.uk; **183** BBC-NHU; **184 left and right** Kevin Downey; **185 left and right** Gavin Newman; **186 top left and centre** Kevin Downey; **186 top right** Gavin Newman; **186 middle left to right** Kevin Downey; **186 bottom left to right** Kevin Downey; **188** Stephen Alvarez / National Geographic Image Collection; **189** Gavin Newman; **190–1** Kevin Downey; **192** Kevin Downey; **193** Gavin Newman; **194–5** Chauvet / Brunel / Hillaire; **196–7 top** Kevin Schafer; **196–7 bottom** Peter Scoones; **198** Mark Brownlow; **199** Mark Brownlow; **200** David Hosking / FLPA; **201 top** Peter Scoones; **201 bottom** BBC-NHU; **202** Michio Hoshino / Minden

Pictures; **203 top** Brandon Cole; **203 bottom** Chris Huss / SeaPics.com; **204** NASA-BDH / BBC-Planet Earth; **205 top** BBC-NHU; **205 bottom** Anup Shah / naturepl.com; **206** Anup Shah; **207** NASA-BDH / BBC-Planet Earth; **208 top** NASA-BDH / BBC-Planet Earth; **208 bottom** Mark Brownlow; **209 top and bottom** Ad Konings; **210 left** Konrad Wothe / Minden Pictures / FLPA; **210 right top and bottom** BBC-NHU; **211 left** Didier Noirot; **211 right** Mark Brownlow; **212 top** Tony Martin; **212 bottom** Pete Oxford / naturepl.com; **213** Frans Lanting; **214** Sergio Brant Rocha; **215** Suthep Kritsanavarin / OnAsia.com; **216 bottom** Peter Scoones; **216–17** Pete Oxford / naturepl.com; **218 left and right** Peter Scoones; **219** Michel Loup; **220** Mark Brownlow; **221** Doug Wechsler / naturepl.com; **222–3** NASA-BDH / BBC-Planet Earth; **224–5 top and bottom** Christian Ziegler; **226** Nick Garbutt; **227** M&P Fogden; **228** Christian Ziegler; **229** Christian Ziegler; **230** Christian Ziegler; **231 top** Luiz Claudio Marigo / naturepl.com; **231 bottom** Martin Wendler / NHPA; **232–3** NASA-BDH / BBC-Planet Earth; **234** Christian Ziegler; **235 top** M&P Fogden; **235 bottom** Pete Oxford / naturepl.com; **236 left** M&P Fogden; **236 right** Tim Laman / National Geographic Image Collection; **237** M&P Fogden; **239 top and bottom** Christian Ziegler; **240** Christian Ziegler; **241 left** Christian Ziegler; **241 right** Staffan Widstrand / naturepl.com; **242** Christian Ziegler; **243** Christian Ziegler; **244 top left** M&P Fogden; **244 bottom left** Christian Ziegler; **244 right** Tim Laman / National Geographic Image Collection; **245** Christian Ziegler; **246** Barrie Britton; **247 left** BBC-NHU; **247 right** Barrie Britton; **248** Tim Laman / National Geographic Image Collection; **249** Kevin Schafer; **250** Nick Gordon / osf.co.uk; **251** Christian Ziegler; **252–3 top** Todd Pusser / naturepl.com; **252–3 bottom** Chris Newbert / Minden Pictures; **254** Kenneth D Knezick; **255** Doug Allan & Sue Flood; **256** Chris Newbert / Minden Pictures; **257 top** Fred Bavendam / Minden Pictures; **257 bottom** Kenneth D Knezick; **258–9** Chris Newbert / Minden Pictures; **259 bottom** Didier Noirot;

260 Fred Bavendam / Minden Pictures; **261** Adam White / naturepl.com; **262–3** Peter Scoones; **264–5** Altitude / Yann Arthus-Bertrand; **265 top** Georgette Douwma; **266** Jurgen Freund; **267 top** Bill Curtsinger / National Geographic Image Collection; **267 bottom** Sam Abel / National Geographic Image Collection; **268** Richard Herrmann / SeaPics.com; **269** Fred Bavendam / Minden Pictures; **270** Ben Osborne; **271** Masa Ushioda / CoolwaterPhoto.com; **272–3** Doug Perrine / SeaPics.com; **274** Dan Burton / naturepl.com; **275 top and bottom** Fred Bavendam / Minden Pictures; **276** Norbert Wu / Minden Pictures; **277** Jurgen Freund / naturepl.com; **278** Brandon Cole; **279** Doug Perrine / SeaPics.com; **280–1 top** Norbert Rosing / National Geographic Image Collection; **280–1 bottom** Howard Hall; **282** Peter Parks / imagequestmarine.com; **283** Mark Conlin / SeaPics.com; **284** David Wrobel / SeaPics.com; **285 left** Peter Parks / imagequestmarine.com; **285 right** Paul A Sutherland / SeaPics.com; **286** Phillip Colla / SeaPics.com; **287** Peter Parks / imagequestmarine.com; **288–9** Francis Gohier / Ardea.co.uk; **289** David B Fleetham / SeaPics.com; **290** BBC-NHU; **291** David B Fleetham / SeaPics.com; **292** Doug Perrine / SeaPics.com; **293 left** Masa Ushioda / SeaPics.com; **293 right** Mike Parry / Minden Pictures; **295 top and bottom** David Shale / naturepl.com; **296 top left** David Shale / naturepl.com; **top centre** David Shale / naturepl.com; **296 top right** Ingo Arndt / naturepl.com; **296 middle left and right** Peter Herring / imagequestmarine.com; **296 bottom left to right** David Shale / naturepl.com; **298** David Shale / naturepl.com; **299** Peter Herring / imagequestmarine.com; **301 top left and right** David Shale / naturepl.com; **301 middle left and right** David Shale / naturepl.com; **301 bottom left** BBC-NHU; **301 bottom right** David Shale / naturepl.com; **302** Ian Hudson / Serpent Project; **303** Ian Hudson / Serpent Project; **304 left** image courtesy of University of Washington; **304 right** Peter Batson / imagequestmarine.com; **305 top and bottom** BBC-NHU; **310–11** Daniel Gomez / SplashdownDirect.com